AIR COMBAT

An Oral History of Fighter Pilots

Air Combat

ROBERT F. DORR

BERKLEY
CALIBER

THE BERKLEY PUBLISHING GROUP
Published by the Penguin Group
Penguin Group (USA) Inc.
375 Hudson Street, New York, New York 10014, USA
Penguin Group (Canada), 90 Eglinton Avenue East, Suite 700, Toronto, Ontario M4P 2Y3, Canada
(a division of Pearson Penguin Canada Inc.)
Penguin Books Ltd., 80 Strand, London WC2R 0RL, England
Penguin Group Ireland, 25 St. Stephen's Green, Dublin 2, Ireland (a division of Penguin Books Ltd.)
Penguin Group (Australia), 250 Camberwell Road, Camberwell, Victoria 3124, Australia
(a division of Pearson Australia Group Pty. Ltd.)
Penguin Books India Pvt. Ltd., 11 Community Centre, Panchsheel Park, New Delhi—110 017, India
Penguin Group (NZ), Cnr. Airborne and Rosedale Roads, Albany, Auckland 1310, New Zealand
(a division of Pearson New Zealand Ltd.)
Penguin Books (South Africa) (Pty.) Ltd., 24 Sturdee Avenue, Rosebank, Johannesburg 2196,
South Africa

Penguin Books Ltd., Registered Offices: 80 Strand, London WC2R 0RL, England

AIR COMBAT

This book is an original publication of The Berkley Publishing Group.

First edition: September 2006

ISBN: 0-425-21170-3

An application to register this book for cataloging has been filed with the Library of Congress.

PRINTED IN THE UNITED STATES OF AMERICA

10 9 8 7 6 5 4 3 2 1

Contents

Author's Note

These first-person accounts of American "Combat Air" pilots in battle are the result of sixty-one interviews and several flights aboard aircraft completed in 2004 and 2005. Any errors are the fault of the author. However, this book would have been impossible without the help of many.

The following Combat Air combat veterans were interviewed for this book:

Roger Ames, Gordon H. Austin, Bill Barron, William A. Bloomer, Eldon Brown, William E. "Earl" Brown, "Capt. John," George Chandler, Eugene P. Deatrick, Karl Dittmer, Rhory Draeger, Dan Druen, Curt Durocher, Arnie Franklin, Thomas C. Gill, Bill Ginn, Kelly Gross, Charles W. Hawley, Thomas L. "Tommy" Hayes, Hank Hoffman, Eugene "Mule" Holmberg, Richard Kirkland, Ron Kron, James F. Low, Hamilton "Mac" McWhorter III, Milt Moore, Joseph J. "Jay" Morrissey, Albert E. Motley Jr., Curtis C. Nelson, Jerry T. O'Brien, Gerald G. O'Rourke, Leonard Plog, Curtis Richards, Jay A. Stout, Evans G. Stephens, Harley Thompson, Charles Vasiliadis, Wayne Whitten, and Dale Zelko

The following people also provided interviews and assistance for *Air Combat*:

Bill Eaton, John Gresham, Robert A. Hadley, Timothy R. Keck, Jack Lambert, Forrest L. Marion, Norman Polmar, Roy Potter, and Norman Taylor.

I also want to thank Bill Fawcett and Tom Colgan.

Roger Ames provided his personal account of the P-38 Lightning mission to kill Japan's Admiral Yamamoto during a series of interviews in the early 1990s. The best full-length account of that extraordinary mission appears in *Lightning Strike: The Secret Mission to Kill Admiral Yamamoto and Avenge Pearl Harbor,* by Donald A. Davis (New York: Penguin Press, 2005).

Some veterans interviewed for this volume have written their own books. EF-10B Skyknight veteran Jerry T. O'Brien is the author of *Top Secret* (Anaheim, Calif.: Equidata Publishing Co., 2004), a history of Marine Corps electronic warfare squadrons. F6F Hellcat pilot Hamilton McWhorter III is co-author with Jay A. Stout of *The First Hellcat Ace* (Pacifica, Calif.: Pacifica Press, 2001).

An excellent biography of Edward H. "Butch" O'Hare is *Fateful Rendezvous* by Steve Ewing and John B. Lundstrom (Annapolis, Md: Naval Institute Press, 1997). This book's account of the November 8, 1950, air battle benefited from research provided by Roy Potter, the nephew of Capt. Eldon N. "Neil" Colby.

Robert F. Dorr
Oakton, Virginia

Chapter One

Peril Above Pearl Harbor

What Happened

At 8:00 A.M. that morning, second lieutenants George Welch and Kenneth Taylor—both new fighter pilots—were awakened at Wheeler Field, Hawaii, by exploding bombs. They raced outdoors and saw smoke rising over Pearl Harbor. Taylor telephoned the grass airstrip at Haleiwa, ten miles from Honolulu, where the 47th Fighter Squadron had been sent for target practice. He told ground crews to have two P-40B Tomahawks fueled and armed for combat. He had reached the site of the only P-40s that were not, at this instant, under Japanese attack.

A little-known sidelight of the Pearl Harbor attack is the air-to-air fighting that went on in the skies of Hawaii on December 7, 1941—most of them between P-40B Tomahawks of the Army's 47th Fighter Squadron and Mitsubishi A6M2 Zero fighters of Japan's First Air Fleet (1st Koku-Kantai). A tiny handful of Hawaiians actually heard the whine of engines and the chatter of machine guns as Tomahawks and Zeros dueled in the Sunday sky.

At Hickam Field just outside Honolulu, base commander Col. William Farthing said it was "only human ingenuity" that enabled a few Army pilots to climb aloft and engage the attackers. Farthing's boss in the islands was Lt. Gen. Walter C. Short, who expected Japanese sympathizers on Oahu to try to blow up aircraft and equipment. To cope with

Second Lieutenant George Welch
December 7, 1941
Curtiss P-40B Tomahawk
47th Fighter Squadron, 15th Fighter Group
Wheeler Field, Territory of Hawaii

2nd Lts. Kenneth Taylor (left) and George Welch were among the P-40B Tomahawk pilots of the 47th Fighter Squadron who got into the air near Pearl Harbor on December 7, 1941, and shot down Japanese aircraft.

[U.S. Army]

the anticipated sabotage, Short ordered his Army Air Forces, or AAF, commanders to park P-36s, P-40s, A-20s, and B-18s wingtip-to-wingtip on the flight lines at Hickam, Wheeler, Bellows, and other airfields. At Short's direction, the island's radar sites operated only part-time and were scheduled to shut down at 7:00 A.M., fifty-three minutes before the attack. On December 7, Farthing was in the control tower early, awaiting the arrival of a flight of B-17 Flying Fortresses from the mainland scheduled for 0600 hours. They were delayed. Farthing saw the first Japanese aircraft hit ships in the harbor before coming on to strafe the airfield.

Farthing was not in the loop when the radar technicians decided they were watching the B-17s. There were, in fact, four B-17Cs and eight B-17Es approaching, just three degrees off the heading of the Japanese warplanes. But 170 torpedo bombers, dive-bombers, and fighters also were arriving over Oahu from six Japanese aircraft carriers.

GORDON AUSTIN. If we'd known the Japanese were going to attack us that morning, I'd have been in the cockpit of a P-40 and I wouldn't have won a coin toss with my operations officer.

I wasn't at Wheeler Field on the morning of December 7, 1941, because of that coin toss, but others in my squadron got into the air and the P-40 served them well. The truth is, the P-40 we had at Pearl Harbor was a big improvement over what we were accustomed to. I would say it had a damn fine cockpit. Our models had two machine guns in the nose, firing through the prop, and they worked pretty well.

One of those pilots was George Welch. Welch was a fabulous pilot. I never saw Welch drink too much, but he loved to have a cool drink or two. And he really knew how to handle the P-40. But that gets ahead of the story.

I graduated from West Point in 1936. I was in Hawaii when they made the decision in December 1940 to double the size of the Air Corps. They told me I would take command of the 47th Pursuit Squadron, part of the 15th Pursuit Group. [Author's note: The term "Pursuit Squadron" was changed to "Fighter Squadron" on May 15, 1942].

I had two flight commanders. One of them was Capt. George S. Welch and the other was 2nd Lt. Kenneth "Ken" Taylor. They got quite famous because of their feats at Pearl Harbor. My squadron operations officer was Capt. Jim Beckwith for a while and then 1st Lt. Robert J. "Bob" Rogers, who eventually achieved the remarkable distinction of flying in combat on the first and last days of World War II.

We trained hard. During this time period in 1941, we in the fighter business at Wheeler thought that war was coming. There was a lot of training. The Navy normally simulated the attacking Japanese force. Our Army Air Corps squadrons defended Oahu.

There was an awful lot of that training. I remember we used to go round and round, our P-40s and the F4F Wildcats of the Navy, dog-fighting all over the sky. It was quite a competitive spirit between the Navy and the Air Corps. It was a good spirit. Somewhere along about this time, the eight pursuit squadrons at Wheeler Field were grouped under the 18th Pursuit Wing, commanded by Col. (later Maj. Gen.) Howard C. Davidson.

I must say that from the point of view of a young captain in the Air Corps and a squadron commander, which was a tremendous position for a young officer in those days—my God, being a captain and a squadron commander, you know, was much better than running an air force today. It was tremendous, and there was a lot of competition among the squadrons. I think the 47th Squadron was one of the best. I say so; I guess I am narrow-minded, biased, and prejudiced, but we did a lot of flying. We were well trained and we had competent people. We were ready for war.

Davidson believed that we should be dispersed around the islands.

Now, as you know, Maj. Gen. Frederick L. Martin was the Hawaiian Air Force commander and Lt. Gen. Walter C. Short was the overall Army commander. I do not know where this idea of dispersal originated, from my limited viewpoint as a squadron commander. The idea was to have each squadron have an off-base field, and I remember they built a dispersal field at Mokuleia; Haleiwa had one. There were others under construction.

The Battle of Britain was taking place and we got quite an input into the fighter business from the Royal Air Force. Somebody got information to us about radio procedures, tactical formations, what they were doing. I remember one day they decided we should all stop flying at 10,000 or 12,000 feet [3048 to 3660 meters] in P-40s. The airplane would go higher. "Let's see how high we can go," they said.

I remember this is when I first had a right ear problem. We did not know about flying at altitude. I remember I took off in a P-40 and, as I recall, got to 33,000 feet (10060 m) with a tube in my mouth, just drawing oxygen; and I came down and had an awful ear blockage.

I actually flew off a carrier in a P-40 in Hawaii because the idea was that we might have to deploy our squadrons someday. I had flown in the backseat with the Navy on their landings, and I had flown with a Navy patrol bomber.

Davidson told his subordinate commanders as a group that he had received orders to move his fighter units from all dispersal areas into Wheeler Field and to line them up. There was a danger of sabotage by the local population but no threat from without, he had been told. The words burned in my mind. "No threat from without."

Davidson said, "I don't go along with any of this. I don't think it is correct, and I have told the higher authorities that I will not make any move until I receive my orders in writing." He got the orders in writing and moved all the P-40s to Wheeler Field, to my knowledge, except for my unit, which was at Haleiwa—I was in gunnery camp—and a squadron at Bellows Field, also in gunnery camp.

We continued our training. I do not remember at that time any undue excitement about the Japanese. We all knew that war was imminent. The thought was, and I remember this clearly, that the Japanese were going into Southeast Asia. However, Davidson felt, and we all felt, that it was silly to line up the airplanes. There was no feeling on the part of any

American pilots were ecstatic when the P-40B Tomahawk arrived in the Hawaiian Islands to begin replacing older fighters. This previously unpublished photo shows P 40Bs of the 6th Pursuit Squadron, 18th Pursuit Group, from Wheeler Field over Hawaii on August 1, 1941. The term "pursuit" was changed to "fighter" in the squadron and group names soon afterward.

[U.S. Army]

---

of ourselves that there was any local threat of any consequence. Davidson got the orders in writing and carried them out.

With regard to my squadron, we flew on Saturday, December 6, 1941, and I remember after flying that day talking to Bob Rogers, my ops officer, saying, "Do you think we ought to fly on Sunday?" We could not decide. We got out a new fifty-cent piece and flipped it to see whether we would fly on December 7. It came down, "No, give the boys a day off." [Author's note: Lt. Gen. Walter C. Short, commander of Army forces in Hawaii, had already issued orders giving everyone that weekend off].

B-18 Flight

We stood the squadron down. Naturally, in retrospect, you look back and say, "Oh, my God!" But as we looked at it, there was no stated threat from without. I figured the men had been working pretty hard and maybe they needed a day off. I went back to Wheeler and got Capt. Sherwood E. Buckland, a friend of mine that was a flying officer. We got two other officers from Schofield Barracks that we knew very well from the Artillery. We had about fourteen or fifteen airmen, and we took off in a utility B-18 and went to Molokai. We went to Molokai as guests of Chung-Hoon, who had a son that went to the Naval Academy, Lt. (later Rear Adm.) Gordon P. Chung-Hoon, class of 1935. Chung-Hoon himself was a Chinese American merchant in Honolulu who knew everybody and was close to the military, and he had asked us to come over and go deer hunting.

Off we went. We had a nice evening with Chung-Hoon, and the next day we were all out early in the morning deer hunting when somebody rushed up to us and said, "The Japanese have attacked Pearl Harbor." Of course, you just cannot believe that a war starts like that. We climbed to the car and raced over to the flying field, climbed into the B-18, and took off for home. The only fix I have on the time of day was that we saw the last end of the Japanese airplanes. Otherwise, I cannot remember what time it was.

I remember flying across the channel from Molokai to Oahu, Buckland and I, and we were saying, "Boy, they sure are making this kind of realistic. We've had so many exercises over here." We heard on the radio, "This is not a drill." We just could not believe it. We said, "Well, let's keep this big buggy up under these clouds so we can get up in there if anybody comes after us because we have no guns or anything."

As we approached Pearl Harbor, it was kind of a hazy day. You could see all of the smoke coming out of Pearl Harbor, and I said to Buckland, "They sure are making this look realistic." We turned on the local radio station, and they were asking for doctors to report to the hospital, for people to remain calm. We heard all of this and were just kind of transfixed, looking at Pearl Harbor. I guess we were over Diamond Head, or approaching there, and all of a sudden we were in a sea of flak. The U.S. Navy was firing at us.

I remember my heart jumped up in my mouth. I never got scared like that in the rest of the war. I turned the control wheel on that B-18 and headed for the mountains. We got out of there, and then we called the Wheeler tower. Wheeler tower said the field had been under attack and there were live bombs and bomb craters on the field.

I said to Buckland, "We'd better get out of here and go somewhere else." He said, "No, we'd better land right here." That was a wise decision. We headed off for Wheeler. We saw a few Japanese airplanes, but they had no interest in us. They each must have had their own job to do. We must have been right on the tail end of the last attack.

Pearl Harbor was in flames, and we made a quick pattern around Wheeler and landed with the flight line ablaze. P-40s' tails were gone. They were sitting nose-up, and all were burning. I did not see any craters on the field, but there may have been some. We taxied past the tower, going in I guess an easterly direction, way off the field by the old group headquarters.

Davidson was there in his car. He said, "Austin, I think your squadron did pretty well. Get down there to Haleiwa. Buckland, you get this B-18 serviced and take it back down to Hickam Field." Buck turned to me and said, "Gee, I don't think that's a very good idea. Do you?" Anyway, I took off for Haleiwa by vehicle. My car, a beautiful 1941 Mercury sedan, was sitting down by the hangar and had been burned up and was out of commission, but I got a car—I cannot remember whose car—and got my .45 pistol from my house and took off for Haleiwa.

As I was driving down that road, hell bent for leather, coming up the road was another car. I recognized it as George Welch's, my flight commander, and I blew the horn and stopped. He stopped and asked, "Well, where have you been, Captain?" I replied, "Where have you been?" Welch said, "Well, we've been shooting down Japs. There's one right off the road here." We turned off the road and went a hundred yards, and sure enough there was a Jap plane that he had shot down with three dead in it—apparently a torpedo bomber.

What Happened

The Japanese battle plan placed great importance on neutralizing AAF airfields on Oahu—lest the Americans employ long-aircraft to shadow departing Japanese planes back to their carriers. These airfields boasted the 18th Bombardment Wing at Hickam Field, the 14th Pursuit Wing at Wheeler Field, and a gunnery training detachment at Bellows Field. The Air Force had 754 officers and 6,706 enlisted men on the islands. Its aircraft were out of date—twelve B-17D Flying Fortresses, thirty-three B-18 Bolo bombers, thirty-nine P-36A Mohawks, eighty-seven P-40Bs, and twelve P-40C Tomahawk fighters. On December 7, few of the fighters had fuel or ammunition loaded aboard. "We did not anticipate what came," said Capt. Gordon Austin, commander of the pursuit wing's 47th Pursuit Squadron.

Striking the Airfields

The Japanese may have been more worried about U.S. airfields and aircraft than they needed to be, given the poor state of U.S. preparation, but they attacked the airfields nonetheless. Japanese carrier planes swarmed down on not only Pearl Harbor but also Hickam and Wheeler Fields. The first wave of strafing runs at Wheeler and Hickam destroyed aircraft, maintenance hangars, and other structures. More were wiped out in the second wave an hour after the first. The second attack also hit Bellows Field. By the end of the day, seven hundred AAF personnel were dead and wounded, and two-thirds of the air power on Oahu was damaged or destroyed.

The only B-24A Liberator four-engine bomber within thousands of miles abruptly achieved the distinction of being the first American aircraft to be lost in World War II. First Lieutenant Ted Faulkner was readying the Liberator for a secret photo-reconnaissance mission to the Caroline Islands aimed at detecting any offensive naval movements by Japan. Aichi D3A Type 99 "Val" dive-bomber pilot Lt. Kunikiya Hira from the carrier *Shokaku*, dropped the first bomb on Hickam, hit Hangar 15, and set Faulkner's B-24A ablaze, killing two of its crew.

Arriving from the West Coast on what was supposed to be a routine flight, a dozen Flying Fortress bombers were suddenly scattered all over the skies of Oahu. A cohort of Faulkner's, 1st Lt. Frank P. Bostrom of the 7th Bombardment Group failed during several attempts to land, evaded Zeros, and put down on the Kahuku Golf Course. Bostrom would later achieve fame for carrying out the second phase of Gen. Douglas MacArthur's evacuation from the Philippines to Australia.

Forty-seventh Pursuit Squadron commander Austin later recalled that, "The odds were against any of us getting into the air that morning."

Second lieutenants George Welch and Kenneth Taylor—both new fighter pilots—were awakened at Wheeler Field by exploding bombs. They raced outdoors and saw smoke rising over Pearl Harbor. Taylor telephoned the grass airstrip at Haleiwa, ten miles from Honolulu, where the 47th had been sent for target practice. He told ground crews to have two P-40B Tomahawks fueled and armed for combat.

The two pilots were strafed while they drove at high speed to Haleiwa. They took off in two P-40Bs only partly loaded with machine-gun rounds and attacked a formation of Nakajima B5N2 "Kate" dive-bombers. Welch and Taylor each shot one down. Moments later, Welch's P-40B was hit with rounds from a Japanese tail gunner. Still, he and Taylor shot down another "Kate" apiece.

Welch and Taylor landed at Wheeler to refuel, re-arm, and take off again. Welch ultimately flew three sorties and was credited with shooting down four Japanese aircraft, including a Mitsubishi A6M2 Zero fighter. Among just half a dozen U.S. airmen who fought that day, Welch and Taylor were each awarded the Distinguished Service Cross.

Over the years, the legend has grown that Welch was recommended for the Medal of Honor but that the military squelched it because he took off without authorization. By one account, the brass wanted not to publicize its defeat at Pearl Harbor. In a contradictory version, the award was killed because a hero was needed immediately and "it would have taken too long for Congress to act."

None of this is true. Welch's bravery was real and was recognized with the nation's second highest award. But he was not nominated for the top award, and he needed no authorization to take off in his P-40B. As for shunning publicity, the military awarded Medals of Honor with much fanfare to fifteen others for Pearl Harbor. It required no act of Congress, since the executive branch gives the award. Welch went on to become a 16-kill air ace and a celebrated test pilot who lost his life in an F-100A Super Sabre in 1954.

Rasmussen's P-36
Also at Wheeler, 2nd Lt. Philip M. Rasmussen struggled with fellow pilots to arm and fuel P-36 Mohawk fighters of the 15th Pursuit Group. Rasmussen, too, had awakened abruptly and was still attired in his purple pajamas. Amid noise and chaos, he managed to get airborne in the clunky, obsolete P-36. "We climbed to nine thousand feet and spotted Val dive bombers," Rasmussen said later. "We dived to attack them."

Rasmussen, 1st Lt. Lewis M. Sanders, and two other P-36 pilots tore into a Japanese formation. Though his P-36 was slower than any of the Japanese aircraft in use that day, Sanders got behind one of the raiders and shot it down. Second Lieutenant Gordon H. Sterling Jr. also shot down a Japanese aircraft but then was shot down over water and drowned after getting out of his aircraft. Just before witnessing Sterling's death, Rasmussen charged his guns only to have them start firing on their own. While the pajama-clad pilot struggled to stop his guns from firing, a Japanese aircraft passed directly in front of him and exploded.

Shaking off two Zeros on his tail, Rasmussen got his guns under control, raked another Japanese aircraft with gunfire, then felt himself taking hits from a Japanese fighter.

"There was a lot of noise. He shot my canopy off." Rasmussen lost control of the P-36 as it tumbled into clouds, its hydraulic lines severed, the tail wheel shot off. Rasmussen did not know it yet, but two cannon shells had buried themselves in a radio behind his pilot's seat. The bulky radio had saved his life.

The 47th Squadron's 1st Lt. Bob Rogers, did not go on the Molokai trip. Rogers managed to get into the air to battle the Japanese. Both Austin and Rogers believe that if squadrons had prepared for air attack, instead of ground sabotage, most of his P-40s would have gotten into the sky. In a sidelight to Pearl Harbor, Rogers became a member of 7th Fighter Command in the Pacific and was in the air on August 15, 1945—the only American to fly on the first and last days of U.S. participation in World War II.

Hell at Hickam

First Lieutenant Annie Guyton Fox, chief nurse at Hickam Field, awakened in her quarters that morning to hear a crescendo of noise. That morning, eighty-two Army nurses were serving in the Hawaiian Islands at Tripler Army Hospital, Schofield Hospital, and—at the airfield—Hickam Station Hospital.

Second Lieutenant Monica Conter was one of those nurses. She'd been on a date with Army 2nd Lt. Barney Benning (later to be her husband of more than sixty years) that Saturday night. "We noticed that . . . there were Navy people all over the place," while at a dance at the Pearl Harbor officers club, Conter recalled. "The fleet was in. Barney and I decided to take a walk, so we went down to the harbor. It was the most beautiful sight I've ever seen, all the battleships and the lights with the reflection on the water. We were just overwhelmed."

At 7:00 A.M. on December 7, Conter reported for duty at Hickam with nurse 2nd Lt. Irene Boyd. They were the only nurses on duty. "We heard this plane. It was losing altitude. We both just stopped suddenly and stared at each other. Then—bang!"

In front of Conter's eyes, a 500-pound bomb landed on the front lawn of the hospital and didn't explode. The bomb was sixty or seventy feet from patients. Some detected what they thought was a peculiar smell and began shouting: "Gas! Gas!" Some troops at Hickam had donned gas masks.

Nurse Fox arrived and organized her team of eight nurses to assist

Smoke rises from Hickam Field, near Pearl Harbor, after the first wave of Japanese air attacks on December 7, 1941. Some of the B-17 Flying Fortresses seen here had just arrived from the United States to find themselves in the middle of a fight.

[U.S. Army]

wounded as they were brought in. Conter, Kathleen Coberly, and others improvised, provided a steadying influence, and handled more patients than they had ever expected to see. Later, Fox became the first of many Army nurses to receive the Purple Heart medal, usually given to those wounded by enemy action. Unwounded, Fox received her medal for "her fine example of calmness, courage, and leadership, which was of great benefit to the morale of all she came in contact with."

A flight surgeon who had arrived on one of the B-17 Flying Fortresses, 1st Lt. William R. Schick, sat on the stairs to the second floor of the hospital attired in winter uniform (never worn in Hawaii) and bled profusely from his head and face. Schick repeatedly refused medical care, pointing to casualties in litters on the floor and urging responders to, "Take care of them." Despite his resistance, Schick was put aboard an ambulance for Tripler—but died before arriving there.

P-36 pilot Rasmussen navigated his way to smoke-shrouded Wheeler

Field, where detonations continued to resound and airplanes burned. Rasmussen landed his P-36 without brakes, rudder, or tail wheel, and with dozens of bullet holes in the rear fuselage. There was no other aircraft available, so Rasmussen's day was over.

A second wave of Japanese air attacks came swarming down on Oahu while American pilots took off individually from two different airfields, sometimes joining up after getting airborne. Welch took off on his second P-40B sortie while Taylor waited until what he thought was the last in a line of Japanese aircraft passed overhead, then took off again in a P-40B, seeking to get them in his gunsight.

Welch spotted a Zero locking onto Taylor's tail. He maneuvered behind the Zero, fired short bursts, and racked up his third kill of the day. Subsequently, Welch flew to Ewa, found a lone Japanese aircraft, and shot down his fourth for the day.

Over at Bellows Field, 1st Lt. Samuel W. Bishop and 2nd Lt. George A. Whiteman attempted to take off in another pair of P-40Bs. Bishop got aloft, but Zeros swarmed over him and he went down in the ocean. Whiteman was hit as he cleared the ground and went down in his aircraft off the end of the runway. Bishop was only wounded and swam ashore, but he eventually lost his life.

Six other pilots got aloft from Wheeler in P-36s and P-40s. Second Lieutenant John Dains ended up flying three sorties, two in a P-40B and one in a P-36, and apparently shot down a Zero that was observed falling from the sky by AAF radar operators at Kaaawa. This aerial victory cannot be linked to any other pilot in the air that day, but it is unclear whether Dains was on the scene shortly before he (Dains) was shot down and killed by U.S. antiaircraft fire. First Lieutenant Harry Brown apparently scored the last confirmed kill of the day when he shot down a Zero as it headed out to sea. The second and final wave of the attack was over.

At Hickam, A-20A Havoc attack bombers of the 58th Bombardment Squadron had been battered and burned by Japanese strafing and bombing. As the second wave of Japanese aircraft retired, the 58th went aloft to search for and attack a Japanese carrier reported (incorrectly) to be south of Barbers Point on Oahu. At 11:27 A.M., after bombs and fuel had been loaded with great difficulty, Major William Holzapfel led four A-20As into the air. But it was too late.

The Pearl Harbor attack killed 2,403 people, most of them Ameri-

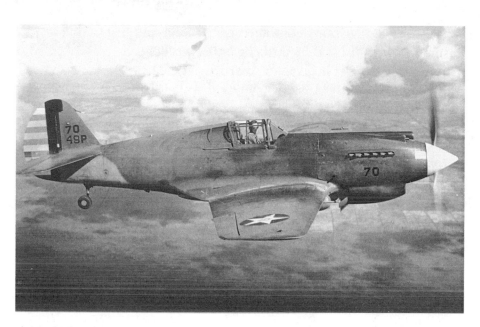

The P-40B Tomahawk seemed like an advanced fighter to the Americans who flew it at Pearl Harbor. They quickly learned, however, that they would have to coax the very best performance out of a P-40 in order to cope with the Japanese Zero, the Mitsubishi A6M2.

[U.S. Army]

can servicemen, and wounded 1,104. The Japanese conceded the loss of twenty-nine aircraft, of which the AAF downed ten (including six by Taylor and Welch). Casualties would surely have been higher but for the initiative of doctors and nurses who improvised on the scene.

GORDON AUSTIN. George Welch was killed many years later test-flying the F-100 Super Sabre. Several of the boys had gotten airborne and had done some good individually. The Japs had not hit Haleiwa. There had not been any organized flying. When we got there, our control center was beginning to get into operation. We really thought the Japs were around, as I recall, for about two days before we recognized that they were gone. Still on December 7, we organized a flight and got fifteen airplanes airborne. Again—it is hard to grasp time—it seems to me that it was about ten o'clock in the morning. We climbed into our P-40s and took off for the Japanese fleet, which was supposed to be in the Kauai Straights. That was to the northwest toward Kauai.

Who's Who

Capt. (later, Maj. Gen.) Gordon Austin, P-40 Tomahawk pilot and commander, 47th Pursuit Squadron

1st Lt. (later, Col.) Robert J. "Bob" Rogers, P-40 Tomahawk pilot and operations officer, 47th Pursuit Squadron

2nd Lt. George S. Welch, P-40 Tomahawk pilot and flight leader, 47th Pursuit Squadron

2nd Lt. (later Brig. Gen.) Kenneth Taylor, P-40 Tomahawk pilot and flight leader, 47th Pursuit Squadron

We went out around the Kauai Straits and flew all over the place and never saw anything. We attracted a lot of ground fire from the infantry at Schofield. We came back and landed. We had one boy shot down, named Dains, by our own ground fire. Over the next couple of days we flew a good deal, but we never found anything. The Japs had gone.

Curtiss P-40B/C Tomahawk

They cursed it. They vilified it. The P-40 fighter came from the company founded by aviation pioneer Glenn Curtiss and named, also, for the Wright brothers, but despite the distinguished pairing of names at the Curtiss-Wright Corporation the aircraft was controversial. It was actually a division of a larger corporation, the Curtiss Airplane and Motor Company, of Buffalo, New York, that developed the P-40 for the Army Air Corps, and there were very smart aircraft designers in Buffalo, but many regarded the P-40 as obsolescent before it ever flew, and even Capitol Hill lawmakers raised questions about it.

Most aircraft are given a popular name. The P-40 received three. It was the Tomahawk (P-40B, P-40C); the Kittyhawk (P-40E); and the Warhawk (P-40F). In later years, after it was forgotten that the P-40 was the most numerous American fighter at the time of Pearl Harbor, it became fashionable to go back and criticize the P-40, especially when comparing it to Japan's Mitsubishi A6M Zero fighter. But the mere fact that the P-40 remained in production until 1944 and that 13,378 were built (as compared to 10,037 P-38 Lightnings, 9,529 P-39 Airacobras) is testimony that, early in the war at least, the P-40 was exactly what Capt. Gordon Austin called it—a damn good airplane.

Earlier Curtiss fighters, including the P-36 Mohawk—also in attendance at Pearl Harbor—were powered by radial engines that created significant aerodynamic "drag." In the late 1930s, Curtiss's general manager Burdette "Birdy" Wright (no relation to the Wright brothers) and its top fighter designer Don Berlin were both impressed by fighters being built in other countries that used in-line, or liquid-cooled engines, among them the British Spitfire and the German Messerschmitt Bf 109. Berlin wanted to try one of his basic fighter designs with an in-line engine, the Allison V-1710.

Curtiss installed the V-1710-19/C-13 engine on a P-36 and it became the XP-40, the very first fighter in a long series of Tomahawks, Kittyhawks, and Warhawks. Curtiss delivered the plane to the Army Air Corps in October 1938. Test pilot Edward Elliott took the aircraft aloft for its first flight on October 14. Two days later, the first plane was flown to Wright Field, Ohio, the Army's flight test center. An evaluation of the XP-40 was encouraging enough that in April 1939, the War Department announced a contract for 524 production P-40 fighters at a price of $ 22,929 each. The manufacturer moved quickly and the first production P-40 Tomahawk was flown on April 4, 1940, with test pilot Lloyd Child at the controls.

The P-40 may not have been in the same category as the Spitfire, Bf 109, or Japanese Mitsubishi A6M Zero, but there was plenty of interest in it. France ordered 140 export models. After the French collapse in June 1940, Britain's Royal Air Force took delivery of many. Britain eventually acquired more than a thousand P-40s. Many fought in North Africa, initially with the RAF's No. 112 Squadron in Sidi Heneish, Morocco, in October 1941.

Plentiful P-40

Curtiss continued to turn out P-40Bs and P-40Cs in Buffalo. In September 1940, the Army ordered the slightly improved P-40D model. Some P-40Bs and P-40Cs began reaching Hawaii in 1940, and a few were able to get into the air during the December 7, 1941, Pearl Harbor attack. When the Japanese struck the Philippines six hours later, where it was December 8 west of the international dateline, there were 107 P-40s and

P-40Bs on duty, but such was the measure of surprise achieved that only four got airborne. "We are doomed at the start," wrote P-40B pilot Max Louk in a letter to his mother a few days before the attack. He became the first American pilot to die in the Philippines when his P-40B ground-looped during a response to an air raid. Within four days, the number of P-40s in the Philippines (operated by the 20th and 34th Pursuit Squadrons) plummeted to twenty-two.

By then, about a hundred export versions of the P-40 had been diverted to Burma for service with the American Volunteer Group, the Flying Tigers. The group, headed by Brig. Gen. Claire Chennault in China and Burma in 1941, provided a success story for Americans at a time when the war was going poorly.

One of the men who became an air ace with the AVG, David Lee "Tex" Hill, claims that Japanese fighters were consistently overestimated and the P-40 too often belittled by those who did not understand it well enough. "You never wanted to dive with a Japanese fighter because he would claw his way up your butt and kill you every time," Hill said. "But at low and medium altitude, especially, the P-40 was as maneuverable as any Jap. And our aircraft were built with armor, self-sealing fuel tanks, and other protections for the pilot that Japanese fliers didn't have."

The Flying Tiger saga began when a freighter unloaded one hundred civilian P-40 equivalents at Rangoon, Burma, in August 1941. In September 1941, Chennault's AVG group of one hundred pilots arrived with promises of $600 per month and a bonus of $500 for every Japanese aircraft destroyed. The first air battle by the Flying Tigers occurred on December 20, 1941 (two weeks after Pearl Harbor), when P-40s flying out of Kunming, China, shot down six enemy planes. On Christmas Day 1941, Duke Hedman became an ace by claiming his fifth victory while he and eighteen buddies flying P-40s, characterized by a shark's mouth painted at the intake, shot down a third of an enemy formation without losing a single aircraft. Gregory "Pappy" Boyington was another of the famous aces who flew along with Hill and others in the Tigers.

It should be emphasized that the Flying Tigers never encountered Japan's best fighter, the Zero. They battled obsolescent fighters, plus the state-of-the-art Nakajima Ki-44, known to Americans as an Oscar. So what did they accomplish? The Flying Tigers' top ace, Bob Neale, was credited with 15.50 aerial victories, closely followed by Tex Hill with

2nd Lts. George Welch (left) and Kenneth Taylor, wearing World War I–style pith helmets and carrying gas masks, are honored at an awards ceremony at Hickam Field near Pearl Harbor, shortly after December 7, 1941. The date of the photo is January 9, 1942.

[U.S. Army]

12.25. Seven more pilots were double aces with ten victories or more. Two pilots—Jim Howard and Greg Boyington—used their AVG experience to earn the Medal of Honor in combat actions that took place after their AVG commitment. The AVG probably shot down 115 Japanese aircraft, not the 286 claimed, against a loss of seventy-eight pursuit ships to all causes. But the numbers are misleading. Using the P-40 with extraordinary skill, the Tigers gave Americans hope.

Progress on the aircraft design continued. With the P-40D model, improvements to the Allison engine enabled the nose to be shortened and the radiator deepened, resulting in the definitive shape for this classic combat machine. Fuselage guns carried by the earlier variants were discarded, and armament of six "fifties" in the wings became standard. The RAF had ordered 560 of these improved fighters in 1940, and they were called Kittyhawk Is. The U.S. Army applied the better-known appellation Warhawk to subsequent P-40 versions.

The first American overseas unit of P-40s in the Atlantic was the 33rd Pursuit Squadron, which was sent to Iceland on July 25, 1941 (all AAF units switched from "pursuit" to "fighter" nomenclature soon afterward). P-40s joined the European war in April 1942, flying out of bases in England until being gradually phased out by next-generation fighters in 1943 and 1944. In Europe, American P-40s destroyed 520 enemy aircraft while losing 553 to all causes—not a bad record for an aircraft always considered inferior to the Luftwaffe's best.

The British-designed Rolls-Royce Merlin 28 engine—also liquid-cooled, but in respects a giant leap ahead of the Allison—went into production in the United States in 1941 (built by Packard as the V-1650) and gave rise to the P-40F variant. Most of the Merlin-powered P-40s were exported to the Soviet Union, the U.S. Army, and the Free French.

Most P-40Fs had a lengthened fuselage that improved directional stability. Subsequent models had a dorsal fin. They reverted to the Allison engine because the much-in-demand Merlin engines (which powered 1,311 P-40s) were going into a new fighter, the P-51B Mustang.

Curtiss P-40B Tomahawk

Type: single-seat fighter

Power plant: one 1,150-hp (860 kW) Allison V-1710-33 Vee inline pistol engine

Performance: maximum speed, 362 mph (580 km/h) at 15,000 ft (4572 m); initial rate of climb, 3,080 ft (938 m) per min; climb to 15,000 ft (4572 m) in 5.2 min

Weights: empty, 5,812 lb (2636 kg); gross weight, 7,459 lb (3378 kg); maximum loaded weight, 8058 lb (3655 kg)

Dimensions: wingspan, 37 ft 3.5 in (11.40 m); length 31 ft 8.5 in (9.54 m); height 12 ft 4 in (3.77 m); wing area, 236 sq ft (21.95 sq m)

Armament: two .50 caliber (12.7-mm) machine guns, with 380 rounds each, mounted in the upper nose and synchronized to fire through the propeller arc; four .30 caliber (7.62-mm) machine guns in each wing with 490 rounds each

First flight: October 1938 (XP-40); April 4, 1940 (P-40); April 10, 1941 (P-40C)

Further developments of this basic design, culminating in the P-40N (4,219 built), were devoted to reducing weight and improving performance, but the whole P-40 family remained fundamentally outclassed by other frontline fighters on both sides. A handful of P-40Ns introduced every weight-saving measure Curtiss could think of, and were quite fast, but still they were outperformed by other fighters.

Experimental versions of the P-40 included the P-40G, which evaluated the six-gun armament, the XP-40K with lightweight features, and the XP-40Q with clipped wing tips and bubble canopy. A few aircraft were converted to TP-40N two-seat trainers.

Chapter Two

Airacobra over the Islands

What Happened

The P-39 Airacobra may have been the least-loved fighter ever flown by American combat pilots. Most flew the P-39 only in training, disliked its quirky traits, and had humiliating experiences. Just ask Bones Marshall, who was trying to begin a routine training flight and couldn't unlock his nose wheel. Marshall once called the P-39 "my own worst enemy."

Evans G. Stephens flew the P-39 in the Louisiana war games before the United States entered World War II and flew it again in difficult fighting in the steamy South Pacific, at a time when Americans were desperate to stave off disaster. Later in his career, Stephens had the distinction of being the U.S. flight leader during history's first battle between jet aircraft. Still later, he flew one of the largest and fastest jet fighters ever built. Every airplane he flew later was better appreciated than the P-39, better performing, and better known. Still, after it was all over, after the twenty-first century had arrived, when it became time to choose an e-mail address for himself, Stephens picked one with a reference to the P-39 in it.

"Yes, I know," said Stephens. "It's the only American fighter that doesn't have a veteran's association. It's the only American fighter that doesn't have a fan club. But . . ."

Second Lieutenant Evans G. Stephens
1942
Bell P-39 Airacobra
40th Fighter Squadron, 35th Fighter Group
Seven Mile Airdrome, New Guinea

2nd Lt. Evans G. Stephens, known as Grant, a P-39 Airacobra pilot in the South Pacific, wearing tropical shorts, web belt, and the fleece-lined Australian boots that wouldn't stay attached during a bailout. Stephens battled the quirks of the P-39, the Japanese, and malaria. In later years, Stephens flew the F-80 Shooting Star.

[Evans G. Stephens]

BONES MARSHALL. One of my greatest embarrassments happened at a training base in the P-39 Airacobra, before I ever reached a combat zone. I was number one for takeoff, on my first gunnery-training mission at Foster Army Air Field, Victoria, Texas. The date was February 15, 1944. My flight was waiting to take off, for a gunnery mission, over the Matagorda Peninsula Gunnery Range, Texas. I was all set to ram the throttle forward and lift my tricycle-gear P-39 off the runway and into the air.

But I wasn't going anywhere because the nose wheel of my P-39 was cocked, 90 degrees to the right. When I increased power to try to straighten out the nose wheel, I just went around and around. It must have looked pathetic to anyone who was watching. Finally, the tower control officer told me to stop and shut my engine down, out of the way of the other taxiing airplanes behind me.

You have to remember. I was new at this. Any tricycle-landing-gear pilot knows how to correct a cocked nose wheel, by increasing power slightly and lightly tapping the opposite brake pedal, until the nose wheel is pointed straight ahead again. Any tricycle-landing-gear pilot except me, that is.

I didn't know anything about the P-39 because I had never attended

Seen on the prowl from above, the P-39 Airacobra looked like a fast, potent war machine. In fact, the Airacobra received mixed reviews from American fighter pilots. It performed well at low altitudes, but could not out-fight its adversaries when higher up. Most American fighter pilots encountered the Airacobra only in training, but some flew it in combat in the Aleutians, New Guinea, and Guadalcanal.

[U.S. Army]

P-39 ground school nor flown the Bell Airacobra before. So here I was, in position for takeoff, with my engine shut down, waiting for my P-39 crew chief friend to come out with a tug to tow me back to the parking ramp.

I was a fighter pilot, having graduated from the Army Air Force's Single Engine (Fighter) Advanced Training Course at Yuma, Arizona, in April 1943. World War II was in full force. We had ten Royal Air Force Battle of Britain pilots as our instructors. We were so pumped up on going to the war in Europe, that we had the insignias of various fighter organizations in Europe posted on our bulletin board. Each evening after flying, we would recommit ourselves to our favorite fighter group by signing our names on that group's list. What dreamers we were, believing that a signature was all that was needed to be assigned to any particular fighter organization in Europe. My personal dream was to fly the P-38 Lightning.

As it turned out, I flew the P-39 rather than the P-38, and I went to Las Vegas rather than to Europe. We'll get back to my experiences. First, it's important to remember that guys were flying and fighting in the Airacobra early in the U.S. involvement in the war.

"Pacemaker of Aviation Progress" was the name Larry Bell's maturing aircraft company in Buffalo, New York, called itself. The commercial message of the Bell Aircraft Co. was that flying a P-39 would assure excitement and victory. One ad told of ". . . the staccato bark of guns. A cannon's cough pierces the rhythmic whine of screaming motors. There's a flash of flame." Blissfully oblivious to the superior fighters being developed by Germany and Japan, a Bell ad proclaimed that the Airacobra "always wins."

Decades later, A. M. "Tex" Johnston, Bell's chief test pilot, would say that the Airacobra "deserved to be considered a top-class fighter" and "was underrated."

None of the praise prevented pilots from berating and defaming the hapless Airacobra, which perhaps can lay claim to being the "least liked" American fighter of World War II.

Tommy Hayes, a pilot at Hamilton Field, California (Chapter 4) hated the plane's flying characteristics but loved its wide-track, tricycle landing gear. So instead of thinking about shooting down Messerschmitts or Zeros, he fantasized about driving a P-39 down the highway all the way from Tonopah to Los Angeles and using its 37-mm nose cannon to stick up a grocery store. Another pilot who didn't like the Airacobra was Kelly Gross, who, like Hayes (and myself, one war later) became an ace.

KELLY GROSS. You do not want to hear about my experience with the P-39 Airacobra at Hamilton Field. The first pilot I ever saw take off in an Airacobra was the commander of the 353rd Fighter Squadron. He was killed in a crash ten minutes later. He spun in. The P-39 had a different center of gravity with that engine in the back, and you had to accustom yourself to it.

We joked about navigation. "How do you find the field?" a new guy would ask. "You look for the column of smoke, and it'll be at the end of the runway," was the answer.

About the only good thing I can say about the P-39 is that it fought well at lower altitudes, as we learned when we occasionally jousted with Navy fighters. Below 5,000 feet we could handle the F4F Wildcat and the F4U Corsair, but we didn't care too much to fight them at high altitude.

BONES MARSHALL. When a British pilot first flew a P-39C on July 6, 1941, he proclaimed himself "dismayed" by the 359-mph (578 km/h) top speed, even though this compared to the speed of many fighters at the time.

To most pilots, the P-39 was a promising fighter that would have been the best had it been equipped to fly and fight at higher altitude. Some say that even if its altitude capability had been enhanced, the P-39 was hindered by its fundamental design and offered almost no potential for further development.

There was no practical way to squeeze more range or greater speed out of the basic airframe. The electrical system was flawed. The long extension connecting the engine with the propeller created too many problems for which a solution was never likely to come. Many pilots questioned why the Army purchased the aircraft. Even more, they wondered why the Army purchased nine thousand of them.

The P-39 Airacobra was on the scene when the 54th Fighter Group confronted Japan's invasion of the Aleutians in June 1942. P-39 pilots escorted bombers and tangled with Japanese floatplanes, Nakajima-built Mitsubishi A6M2N, based on the famous Zero and known as "Rufes." American P-39 pilots were credited with shooting down thirty-nine Japanese aircraft before the Airacobras were withdrawn at the end of 1942.

The P-39 also made a relatively brief appearance in Europe before being replaced with other fighters. In the Mediterranean, Airacobras of the 350th Fighter Group enjoyed modest successes against the Luftwaffe.

At embattled Henderson Field on Guadalcanal, P-39D-2s and repossessed P-400s (export Airacobras) fought Japan's best, including the Mitsubishi A6M Zero. First Lieutenant Wallace L. Dinn Jr. of the 58th Fighter Group pioneered the use of the Airacobra as a dive-bomber to attack Japanese shipping. Col. Charles Falletta, who ultimately downed sixteen Japanese aircraft, scored six victories in the P-39. In the Airacobra's last action at Guadalcanal on June 17, 1943, Capt. William D.

Wells led Airacobras into a formation of thirty to thirty-five Aichi D3A Type 99 "Val" carrier bombers and shot down four.

EVANS G. STEPHENS. I was in the 40th Fighter Squadron, the "Red Devils." I was one of the first dozen officers who went to Selfridge Field, Michigan, in July 1941, six months before Pearl Harbor, to begin flying the Airacobra. At first, the 40th squadron had just a single P-39D for checkout of new pilots, though others began to arrive quickly. The squadron also had BT-14, PT-17, and AT-6 trainers.

Once the Airacobras arrived, we began to move around. During the first week of September 1941, the 40th moved to Jackson, Mississippi, for the famous Louisiana maneuvers. On the first of October, we were at Bolling Field in Washington, D.C. On October 17, we moved to Augusta, Georgia, and on November 16 to Pope Field, North Carolina—all part of the war games that were taking place all over the South.

While at Bolling Field, we flew low sweeps over the nation's capital to test the accuracy of civilian air observers charged with reporting the movements of aircraft to message filter centers. This was part of the air defense system of the period. Operating from grass parking areas at Bolling, our P-39D Airacobras also responded to simulated bombing raids, receiving credit for shooting down thirty attacking bombers. The *Washington Times-Herald* called our fighters "lethal as lightning and swift as thought."

Still participating in the massive war games of the fall of 1941, our 40th squadron Airacobras continued south, where poor weather stranded several pilots at the Knoxville, Tennessee Municipal Airport. Our brief stop coincided with a visit by Army Air Forces boss Maj. Gen. Henry H. "Hap" Arnold, who chatted with us. I don't remember much about Arnold, who went on to become the great air power leader of World War II, but our attitude toward Arnold was reported this way in the *Knoxville News-Sentinel*: "It was easy to tell that they knew about him [and] worshipped him."

On October 18, 1941 the *Augusta Herald* headlined TWENTY ARMY FIGHTERS ARRIVE HERE FOR MANEUVERS. The news story noted that "pilots, all commissioned officers averaging only 23 years of age" were "flying the new Bell Airacobra interceptor planes, the Army's fastest and deadliest fighting ships."

Twenty-three-year-old 1st Lt. Fred Dean, commander of the 40th, was depicted emerging from the car-style door of his P-39D at Augusta's Daniel Field, looking remarkably innocent when we consider what awaited us just a few months in the future. When *Herald* shutterbug Frank Christian went up in a C-47 to photograph Airacobras flying over the Augusta canal, the newspaper reported that the fighters were "protecting Augusta."

Lt. Gen. D.C. Emmons, the boss of the maneuvers, dropped in at Daniel Field to watch our Airacobras perform. Emmons and his entourage watched as Dean led us aloft to intercept a mock enemy threat. Soon afterward, however, a pair of B-17 Flying Fortresses participating in the war game managed to bomb Augusta "heavily" while we were patrolling elsewhere. A couple of days later, a miserable tropical storm in the region saved Augusta from further simulated bombing, taking our job away from us.

Once the war games ended, it was time to move on. While the maneuvers were taking place, a new airfield was being made ready for us at Fort Wayne, Indiana. The 40th squadron arrived there on December 6, 1941. The location was Baer Field. That Saturday was the last time Americans would know peace for a long while to come.

Once the attack on Pearl Harbor came, we knew we had the real thing ahead of us.

There were no P-39s at Pearl Harbor when the Japanese attacked on December 7, 1941. A handful of P-36 Mohawks and P-40 Tomahawks managed to get into the air to battle the Japanese attackers. Army 2nd Lieutenants Kenneth Taylor and George Welch (Chapter 1) managed to engage the Japanese in a pair of P-40s. Welch scored four aerial victories. Both men would fly P-39s in the South Pacific later.

The outbreak of war caused many sudden uprootings. At Fort Wayne, there was much confusion. We were ordered to proceed to Port Angeles, Washington. The air contingent with twenty-three P-39s departed on December 8 and arrived at Port Angeles on December 25. The trip was a saga involving weather, mishaps, and lack of experience.

It took us a long time to get our P-39 Airacobras from the eastern United States to the war in the Pacific. Our arrival at Port Angeles was spectacular, with the 40th squadron in close formation at low altitude, buzzing the town at about 11:00 A.M. when many of the people were at church. Some thought a Japanese invasion of the Pacific Northwest had begun.

While at Port Angeles, the 40th was billeted at the county fairgrounds adjacent to the airfield. We flew submarine patrols. We hit some redwood logs with gunfire. This was the first time that most of our pilots had fired a gun in the air. We didn't find any subs.

Pacific Bound

In early 1942, rumors abounded of Japanese aircraft carriers off the west coast, with invasion forces ready to come ashore. We were torn between defending against a phantom enemy at home and preparing for combat abroad.

During the first week of January 1942, commanding officer Fred Dean, now a captain, and his second in command, 1st Lt. S. M. Smith, divided the squadron in half on paper. Then, Smith's half was selected to go to the Pacific area. On January 18, 1941, the squadron's supply and maintenance officers were sent to the San Francisco port of embarkation to obtain equipment and supplies to bring our "half squadron" up to full mobility.

We left San Francisco the first week in February and arrived in Australia the first week in March. Upon arrival at Brisbane, the squadron was put in tents on the Ascot Race Track for the first night. Our maintenance personnel went to Royal Australian Air Force Station Ipswich to put out aircraft wings back on and flight-test each P-39 to make it combat ready. Each Airacobra was in several pieces when they unloaded it from the ship, and each had to be put back together by hand. On March 17, 1942, we left for Mt. Gambier and gunnery training.

On April 20, 1942, the 39th, 40th, and 41st squadrons became part of the 35th Fighter Group. In addition to the P-39 Airacobra, we had the P-400 Airacobra, which was an export model with a 20-mm cannon instead of a 37-mm gun. We took P-39s and P-400s to New Guinea.

In that island's steaming jungles, we came face-to-face with problems that were alien to most Americans. We were flying in a location where Americans had never served. The few available maps were so riddled with inaccuracies that they were virtually useless. Intelligence reports were so wildly inaccurate that we did not know what we would be facing; rumors ran rife. And, of course, we faced Japanese warplanes with reputations that made them seem invincible.

Our new home on New Guinea was an airfield called Seven Mile. It was pretty primitive. For food, we were under Australian rations. My main meal was bread, peanut butter, jelly, and cheese. The bread was made from flour out of an old bakery at Port Moresby and had weevils in it. You would remove the weevil and eat the bread. We flew with Australian flying boots, which were fleece-lined and very comfortable.

That practice didn't last long. One of our P-39 pilots, named Hall, was shot down over the jungle and had to bail out. He was descending in his parachute, his legs flailing, when those boots came off and vanished. We learned later that the boots just wouldn't stay attached to your feet if you encountered any sort of problem. Hall spent ten days walking out of the jungle, and he was barefoot the whole time.

Because of the heat, we flew in shorts and short-sleeved shirt. I liked flying the P-39 but always kept in mind that it would not be a match for the Japanese Zero in a fair fight.

A well-known air ace, Lt. Col. Boyd D. "Buzz" Wagner, who had fought the Japanese in P-40s in the Philippines on December 8, 1941, came down and flew with our squadron. Wagner went from first lieutenant to lieutenant colonel in just five months during those difficult early days of the war in the Pacific. He had a reputation for being a hot, aggressive pilot. They made him chief of fighter aviation in New Guinea and although he had not previously flown the P-39 in combat, he came down to join us and shot down three Japanese fighters in a single action, bringing his total number of aerial victories to eight. At that point, using a P-39 to shoot down a Zero was almost unheard of.

Initially, we were the only American fighters in the area. We flew some escort, which was very questionable, since it wasn't clear how we were going to react if fighters intercepted the bombers we were escorting. I was one of the first in the squadron to come down with malaria, but I kept flying, escorting B-24 Liberators toward Lae. We also did quite a bit of strafing. We went and strafed Buna. When the Japanese were coming toward the Owen Stanley Range, we tried to knock out some bridges, but with not much success. It was mostly escort to start with, and later on some strafing. No one seriously expected the P-39 to excel in air-to-air combat.

Still on New Guinea, we moved to a strip we called Silly Silly across the valley from Lae. We had some success knocking down Japanese bombers. I encountered them on only one mission: We scrambled four P-39s and engaged them way over on the other side of New Guinea. We made four passes at them. We shot at them. I had a bomber in my gunsight and the rounds were pouring out, but there was no apparent damage.

Airacobra Quirks

The old 37-mm cannon on the Airacobra was not too reliable. It would jam quite often. A shell casing would fly loose and jam up the whole works.

I personally did not contribute a lot, partly because of the malaria and partly because the P-39 wasn't fully up to the job. Our sister squadron, the 39th, which was called the "Cobras" because they'd been first to operate the P-39 Airacobra, switched to the incomparable P-38 Lightning and began shooting down Zeros left and right. The squadron commander, Lt. Col. Tom Lynch, shot down three Japanese aircraft while flying the P-39 but raised his total number of aerial victories to twenty after they converted to the P-38.

The malaria took me from a normal weight of 165 down to 124 pounds. In October 1943, they withdrew me from the 40th squadron, while the unit was still equipped with P-39s. I was assigned to group headquarters. When I was with the 40th, there was no set max on total combat or hours flown. You did the job at hand as long as you could. I think I had about five hundred P-39 hours, most in combat.

Later in the war, I flew fighters with a training unit in Santa Rosa, California. During the Korean War, I commanded the 16th Fighter Interceptor Squadron and was the flight leader in November 1950, during history's first battle between jet fighters—the American F-80 Shooting Star and the Soviet MiG-15.

ROBERT F. DORR. While the 40th Fighter Squadron (and others) battled the Japanese on New Guinea, the 70th Fighter Squadron (and others) fought under similarly grueling circumstances on Guadalcanal. There, a hard-fighting pilot who sometimes seemed to be everywhere at once—2nd Lt. William F. Fiedler—racked up a unique record of achievement. On January 26, 1943, flying a P-39D Airacobra of the 70th Fighter Squadron, 347th Fighter Group, he shot down a Zero over Wagana Island. It was the beginning of a remarkable fighting streak that would claim a remarkable record.

In February 1943, twenty-two Japanese destroyers speeded down the "slot" near Guadalcanal with twenty-five Zeros flying cover. The plan was to evacuate exhausted Japanese troops from Guadalcanal. Led by Capt. James Robinson, the 70th squadron intercepted the Japanese in late afternoon, two hundred miles (320 km) just north of Kolombangara. Fiedler shot down a Zero in the fight. It was his second kill.

Transferred to the 68th Fighter Squadron, Fiedler was in the air again on June 12, 1943, when fifty Zeros made a sweep toward the Russell Islands, and the Americans managed to get an impressive ninety fighters into the air. The American side claimed thirty-one aerial victories, and one of them was a Zero bagged by Fiedler ten miles (16 km) from Cape Esperance—his third victory.

Four days later, an Australian coast watcher on Vella Lavella radioed that thirty-eight Zeros followed by another thirty Zeros escorting fifty Aichi D3A Type 99 "Val" dive-bombers were on their way at noon from the northwest to attack U.S. Navy transports off Guadalcanal. This was a remarkably strong Japanese bid, and the transports were virtually naked to attack.

Six P-39s of the 68th squadron were the last aircraft to take off. They had been held in reserve to meet a threat to the transports, which had now materialized. Fiedler shot down two "Vals," the second with his 37-mm nose cannon inoperable, using only his four small .30 caliber (7.62-mm) wing guns. Altogether, American fighter pilots claimed ninety-seven Japanese aircraft, against a loss of five friendly aircraft. Only a barge and a merchant ship were lost. As happened on both sides throughout the war, these claims later turned out to be exaggerated, but it was a stunning victory and one to feel good about.

William F. Fiedler went into the history books as the only American air ace to rack up five aerial victories in the P-39 Airacobra. It is unclear how much time he had to enjoy the unique status he still holds today in the annals of Air Force history. Sadly, Fiedler was killed two weeks later on June 30, 1943, when his Airacobra was hit by a P-38 Lightning while waiting to take off. No photo of Fiedler is known to have survived.

Another successful Airacobra pilot was 1st Lt. George S. Welch, who had shot down four Japanese aircraft at Pearl Harbor while flying a P-40, and who would become a North American test pilot after the war. On December 7, 1942, exactly one year after he made his combat debut in Hawaii, Welch was leading a flight of four P-39s when they encountered a formation of "Val" dive-bombers that were in the process of attacking

Even on the ground, the P-39 had clear lines. With a supercharger and a more powerful engine, the P-39 would have been a formidable rival to Japan's Mitsubishi A6M Zero fighter. Main armament on the P-39 was a cannon protruding through the propeller hub.

[Robert A. Hadley]

---

the station at Buna. As he was lining up for the attack, he spotted a Zero coming off a strafing pass and dove on it from 4,000 feet (1219 m). He chased the Zero for ten miles (16 km) and finally shot it down.

Welch had the initiative. Next, he climbed to 5,000 feet (1524 m) and latched on to one of the "Vals" and shot it down. Then he went after another "Val" and sent it splashing to the sea. Welch finished the war as a 16-kill triple ace, but this feat of downing three dive-bombers in one engagement may have been a record for the Airacobra.

BONES MARSHALL. After I pinned on my wings in April 1943, I was assigned to the 326th Gunnery Training Command at the Las Vegas Army Air Field, Nevada. That's known today as Nellis Air Force Base. I was supposed to be a fighter pilot but, initially, there were no fighters to fly. The mission of the 326th was to train B-17 Flying Fortress crews in flexible gunnery.

P-39 Airacobra pilot 1st Lt. Winton W. "Bones" Marshall at the Club Atlas in Panama in 1945. (Left to right): Capt. Schmidt, Marshall, Lt. Arnold E. Olson of Minot, North Dakota, and Lt. "Frenchie" Beaudine. Schmidt, Marshall, Olson, and Beaudine had driven eighty miles from the 28th Fighter Squadron base at Chame, Panama, for a scheduled three-day R&R in Panama City. They were guarding the Panama Canal, but the war in the Pacific was going on without them.

[Winton W. Marshall]

My first job was to fly these B-17 gunners in the backseat of an open cockpit in the AT-6 Texan and make runs at a towed banner target, so the gunner could fire at the target with his .50 caliber machine gun. If he was a good guy, I would fly as close as I could to the target and let him hose away for a good score. If he was a smartass, he never saw the target. I would have him hanging by his shoulder straps, in his open cockpit as I flew upside down, did loops and rolls—pretending my AT-6 was a fighter—then made him clean out the rear cockpit, of his own vomit, after we had landed.

I wrote a letter every other week, requesting combat duty in any theater. But the Training Command wouldn't turn me loose. So it was a happy day when I was told that our base was to be equipped with the P-39 Airacobra.

There was more good news. I was selected to attend a fighter gunnery course at Foster Field, Texas, in February 1944. The base was located on an island in the Gulf of Mexico.

After reporting, I was instructed to fill out a personnel form and to indicate the type of aircraft I was qualified in. I was faced with a dilemma. Listed on the sheet were the P-38 Lightning, P-39 Airacobra, P-40 Warhawk, P-47 Thunderbolt, P-51 Mustang, and the goddamn AT-6 Texan. I bit the bullet and said to myself that I would be damned if I would sign up for the AT-6, which was only a training aircraft. After all, I theorized, I was going to go to P-39 school and we would soon be equipped with P-39s, so I signed the form saying, yes, indeed, I was a qualified P-39 pilot.

Before going to bed, we were told to check the schedule board for the next day's flight activities. My God! I was scheduled to fly the P-39 on tomorrow morning's gunnery familiarization mission. I had not yet, ever touched a P-39 nor sat on the lap of that throbbing, hot, smelly engine. To add to the excitement, I was assigned to be part of a flight of six fighters that would include a P-38, two P-40s, a P-51, and the instructor in a P-47.

When everyone was bedded down, I rushed to the flight line, hoping to find information, any information, on the P-39. It was my lucky day. The P-39 crew chief was still there, working on the aircraft that I would be flying at dawn tomorrow. With everything to lose, I explained my dilemma to that great and noble sergeant and friend. He stayed up all night with me and with buckets of coffee, helped me to go over every page of the P-39 operating manual.

The next day, I started the engine, with the help of my crew chief friend and became number-two position, in the flight of six fighters, taxiing out for takeoff behind the instructor's P-47.

That's when it all went wrong. The instructor's P-47 stopped on reaching the runway, I hit the brakes too hard and the nose wheel of my P-39 went into a full cocked position, 90 degrees to the right. I could do nothing but go around and around, in spite of my efforts with the engine and brakes.

Our instructor and his P-47 took off, but because I was blocking the entrance to the runway, the other fighters with their inline engines, were starting to overheat and needed to get into the air quickly. To pass me they would have to taxi off the taxiway, out on the dirt, to get to the runway and take off.

The tower control officer told me to shut down, clear of the taxi strip. The fighters taxied on to the runway and took off. My crew chief friend arrived immediately, with his tug and tow bar, before my prop stopped rotating. He had followed me out to the runway, to be available in the event of a problem. This was a problem. He quickly straightened the nose wheel and helped me to start the engine again. I reported to the control tower and took off for the gunnery range. This was my first flight in the P-39. The date was February 15, 1944.

I spent that evening at the officer's club, bragging about how much better the P-39 was, over the P-40 and P-51. Little did I know. The rest of the course was uneventful, and I became quite good at keeping the nose wheel straight and sticking with my flight instructor.

On graduation night at the officer's club, the group commander climbed on top of a table and directed that Lieutenant Bones Marshall stand on top of another table. There in front of an amazed audience, the group commander told the story of my P-39 inaugural. The next morning, I'm standing at tight attention in the group commander's office while he tried to decide what to do about me.

Instead of sacking me, they sent me to ferry P-39s from a base in Georgia to Las Vegas. During one of those flights, I was on the deck, being escorted by a B-26 Marauder, and he was telling me on the radio, about the Civil War trenches below us as we flew over Mississippi.

Suddenly, my engine exploded in a ball of fire. I couldn't call "May Day" because the radio was clogged with talk about Vicksburg. The B-26 flew almost a hundred miles farther west before they discovered that my P-39 was no longer on their wing.

With the engine mounted behind me, I felt the heat. The cockpit was full of smoke. I was crashing straight ahead, into the trees. I suddenly remembered that I had an external fuel tank and jettisoned it just as I hit the trees. Luckily both wings sheared off or I would have cartwheeled through that forest, with no hope of getting out of the cockpit.

Crash Landing

The cockpit was now a missile that somehow held together, until it lurched to a crashing stop. I rolled out of the right door and ran from the burning aircraft. I must have had superhuman strength: I rolled out of that small cockpit and ran, still wearing my seat parachute.

I was bruised and had numerous cuts on my back, neck, and hands from glass, but I was alive and had no burns. The entire town of Vicksburg came rushing out to my rescue. Milk and laundry trucks were the

Who's Who

2nd Lt. (later Lt. Gen.) Winton W. "Bones" Marshall, air ace who flew the P-39 Airacobra in the 28th Fighter Squadron, Chame Air Base, Panama

2nd Lt. (later Col.) Evans G. Stephens, P-39 Airacobra pilot, 40th Fighter Squadron, in the United States and on New Guinea

Capt. (later Brig. Gen.) Thomas L. "Tommy" Hayes Jr, air ace who flew the P-39 Airacobra in training, Hamilton Field, California

2nd Lt. (later Capt.) Clayton Kelly Gross, air ace who also flew the P-39 Airacobra at Hamilton Field, California

first. Up roared a jeep with a girl driving. She was the Vicksburg radio operator that had been giving me position reports. In spite of my filthy and bloody flight suit, I asked her for a date and she agreed.

Soon, an Army L-1 appeared overhead. And then an Army doctor rushed up to take me to the Army Medical Center at Jackson, Mississippi. I convinced him that I was okay and promised to check in to the hospital soon, so he left.

My air-traffic-control girl took me to her parents' home to clean up. In dirty flight suit and all, we went to the local movie house. When we walked in, they stopped the movie, turned on the house lights, and everyone cheered as I hobbled down the aisle.

The next day, I was ordered to fly to another base, to pick up another P-39. This one was in good shape, but I remember how painful it was to crawl into that cramped, hot, smelly cockpit again and head for home.

I made many emergency landings in the P-39 at Las Vegas, usually due to the high temperatures in the summer. One day, I land a P-39 dead-stick, into a small dry lake south of Las Vegas. It's the middle of summer. The temperature is easily 130 degrees. So I sit under the wing and wait to be rescued. There isn't a sign of life in any direction and my radio failed when the engine quit. So no one knows of my situation. No one knows that I'm on a dry lake, outside the Las Vegas local flying area.

After five hours in that unbearable heat, I climb back into the cockpit. To my surprise, the engine starts on my first try. I might be a dumb lieutenant, but not so dumb that I'll attempt to take off with a bad engine, on that small dry lake, on that hot day. So I start taxiing toward a dirt road I saw earlier. I get to the road, and there's nothing in either direction. So I taxi up the road, heading north.

After thirty minutes taxiing, with the engine overheating, I spot an old deserted gas station. So I taxi up, shut down, and look for a telephone. None. While I'm standing there, up drives an old pickup truck. I ask the driver if he'll take me to a telephone. He nods. He's a funny old guy. He never says anything. Never says, "Hey, look at the P-39 Airacobra parked in the gas station!" He takes me to a Texaco station, where I call the base. They come and get me, in a jeep. Later in the week, a huge truck with a crane picks up the P-39.

Still trying to get into the war, I finally received orders—to the 28th Fighter Squadron at Chame Air Base, Panama. The war in Europe was winding down. They told me we were building up for action in the Pacific, including the invasion of Japan.

Chame Air Base was a hundred miles (161 km) north of the Panama Canal Zone, ringed on one side by the Pacific Ocean and the other by thick jungle and the Chame Mountain. There was no chance to survive if you crashed into the ocean, with its 26-foot sharks and barracuda. There was also no chance if you crashed into the triple-canopied jungle. The jungle was so dense that you would never be found, except by the headhunters.

The heat and humidity were terrible, especially sitting in the lap of that P-39 engine. We all had heat rash and boils. The food was terrible. I had a bad case of malaria, which was never entered on my medical records.

It was spring—not Christmas—when Santa Claus brought us a present, consisting of the P-38 Lightning, the plane I had always wanted to fly. We never got any closer to the war than Panama, but I began flying the P-38 in May 1945. Finally, finally, my P-39 Airacobra days were over.

Bell P-39 Airacobra

Almost every American fighter pilot in World War II flew the Bell P-39 Airacobra. Yet the P-39 is largely ignored because most flew it only in training. Even the handful who took the Airacobra into battle also piloted some other fighter and always liked it better.

The P-39 was defined by Bell's decision to mount an American Armament Corporation T-9 37mm cannon in the propeller hub, making it necessary to locate the engine in the rear fuselage. The Airacobra was the first Army single-seat fighter with tricycle landing gear.

The 37mm gun became standard on all production models except the P-39D-1 and the export P-400, which employed a 20mm weapon and can be readily identified by the longer barrel extending from the propeller hub. Early Airacobras also had two .50 caliber (12.7-mm) Colt nose machine guns, with 270 rounds each, and four .30 caliber (7.62-mm) Colt wing-mounted machine-guns, with 1,000 rounds per gun.

The Airacobra's retractable tricycle landing gear included a non-steering, self-castoring nose wheel that retracted straight up and aft into the forward fuselage—"my nemesis," said retired Lt. Gen. Winton W. "Bones" Marshall, who became an air ace in Korea but spent World War II cursing the P-39. The pilot raised or lowered the gear using a toggle switch in the cockpit. Contrary to myth, the tricycle configuration was no less robust than a conventional undercarriage would have been. When 1st Lt. George A. Ziendowski ran out of fuel on a routine flight in early 1942, he landed easily on Highway 501 near Latta, South Carolina, a secondary highway just twenty feet (6.09 m) wide.

The Allison V-1710 engine was a liquid-cooled, 12-cylinder, vee-type, in-line engine equipped with a single-stage, single-speed supercharger.

The pilot of the P-39 Airacobra sat in a bucket-type, metal seat. Despite braces on the canopy, the pilot enjoyed excellent visibility, especially for taxiing and ground handling. In the air, visibility was hindered to the rear.

With auto-style doors on both sides of the cockpit, the Airacobra's cockpit was cramped and space was at a premium. Improperly secured, the door had a tendency to fly off in high-speed dives, and pilots somehow ignored a latch retrofitted by Bell to prevent separation. Ironically, pilots also reported the door difficult to remove after a ditching at sea.

The XP-39 completed its maiden flight on April 6, 1939, flown by Bell test pilot James Taylor. The silvery, shiny XP-39 looked much like the shiny-metal children's toys of the era—left in natural metal finish, with a dark anti-glare shield painted between the forward canopy and the propeller. Red and white American stripes appeared horizontally on the rudder in the style typical during the late 1930s.

Most Americans flew the P-39 Airacobra only in training, but a few reached the airfield called Seven Mile on New Guinea—seen here—where the enemy was sometimes the Japanese, sometimes the weather, and sometimes malaria. This view of a squadron taking off suggests a larger mission than usual for the thinly spread Airacobra pilots on New Guinea.

[Bell Aircraft Corp.]

Bell P-39M Airacobra

Type: single-seat fighter

Power plant: one 1,200-hp (895-kW) Allison V-1710 in-line engine driving a 10-ft 4-in (3.14-m) Curtiss Electric propeller

Performance: maximum speed 386 mph (621 km/h); cruising speed 378 mph (608 km/h), climb to 16,400 ft (5000 m) in 6.5 minutes; service ceiling 36,000 ft (10970 m); range 650 mi (1046 km)

Weights: 5,610 lb (2545 kg); normal gross weight 8,400 lb (3810 kg); maximum takeoff weight 10,500 lb (4,763 kg)

Armament: one American Armament Corporation T-9 37-mm cannon in the propeller hub, plus four .30 caliber (7.62-mm) machine guns

Dimensions: included wingspan 34 ft (10.36 m); length 30 ft 2 in (9.19 m); height 11 ft 10 in (3.61 m)

First flight: April 6, 1939 (XP-39); November 25, 1939 (XP-39B); September 13, 1940 (YP-39)

Bell turned out 9,589 Airacobras, of which 4,779 were exported to the Soviet Union. The British used the Airacobra only briefly and rated it as unsuitable. The Airacobra also flew with the Portuguese, Free French, and co-belligerent Italian air arms.

Chapter Three

Yanks Against Yamamoto

What Happened

When air ace Maj. John Mitchell led sixteen P-38 Lightnings on the longest combat mission yet flown (420 miles, or 670 kilometers, one way) on April 18, 1943, Mitchell's target was the Japanese admiral considered the architect of the Pearl Harbor attack.

Mitchell's P-38 pilots, using secrets from broken Japanese codes, were going after Yamamoto Isoroku, the poker-playing, Harvard-educated naval genius of Japan's war effort. As almost everyone now knows, Mitchell's P-38s intercepted and shot down the Mitsubishi G4M "Betty" bomber carrying Yamamoto. After the admiral's death, Japan never again won a major battle in the Pacific war.

No band of brothers ever worked together better than the men who planned, supported, and flew the Yamamoto mission. Yet after the war, veterans fell to bickering over which P-38 pilot actually pulled the trigger on Yamamoto.

One thing they never disagreed on. Like most young pilots of their era, they believed the P-38 Lightning was the greatest fighter of its time. Whether they were in Mitchell's 349th Fighter Group or another P-38 outfit, they believed in the P-38 and were confident at its controls.

First Lieutenant Rex T. Barber
April 18, 1943
Lockheed P-38G Lightning
(43-2264)
347th Fighter Group
Henderson Field, Guadalcanal

1st Lt. Rex T. Barber of the 12th Fighter Squadron in about 1944. Historians no longer doubt that Barber was the P-38 Lightning pilot who shot down the Mitsubishi G4M Betty bomber carrying Japan's Adm. Isoroku Yamamoto.

[George Chandler]

RICHARD KIRKLAND. The P-38 Lightning was the aircraft every young kid wanted to fly. I know we all say that, but it's true. Talk all you want about the other great fighters of World War II—Thunderbolt, Mustang, Corsair—but if you were a young man in 1940 and your imagination was up in the clouds, the only cockpit you wanted to occupy belonged to the P-38 Lightning.

It had this beautiful little gondola that you sat in, with beautiful engines on the side and a lot of power. The way you sat in the cockpit between those two powerful engines was really something. The P-38 was just a dream to fly. In its time, it was the fastest airplane in the sky. It was easy to fly, easy to land, easy to take off. It had no bad characteristics, except that in early models you had to be careful in a dive or you could exceed the limits of the aircraft. It had counter-rotating props, so there was no torque. It was so easy to take off, you could be lighting your cigarette or winding your watch. But if you lost an engine on take-off, you had instant torque on one side, so you had to be on it and act quickly. It was a thing of beauty to fly.

I flew in the 49th Fighter Group with several of the top aces in the South Pacific, including America's top air ace, Richard I. "Dick" Bong, who was credited with forty aerial victories. None of us would have traded any other fighter for the P-38.

Richard Kirkland flew the P-38 Lightning with the 49th Fighter Group. This portrait was taken on New Guinea in December 1943.

[U.S. Air Force]

Bong was different from McGuire, Johnson, and the other famous aces of the Pacific war. If you met him, you would say, "To me, this is not a red-hot fighter pilot." Bong was reserved. He could be talkative, but he was strangely quiet most of the time and not outgoing at all. He didn't like to talk to war correspondents.

But both in the cockpit and out, Bong was absolutely fearless. When the rest of us were scrambling out of bunks as Japanese warplanes came to bomb our airfield, Bong wouldn't get out of bed. He simply wasn't afraid of anything.

At the controls of a P-38, he was a terror. The other aces looked and acted like the spirited, aggressive pilots they were. Bong was as spirited and aggressive as they were, but he didn't look or act the part.

I suppose I didn't necessarily look like a fighter pilot, either. I didn't start out knowing that I would fly with America's top ace, in what I consider to be World War II's greatest fighter. Today, most of my friends know me as an early helicopter pilot, who flew helicopters in the Korean

War and helped develop helicopters that served in Vietnam. But I didn't start out expecting to do that, either. I was born in 1923 and had a fairly ordinary American upbringing. I do, however, plead guilty to wanting to fly and, more than anything else, wanting to fly the P-38.

I came on active duty on August 28, 1942, and graduated with Flying Class 43-F in June 1943. I went to the southwest Pacific. I reached Hollandia, New Guinea, and joined the 9th Fighter Squadron, part of the fabled 49th Fighter Group, in October 1943. The squadron later moved to Biak and then to the Philippines. I flew sixty-one combat missions in the P-38 Lightning and forty-two combat missions in the P-47 Thunderbolt. Many of these were escort and fighter sweep missions.

I flew the sleek, powerful P-38 in combat with some of America's great aces, including Major Richard I. Bong, our all-time top ace with forty aerial victories. I was in a slew of dogfights myself and got credit for shooting down one Japanese Zero fighter, a Mitsubishi A6M, although I believe I actually got two. I also flew a combat sortie with Charles Lindbergh, when he was advising P-38 pilots on how to conserve fuel on long-range missions over those vast waters. Lindbergh got a Zero, too, although it isn't listed officially anywhere.

My aerial victory came when my flight of four P-38s flew into a swarm of Zeros during a sweep over Manokwari, on the north coast of New Guinea. The Japanese fighters started with the advantage of higher altitude and came swarming down on us in a head-on pass.

That wasn't smart. With its heavy 20mm nose cannon and four .50 caliber machine guns on the nose centerline, the P-38 Lightning is a formidable enemy from dead ahead. Nevertheless, our two aerial formations rushed into each other, converging at more than a thousand miles per hour, both sides firing furiously. This mid-air merger quickly became a madhouse, with P-38s and Zeros careening in all directions. Now, the Zeros had a better chance to take advantage of their extreme maneuverability during a close-quarters fight.

Zero Kill

I saw a Zero pop up in front of me. I fired a burst but, not surprisingly, he whipped into a tight turn. He was now shooting at me, but his tracers were vaulting overhead. I turned into him, and he broke off. I swung back into my climb and discovered that my wingman was missing. "Red Two! Red Two, get back in formation!" I shouted.

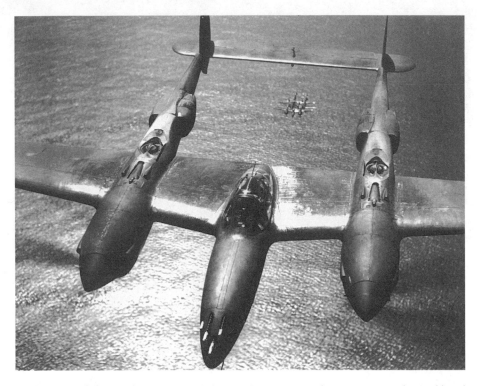

At the time of the April 18, 1943, mission against Japan's Adm. Yamamoto, the Lockheed P-38 Lightning was the only fighter with the fuel capacity and long range needed to cross 420 miles (or 672 kilometers) of ocean, carry out an intercept mission, and return safely. This overwater formation is similar to the one that bagged Yamamoto.

[U.S. Air Force]

My earphones were silent. I looked around. The shavetail second lieutenant who was supposed to be covering my wing was nowhere in sight.

A moment later, I heard his voice: "Get 'em off! Get these Zeros off my tail!" I stood my Lightning vertically on its 52-foot wing, looked down, and saw my guy in a dive with two Zeros closing in behind him.

I didn't have time to get into the fight. The only chance to help my wingman was to attempt a tactic I'd tried once before without success. I dipped the nose and fired a long burst—shooting from much too far away. Somehow, the unbelievable happened. My tracers fell between my wingmen and the pursuing Zeros, and one of the Japanese fighters took hits and rolled out of control, smoking. That was a moment of triumph. I was shooting from too far out and I got him.

In order to attack the bomber carrying Adm. Yamamoto, P-38 Lightning pilots expected to fight their way through a swarm of Japanese Mitsubishi A6M Zero fighters like this one. The P-38 was a match for the Zero in most situations, but this was one time the Americans did not want to spend a lot of time in fighter-versus-fighter combat.

[U.S. Navy]

Our nemesis, always, was the Japanese Zero fighter. The Zero was held in awe when Americans first heard about it at the time of Pearl Harbor. By 1944 and 1945, we knew a lot about the Zero, and it was no longer a sinister, brooding mystery, but we never stopped respecting it. The guys who went after Admiral Yamamoto in the P-38 undoubtedly respected the Zero as much as anyone.

ROGER AMES. It may have been the most studied fighter engagement of the Pacific war. Adm. Isoroku Yamamoto, 56, was commander in chief of the Japanese combined fleet and the architect of the Pearl Harbor attack. He called himself the sword of Japan's Emperor Hirohito. He claimed he was going to ride down Pennsylvania Avenue on a white horse and dictate the surrender of the United States in the White House.

Yamamoto studied at Harvard, traveled around America, and understood as much about the United States, including U.S. industrial power, as any Japanese leader. In April 1943, Yamamoto was trying to prevent the Allies from taking the offensive at Guadalcanal and the other Solomon Islands. He made a visit to Japanese troops in the Bougainville area.

On the afternoon of April 17, 1943, Maj. John Mitchell, commander of the 339th Fighter Squadron, was ordered to report to our operations dugout at Henderson Field on Guadalcanal. The 1st Marine Division had captured the nearly completed field the previous summer and named it for Maj. Lofton Henderson, the first Marine pilot killed in action in World War II, when his squadron engaged the Japanese fleet that was attacking Midway. Now, Mitchell found himself surrounded by high-ranking officers. They told him the United States had broken the Japanese code and had intercepted a radio message advising Japanese units in the area that Yamamoto was going on an inspection trip of the Bougainville area.

The message gave Yamamoto's exact itinerary and pointed out that the admiral was most punctual. They told Mitchell that Frank Knox, secretary of the navy, had held a midnight meeting with President Franklin D. Roosevelt regarding the intercepted message. It was decided that we were going to get Yamamoto if we could. The report of the meeting was probably inaccurate because Roosevelt was on a rail trip away from Washington, but the plan to get Yamamoto unquestionably began at the top.

The Navy would never have admitted it, but the Army's P-38 was the only fighter with the range to make the approximately 1,100-mile (1760-km) round trip. We were under the command of the Navy at Guadalcanal, so you can bet they'd have taken the job if they were able.

According to the intercepted message, Yamamoto and his senior officers were arriving at the tiny island of Ballale, just off the coast of Bougainville at 9:45 A.M. the next morning. The message said that Yamamoto and his staff would be flying in Mitsubishi G4M "Betty" bombers, escorted by six Zeros. The Yamamoto trip was to include a visit to Shortland Island and Buin base Kahili airstrip on Bougainville.

Mitchell was to be mission commander of eighteen P-38s that would intercept, attack, and destroy the bombers. That's all the P-38s we had in commission.

Led by Mitchell, we planned the flight in excruciating detail. Nothing was left to chance. Yamamoto was to be at the Ballale airstrip, just off Bougainville, at 9:45 A.M. the next morning, and we planned to intercept him ten minutes earlier, about thirty miles out. To ensure complete surprise, we planned a low-level, circuitous route, staying below the horizon from the islands we had to bypass, because the Japanese had radar and coast watchers just as we did.

We plotted the course and timed it so that the interception would take place upon the approach of the P-38s to the southwestern coast of Bougainville at the designated time of 9:35 A.M. Each minute detail was discussed and nothing was taken for granted. Takeoff procedure, flight course and altitude, radio silence, when to drop belly tanks, the tremendous importance of precise timing, and the position of the covering element: All were discussed and explained until Mitchell was sure that each of his pilots knew his part and the parts of the other pilots from takeoff to return.

Mitchell chose pilots from the 12th, 70th, and 339th fighter squadrons. These were the only P-38 squadrons on Guadalcanal. The only belly tanks we had on Guadalcanal were 165-gallon (630-liter) tanks, so we had to send to Port Moresby for a supply of the larger 310-gallon (1300-liter) tanks. We put one tank on each side of each plane. This gave us enough fuel to fly to the target area, stay in the area where we expected the admiral for about fifteen minutes, fight, and come home. The larger fuel tanks were flown in that night, and ground crews worked all night getting them installed, along with a Navy compass in Mitchell's plane.

Four of our pilots were designated to act as the "killer section," with the remainder as their protection. Mitchell said that if he had known there were going to be two bombers in the flight, he would have assigned more men to the killer section. The words for bomber and bombers are the same in Japanese. (Author's note: Ames is incorrect on this point about the Japanese language).

Capt. Thomas G. Lanphier Jr. led the killer section. His wingman was 1st Lt. Rex T. Barber. First Lieutenant Besby F. "Frank" Holmes led the second element, with his wingman being 1st Lt. Raymond K. Hine.

The cover section was led by Mitchell and included myself and eleven other pilots. Eight of the sixteen pilots on the mission were from the 12th Fighter Squadron, which was my squadron.

Although eighteen P-38s were scheduled to go on the mission, only sixteen were able to participate because one plane blew a tire on the runway on takeoff and another's belly tanks failed to feed properly.

It was Palm Sunday, April 18, 1943. But since there were no religious holidays on Guadalcanal, we took off at 7:15 A.M., joined in formation, and left the island at 7:30 A.M., just two hours and five minutes before the planned interception. It was an uneventful flight but a hot one, at from ten to fifty feet above the water all the way. Some of the pilots counted sharks. One counted pieces of driftwood. I don't remember doing anything but sweating. Mitchell said he may have dozed off on a couple of occasions but received a light tap from The Man Upstairs to keep him awake.

Marathon Mission

Mitchell kept us on course, flying the five legs by compass, time, and air-speed only. As we turned toward the coast of Bougainville and started to gain altitude, 1st Lt. Douglas S. Canning—Old Eagle Eyes—broke radio silence with a quiet, "Bogeys! Eleven o'clock, high!" It was 9:35 A.M. The admiral was precisely on schedule, and so were we. It was almost as if the affair had been prearranged with the mutual consent of friend and foe. Two Betty bombers were at 4,000 feet (12192 m), with six Zeros at about 1,500 feet (4572 m) higher, above and just behind the bombers in a "V" formation of three planes on each side of the bombers.

We all dropped our belly tanks and put our throttles to the firewall and went for altitude. The killer section closed in for the attack while the cover section stationed themselves at about 18,000 feet (5486 m) to take care of the expected fighters from Kahili. As Mitchell said, "The night before, we knew the Japanese had seventy-five Zeros on Bougainville, and I wanted to be where the action was. I thought, 'Well, I'm going on up higher and we're going to be up there and have a turkey shoot.'" We expected from fifty to seventy-five Zeros should be there to protect Yamamoto, just as we had protected Secretary of the Navy Frank Knox when he came to visit a couple of weeks before. We'd had as many fighters in the air to protect Mr. Knox as we could get off the ground. I guess the Japanese had all their fighters lined up on the runway for inspection. Anyway, none of the Zeros came up to meet us.

Lanphier and Barber headed for the enemy, and when they were about a mile in front and two miles to the right of the bombers, the Zeros spotted them. Lanphier and Barber dropped their belly tanks and headed down to intercept the Zeros. The Bettys nosed down in a diving turn to get away from the P-38s. Holmes, the leader of the second element, could not release his belly tanks, so in an effort to jar them loose, he turned off down the coast, kicking his plane around to knock the tanks loose. Ray Hine, his wingman, had no choice but to follow him to protect him. So Lanphier and Barber were the only two going after the Japs for the first few minutes.

From this point onward, accounts of the fight get mixed up about who shot down whom. Briefly, here is probably what happened, based on the accounts of all involved. I did not see what was happening 18,000 feet (5486 m) below me.

As Lanphier and Barber were intercepted by the Zeros, Lanphier turned head-on into them and shot down one Zero and scattered the others. This gave Barber the opportunity to go for the bombers. As Barber turned to get into position to attack the bombers, he lost sight of them under his wing, and when he straightened around he saw only one bomber, going hell bent for leather downhill toward the jungle treetops. Barber went after the Betty and started firing over the fuselage at the right engine. And as he slid over to get directly behind the Betty, his fire passed through the bomber's vertical fin and some pieces of the rudder separated from the plane. He continued firing and was probably no more than a hundred feet (30 m) behind the Betty, when it suddenly snapped left and slowed down rapidly, and as Barber roared by he saw black smoke pouring from the right engine.

Barber believed the Betty crashed into the jungle, although he did not see it crash. And then three Zeros got on his tail and were making firing passes at him as he headed toward the coast at treetop level, taking violent evasive action. Luckily, two P-38s from Mitchell's flight saw his difficulty and cleared the Zeros off his tail. Holmes said it was he and Hine that chased the Zeros off Barber's tail. Barber said he then looked inland and to his rear and saw a large column of black smoke rising from the jungle, which he believed to be the Betty he'd shot.

As Barber headed toward the coast, he saw Holmes and Hine over the water with a Betty bomber flying below them just offshore. He then saw Holmes and Hine shoot at the bomber with Holmes' bullets hitting the water behind the Betty and then walking up and through the right engine of the Betty. Hine started to fire, but all of his rounds hit well ahead of the Betty. Then Holmes and Hine passed over the Betty and headed south.

Barber said that he then dropped in behind the Betty flying over the water and opened fire. As he flew over the bomber it exploded and a large chunk of the plane hit his right wing, cutting out his turbo super-

Who's Who

2nd Lt. (later, Major) Richard Kirkland, P-38 Lightning pilot, 9th Fighter Squadron, 49th Fighter Group

Maj. (later, Col.) John Mitchell, P-38 Lightning pilot and commander, 339th Fighter Squadron, 347th Fighter Group

Capt. Thomas Lanphier, P-38 Lightning pilot, 12th Fighter Squadron, 347th Fighter Group

1st Lt. (later Lt. Col.) Roger Ames, P-38 Lightning pilot, 12th Fighter Squadron, 347th Fighter Group

1st Lt. Rex Barber, P-38 Lightning pilot, 12th Fighter Squadron, 347th Fighter Group

charger intercooler. Another large piece hit the underside of his gondola, making a very large dent in it. After this, he, Holmes, and Hine fired at more Zeros. Barber said that both he and Holmes shot down a Zero, but Hine was seen heading out to sea, smoking from his right engine. As Barber headed home, he saw three oil slicks in the water and hoped that Hine was heading for Guadalcanal, but that was not the case.

Lanphier, having scattered the Zeros, found himself at about 6,000 feet (1830 m). Looking down, he saw a Betty flying across the treetops, so he came down and began firing a long, steady burst across the bomber's course of flight, from approximately right angles. In another account, Lanphier said he was clearing his guns. By both accounts, he said he felt he was too far away, yet to his surprise, the bomber's right engine and right wing began to burn, and then the right wing came off and the Betty plunged into the jungle and exploded.

Lanphier said that three Zeros came after him, and he called Mitchell to send someone down to help him. Then, hugging the earth and the tree-tops while the Zeros made passes at him, he unwittingly led them over a corner of the Japanese fighter strip at Kahili. He then headed east, and with the Zeros on his tail, he got into a high-speed climb and lost them at 20,000 feet (6096 m). He got home with only two bullet holes in his rudder. Contrast this to the 104 bullet holes in Barber's plane, plus the knocked-out intercooler and the huge dent in his gondola.

Flying back to Guadalcanal, I heard Lanphier get on the radio and say, "That SOB won't dictate peace terms in the White House." This really upset me because we were to keep complete silence about the fact that we had gone after Yamamoto. The details of this mission were not to leave the island of Guadalcanal.

Lockheed P-38 Lightning

In the late 1930s, every youngster who wanted to fly dreamed of piloting the P-38 Lightning, a silvery pursuit ship with a sleek, futuristic look.

"In my mind, the P-38 Lightning was the most beautiful thing I had ever laid my eyes on," said retired Lt. Gen. Winton W. "Bones" Marshall, 86, of Incline Village, Nevada, who later achieved his goal in a fighter squadron in Panama. "I saw a P-38 in a movie newsreel. Then, my father took me to an Army airfield, and I got to see a real P-38 taking off, all sleek and streamlined and beautiful. It was the newest and the greatest."

Today, developing a new fighter is a multibillion dollar business. In the 1930s, during the Great Depression, key decisions about new fighters were made at Wright Field, Ohio, by a first lieutenant, Benjamin Kelsey. In 1937, Kelsey had helped define a requirement for a new pursuit plane that would have a maximum speed of 400 mph (640 km/h) and the ability to climb to 20,000 feet (6096 m) in six minutes. Fighters with these capabilities were flying in Britain, Germany, and Japan but not in the United States.

In June 1937, the Army Air Corps ordered a single XP-38 test ship from Lockheed. Kelly Johnson performed initial design study. James Gerschler headed the team that completed detailed engineering work.

The designers came up with a twin-engined, twin-boomed aircraft "that looked like the spaceships being flown by Buck Rogers in the Saturday movie serials," said Warren M. Bodie, author of *P-38 Lightning*. The government paid $161,795 for the design and development of the sole XP-38.

Lockheed disassembled the XP-38 at its Burbank, California, plant and trucked it to March Field, California. There, on January 27, 1939, Kelsey made the first flight of the new plane. As he described it years later, it was a false start.

Just after takeoff, vibrations shook the plane. The flaps were moving up and down, out of control. Kelsey solved that problem by retracting the flaps. This meant he would have no flaps for landing and would land at high speed. Observers in a chase plane, a Ford Tri-Motor, assured Kelsey that everything looked all right. It was later learned that control rods connecting the pilot to the flaps had broken. Kelsey made a "hot" landing after thirty-four minutes, unharmed.

Pictures of the XP-38 were circulated. The plane became an inspiration to young air enthusiasts. Kelsey made five successful flights, beginning February 5, 1939. It was then decided to take the plane on a showcase tour to Mitchel Field, New York, with refueling stops in Amarillo, Texas, and at Wright Field. After a brief appearance on the east coast, the plane would go to Wright Field—Kelsey's base and the service's flight test center—for exhaustive tests.

After two successful legs on the planned transcontinental journey, Kelsey was attempting to land at Mitchel Field, when he crashed on a golf course 2,000 feet (610 m) short of the runway.

Kelsey was unhurt, but the beautiful XP-38 was totaled.

After assisting with the accident investigation, Kelsey accompanied Air Corps boss Maj. Gen. Henry H. "Hap" Arnold to Washington, D.C., where the two persuaded Secretary of War Louis Johnson to proceed with the P-38 design.

The Army ordered thirteen preproduction YP-38 models. And in September 1939, the service began a long series of purchases, with an order for sixty-six P-38s. One of these was modified to become the only XP-38A, with an experimental, pressurized cabin. The P-38B and P-38C were designs that were never built.

At the time of Pearl Harbor, the Army had begun to receive P-38D Lightnings. Production at Lockheed's Burbank, California, plant soon shifted to the improved P-38E. These "E models" equipped twelve squadrons, and most fought in the Southwest Pacific and in the Aleutian Islands. A P-38E also claimed the first German aircraft to be shot down by a Lightning, a four-engined Focke-Wulf Fw 200 Condor shot down near Iceland only hours after the United States declared war.

Britain's Royal Air Force developed an interest in the P-38. The British considered naming the fighter the Atlanta, but the idea never took hold, so it became the Lightning in the RAF, too. By the end of 1941, Lightnings equipped the RAF's 46, 69, 89, 137 and 123 squadrons. But at this juncture in the war, there was a ban on the export of superchargers to Europe. Without them, the RAF Lightnings lacked the rapid acceleration and turning capability that were taken for granted by American P-38 pilots. Britain was also dissatisfied with U.S. handling of the export of the fighters, and in the end U.S. forces repossessed many of them.

The U.S. air arm, now called the Army Air Forces, or AAF, began in March 1942 to receive deliveries of a reconnaissance version of the Lightning, called the F-4 (a converted P-38E), in which all armament had been replaced by four K-17 cameras. A drift sight and autopilot were also introduced as standard. The AAF took delivery of F-4s, which served with the 5th and 7th Photo Reconnaissance squadrons.

By late 1942, Burbank was churning out P-38F models, which had more powerful versions of the now familiar V-1710 in-line engine and were capable of a top speed of 395 mph (636 km/h). The P-38F was slightly heavier than previous Lightnings, thanks to the introduction of underwing bomb shackles for two 1,000 pound (454-kg) bombs. These wing stations could also be used to mount long-range drop tanks or smoke-laying equipment. At least one P-38F was test flown with a pair of 22-inch (560-mm) torpedoes on the underwing racks. Some P-38Fs were equipped with a second seat, but without controls, as a way of providing air experience to pilots who lacked nosewheel handling skills, as well as incentive rides for crew chiefs and armorers.

The P-38G introduced a boost-driven version of the V-1710 engine and improved superchargers. Drop-tank equipped P-38G models of the 347th Fighter Group on Guadalcanal, led by Lt. Col. John Mitchell, carried out the long-range, 550-mile (880-km) Pacific mission that killed Japan's Adm. Isoroku Yamamoto, the architect of the Pearl Harbor attack. Debate over which P-38 pilot actually shot down Yamamoto has raged since the war, but studies completed decades later make it almost certain that the pilot was 1st Lt. Rex Barber. Of the 1,082 P-38G models built, 181 were converted to become F-5A reconnaissance aircraft and 200 became F-5Bs.

Like most combat planes, the Lightning kept getting heavier as new models were introduced. Maximum takeoff weight went up to 19,200 pounds (8709 kg) on the P-38G model, which began reaching squadrons in Europe in June 1943. The increased weight of the P-38G had no effect on its performance. By the time it appeared, some Lightnings were flying long-range escort missions in Europe. In the literature of the era, the P-38 was outshined by the P-51 Mustang when it came to escorting bombers to the deepest targets in Europe, including Berlin, but

This is a formation of P-38 Lightnings in flight. Once the American P-38s reached Adm. Yamamoto's aircraft, they broke into smaller units and a "killer unit" of P-38s went after the Japanese admiral.

[U.S. Air Force]

---

bomber crews had a special feeling for the Lightning anyway. A gunner aboard a 15th Air Force bomber, Technical Sgt. Robert H. Bryson wrote a widely quoted poem about the fighter before his own death in combat. The most memorable passage refers to airmen who were in action because they hadn't been rejected by their draft boards:

> Sure we're braver than hell
> On the ground all is swell
> In the air it's a different story
> We sweat out our track through the fighters and flak
> We're willing to split up the glory
> Well, they wouldn't reject us, so heaven protect us
> And until all this shooting abates
> Give us the courage to fight 'em and—one other small item—
> An escort of P-38s.

In Europe, the P-38 rarely escorted bombers to their farthest destinations, Berlin included. Still, the P-38 was visible in almost every battle in Europe. German troops supposedly called it *der gabelschwanz Teufgel*, or the fork-tailed devil. On the Mediterranean front, F-5 Lightnings mapped some 80 percent of the Italian mainland before the invasion at Anzio. The P-38H model was the inspiration for 128 Lightnings that were converted to F-5C models.

The P-38J model introduced in August 1943 had a distinguishing feature that set it apart from earlier Lightnings. This was the chin-shaped fairing under the nose to enclose the intercooler intakes sandwiched between the oil radiator intakes. This freed an area of the wing's leading edge to accommodate two additional 55-gallon (208 liter) fuel tanks, increasing the Lightning's total fuel capacity to 410 gallons (1552 liters). When carrying drop tanks, the P-38J had a range of 2,300 miles (3701 km). The next term in the series, P-38K, applied to an experimental version of the Lightning with larger propellers.

The final and best-known combat version of the Lightning was the P-38L, which had an improved version of the V-1710 engine and provision for rocket projectiles under the wings. Lockheed manufactured

---

Lockheed P-38L Lightning

Type: single-seat fighter

Powerplant: two 1,600-hp (1194-kW) Allison V-1710-111/113 in-line piston engines driving three-bladed, 9-ft (2.74-m) Curtiss Electric propellers

Performance: maximum speed 414 mph (666 km/h) at 25,000 ft (7620 m); climb to 20,000 ft (6095 m) in 7.0 minutes; service ceiling 44,000 ft (13410 m); range 450 miles (724 km); maximum ferry range 2,600 miles (4184 km)

Weights: empty 12,800 lb (5806 kg); maximum takeoff 21,600 lb (9798 kg)

Dimensions: wingspan 52 ft (15.85 m); length 37 ft 10 in (11.53 m); height 9 ft (2.74 m); wing area 327.5 sq ft (30.42 sq m)

Armament: one 20-mm cannon and four .50 caliber (12.7-mm) machine guns, plus up to two 2,000-lb (907-kg) bombs or two 1,600 lb (726 kg) bombs and ten 5-in (127-mm) rocket projectiles under the wings

First flight: January 27, 1939 (XP-38)

3,810 P-38L models at Burbank, and Vultee completed 113 more at Nashville, Tennessee.

The favorable opinion of the Lightning that began with Ben Kelsey's first recommendation of the plane never changed throughout the lifetime of the Lightning. The P-38 became the only U.S. fighter that was in production at the start of World War II and at the end. Lockheed and other companies manufactured 10,037 Lightnings of all models. The two top U.S. aces of the war, Majors Richard I. Bong and Thomas McGuire, flew P-38s and were awarded the Medal of Honor.

In 1945, Lockheed had two production lines in Burbank building P-38s and P-80 Shooting Stars, one of the few times propeller and jet aircraft were being assembled side by side.

Chapter Four

Hellcats of the Navy

HAMILTON McWHORTER. Imagine you're in a metal shed and somebody throws rocks against the outside.

That's what it sounds like when machine gun fire hits your plane. I looked around and, sure enough, there were a pair of Japanese Zero fighters right behind me. A long stream of tracers was coming at me.

I was the pilot of a magnificent Grumman F6F Hellcat, probably the best fighter of World War II, as a member of Navy fighter squadron VF-9, operating from the USS *Essex* (CV 9). We were escorting our carrier's bombers on a strike to Rabaul, New Britain, in the South Pacific on November 11, 1943, attempting to relieve pressure on the U.S. troops who'd landed at nearby Bougainville a few days earlier.

This was a big battle, high over Rabaul, with maybe a hundred Zeros and fifty Hellcats fighting each other and planes tumbling all over the sky. When I heard those slugs hitting my Hellcat, I wondered if this huge, sprawling dogfight was going to be the end of my very brief (so far) Navy career, which had begun shortly after Pearl Harbor. Like many before me, I had begun my Navy flying not in the Hellcat but in the older and less capable F4F Wildcat.

Lieutenant Hamilton McWhorter
November 11, 1943
Grumman F6F-3 Hellcat
Fighter Squadron Three (VF-9)
USS *Essex* (CV 9)
Rabaul, New Britain

Hamilton "Mac" McWhorter poses in his F6F-3 Hellcat fighter on February 16, 1944, after it was painted with ten Japanese naval flags to represent his ten aerial victories. The portrait was taken when he became the first Hellcat double ace, after earlier becoming the first Hellcat ace. McWhorter later brought his total of enemy aircraft destroyed to twelve.

[U.S. Navy]

What Happened

In the weeks following the Pearl Harbor attack of December 7, 1941, Japanese forces seized huge chunks of Southeast Asia and the South Pacific, swarming over Hong Kong, Singapore, and the Philippines, bearing down on Java, and threatening Australia. In February 1942, the bleakest month of a period when Americans experienced only defeat, Vice Adm. Wilson Brown led Task Force Eleven into South Pacific waters dominated by Japan. Brown's flagship was the aircraft carrier USS *Lexington* (CV 2). One of his pilots was a 1937 Naval Academy graduate, Lt. Edward H. "Butch" O'Hare.

The Pearl Harbor attack had missed U.S. carriers. Now, the flattops offered hope to beleaguered Americans. Brown's bold plan was to elude Japanese surveillance and sneak close to the bastion on Rabaul, New Britain, to launch a strike that would be the first offensive action of the war.

Brown was fully 3,000 miles (4800 km) from the fleet support base at Pearl Harbor. Fuel was a serious concern, since his slow-moving fleet oilers were vulnerable to submarine attack. And Japanese airpower at Rabaul commanded the region.

On February 20, 1942, as "Lady Lex" passed near Bougainville, stubby Grumman F4F-3 Wildcat fighters of Fighting Three squadron, or VF-3, intercepted and shot down two scouting Japanese flying boats. VF-3 skipper Lt. Comdr. John "Jimmy" Thach claimed one of the big seaplanes after nearly colliding with it first. Thach assured his pilots that shooting during this baptism of fire was "no more difficult than shooting on the gunnery range." Looking on from the carrier was O'Hare—disappointed at missing the first combat.

Brown was certain the flying boats had radioed Rabaul to report his presence. Still, he continued toward Rabaul. The Japanese responded by launching a two-wave attack by seventeen Mitsubishi G4M1 "Betty" bombers. In late afternoon on February 20th, Lexington's radar (an invention the Japanese did not have) detected the first nine Bettys pressing in.

Lt. Noel Gayler led a flight of F4F-3s that rose to intercept the bombers. Sailors cleared the Lexington's deck and launched other planes, mostly to get the planes—and volatile fuel and ammunition—out of the way before bombs started falling. Brown said later that, "Our fighters electrified all of us by making their kills mostly within sight of our ships." Gayler's Wildcats shot down several intruders, but bombs started exploding dangerously near the Lexington. Task Force Eleven was in danger of sustaining serious damage and casualties.

The carrier sent O'Hare's Wildcat aloft. Unaware that a second wave of eight Betty bombers was approaching, the immediate motive was simply too get O'Hare and his wingman, Lt. Marion W. "Duff" Dufilho, out of the way. O'Hare scanned the ocean and wondered where he might land if the Lexington wasn't still there an hour later. He had nowhere else to go.

Surveying the air and sea around the carrier, O'Hare discovered that he and Dufilho were above and to the right of a second wave of eight attacking Betty bombers (though both he and those on the ship believed there were nine). Communicating with Dufilho by using hand signals, O'Hare gestured to attack.

Dufilho's guns jammed. It was a moment of horrendous frustration. He couldn't shoot, and although sixteen Wildcats were now in the air, only he and O'Hare were close to the second bomber formation. O'Hare dived toward a Betty and fired into one of its fuel tanks. He saw the bomber burn and veer out of control.

O'Hare lost sight of his wingman and pressed on with his attack, stalked by bursts from the machine guns aboard the Betty bombers. He put lethal shots into a second bomber, crossed over the Japanese formation, rolled, and began firing at a third. A Japanese crew member later recounted "numerous" American fighters attacking "from all directions." In fact, only O'Hare and Dufilho were there. Even though he could not shoot, Dufilho courageously diverted gunfire from the bombers.

As the air battle raged, it drew closer to the carrier. Watching sailors had a close-up look at the air fighting. They watched and listened as O'Hare returned again and again to rip through the formation of bombers while their gunfire swirled around him. In a matter of just minutes, O'Hare made four firing passes.

Bombers vs. Carrier

A damaged bomber attempted to crash into the *Lexington* but splashed 1,500 yards off the carrier's port bow, without success.

The outcome of the fighting was one-sided. The Japanese air attack ended as a total failure. The Americans were credited with destroying fifteen Betty and two Mavis (Kawanishi H6K) flying boats. Thach's VF-3 lost two Wildcats. Ensign John Wilson was killed, while Lt. (jg) Howard Johnson was shot down and rescued.

O'Hare was credited with shooting down five aircraft and recognized as an ace—only the second Navy ace ever, following Lt. David S. Ingalls, who had shot down six German planes in World War I. O'Hare's biographers Steve Ewing and John B. Lundstrom, in the book *Fateful Rendezvous* (Annapolis, MD: Naval Institute Press, 1997) argue that O'Hare actually shot down three planes immediately, inflicted mortal damage that caused a fourth to ditch, and damaged two others.

It was a victory at a time when Americans had not known victory. For the Japanese, it was a strategic defeat: the bomber force at Rabaul was gutted and would have to be replaced. The Japanese were forced to delay planned landings on the north coast of New Guinea for five days. Weeks later, in May 1942, American sailors won the Battle of Coral Sea, although at the price, in that battle, of mortal torpedo damage to the *Lexington*.

Dufilho was later lost in an action in the Solomon Islands, for which he was awarded a posthumous Navy Cross. Thach perfected the air combat tactics used by the Navy in the Pacific, including a fighting maneuver called the "Thach weave." Gayler became head of the National Security Agency and, later, commander in chief of U.S. Pacific forces.

O'Hare, who had been born in 1914 in St. Louis, Missouri, and had strong links to both that city and Chicago, Illinois, became the first popular hero of the naval war in the Pacific—a status the easygoing O'Hare greeted with embarrassment. With his wife, Rita, O'Hare was summoned to the White House, where, on April 21, 1942, President Franklin D. Roosevelt awarded him the Medal of Honor. Three days later, a parade was held in his honor in St. Louis. But O'Hare was uncomfortable as a public figure, felt his flying skills were needed, and asked to return to combat.

In November 1943, aboard the *Enterprise*, O'Hare was leading the first night fighters to fly from a ship against Japanese warplanes. Now, he was flying the Grumman F6F Hellcat, the magnificent fighter that replaced the Wildcat and turned the tide against the Japanese. But on this night mission, O'Hare was mistakenly shot down and killed by a U.S. aircraft. Posthumously, O'Hare was recommended for a second Medal of Honor and awarded the Navy Cross.

In postwar years, Chicago newspaper publisher Col. Robert H. McCormick led a civic campaign to Orchard Field in honor of the flyer; it became O'Hare Airport in 1949.

NOEL GAYLER. Being the pilot of a Wildcat was an unforgettable experience. The ship's stalky landing gear gave it dubious ground- or deck-handling characteristics. It could be "mushy" when maneuverability counted most. There was a violent draught if the cockpit hood was slid open in flight, and there existed no provision at all for jettisoning the hood in an emergency. The pilot's seat was cramped and too low, relative to the location of your head. In short, much as pilots were to praise it, the Wildcat could be tricky and unforgiving.

The Wildcat was, by dint of its time and place, the fighter in which American naval officers and Marines made their stand against the Mitsubishi A6M Zero, and while the Japanese fighter enjoyed numerous advantages in its performance and capabilities, the Wildcat achieved a measure of greatness in part due to circumstance, in part because some exceptional men flew it.

Fighting the Zero was not, to be sure, a task to be envied. Navy flyers and Marines learned early in the war not to dogfight with the more nimble Zero any time that the contest could be resolved in some other fashion. Where possible, they sought to break through a screen of Mitsubishis and attack the enemy's big bombers directly. At times, a brace of Zeros could be lured into an overshoot, making it easier to break through to the bombers.

Foster Hailey, correspondent for the *New York Times*, summed up the results in 1943. "The Grumman Wildcat, it is no exaggeration to say, did more than any single instrument of war to save the day for the United States in the Pacific," Hailey wrote. He was right.

HAMILTON McWHORTER. I can't emphasize how important it was to us to have the F6F Hellcat in the fighting in the Pacific. I flew the earlier F4F Wildcat in the fighting in North Africa before I went to the Pacific, and you have to respect the men who stood up against the Japanese war machine in the F4F. But the Grumman F6F Hellcat was the key to turning the tide and defeating Japan.

I was in squadron VF-9 at Oceana, near Norfolk, Virginia. In January 1943, we became the first squadron to get the Hellcat. It was like going from a Model T Ford to a Cadillac. The Hellcat was more powerful, about sixty miles per hour (90 km/h) faster, roomier, had a faster rate of climb, and carried more ammunition.

Consider the simple matter of taking off from the runway or the carrier deck. The F4F Wildcat was a real bear during takeoffs and landings. The Hellcat was easy to keep straight going down the runway. The Hellcat was so much more stable and was a beautiful gun platform. My practice gunnery scores went up when we got the Hellcats. It was very maneuverable. It probably had the biggest wing area of any of the American fighters. It was the best carrier plane we had. It would darn near land itself on the carrier without any help from the pilot.

My squadron, VF-9, went aboard the new *Essex* in May 1943. We went down through the Panama Canal and out to Pearl Harbor. Soon afterward, we were fighting the war in the western Pacific. Our first combat strike was on Marcus Island in August 1943.

I flew eighty-nine combat missions. The most memorable was the strike against Rabaul on November 11, 1943. The Marines had just landed on Bougainville on November 1. The Japanese were massing a lot of warships in Rabaul harbor, so they sent us down. We were apprehensive that morning. We were launched from 150 miles (240 kilometers)

The Grumman F6F Hellcat was the fighter that turned the tide in the naval air battles of the Pacific war. Robust, powerful, and maneuverable, it was the first U.S. fighter that was truly a match for the Japanese Zero. "Mac" McWhorter described it as a "Cadillac of the skies."

[U.S. Navy]

southeast of Rabaul, escorting our task force's SBD Dauntless dive bombers and TBF Avenger torpedo bombers. We started toward Rabaul flying the standard cover, with the bombers in a box formation and us about a thousand feet above them. The clouds topped at 10,000 feet (3048 meters), so we stayed above them. About fifty miles (75 km) from Rabaul, we were boring through the sky when a dozen or so Zeros showed up.

They were above us about 2,500 feet (765 meters). Every few moments, one of the Zeros peeled away and appeared to start a diving run on us and on our bombers below us. A couple of our planes would turn into them and they would turn back. At this point, they did not press us, and as we got closer to Rabaul, the Zeros disappeared and the flak started popping all around us. There was a lot of flak all around our formation. It was impressive, but none of it was close enough to hit us. We passed that and reached the Rabaul harbor area, and the clouds started breaking.

The first thing I saw was a long white streak behind the Japanese warships as they were speeding out of Rabaul harbor in a long column.

We were at about 12,000 feet (3650 m) or so. We dived. We went down to the surface, preparing to strafe them.

My division went in ahead of the torpedo planes. I got down to an altitude of just 150 or 200 feet above the water. I was now heading at high speed straight toward a long line of Japanese warships—heavy cruisers and destroyers.

For some reason, I picked the biggest one of the ships. It was one of their early, large cruisers—the one with the big, pagoda-like mast. I set up my firing pass so as to approach him from his starboard side.

When we were still about a mile out from the line of Jap warships, every one of them started opening fire at us. As we got in closer, my target, the big heavy cruiser, opened up with its 8-inch batteries. I can testify that you can actually see an 8-inch shell when it's coming toward you. If it looks like it's going to hit you, you might even have time to move out of the way. I stayed on course, and when my Hellcat was within range, I began firing.

I can still see the impact of my .50 caliber (12.7-mm) machine gun bullets hitting the Jap ship. In our ammunition supply, every fifth round was an armor piercing round, and it made a bright flash. We had six machine guns, and each gun fired about ten rounds per second. With that many brightly lit rounds pouring into it, the Jap cruiser lit up like a Christmas tree. The nice thing was, every one of those bright flashes meant that four additional rounds, which weren't visible, were also hitting in the same area.

When I was mast-high over the cruiser, I was flying through an incredible barrage while looking down at the faces of the Jap crewmembers. I could see them clearly, some looking at me, some shooting, some scrambling for cover, and I know my rounds hit some of them.

I passed over the cruiser. I pulled out and started for the rendezvous point, when I saw a huge melee going on in the air above a Japanese air base. There were planes all over the sky, planes exploding, and parachutes falling. There were about fifty Zeros and about thirty Hellcats. I looked over and saw a Hellcat flying straight and level, and a Zero right behind him, shooting. The 20-mm cannon shells from the Zero were hitting the Hellcat and blowing pieces of metal off. The Hellcat was smoking badly. The pilot was not taking evasive action. Maybe he was wounded.

I banked sharply, maneuvered into position, and got underneath the Zero. From three hundred feet or so, I fired a short burst and got hits all along its fuselage. On the verge of a midair collision, I had to pull up slightly to go over the top of the Zero. As I did, I looked right down into the cockpit.

I actually saw flames coming out from under the instrument panel inside the Zero's cockpit. The Zero pilot had no chance whatsoever. The Zero had no armor plate in its cockpit.

I started after another Zero, when a very, very loud noise occurred. Like I said earlier, imagine you're in a metal shed and someone throws rocks against the outside. That's what it sounded like when machine gun fire ripped into my Hellcat.

I looked around and, sure enough, a pair of Zeros was right behind me and a long stream of tracers was coming at me. I looked up and saw another Zero crossing in front of me. I barely had time to put the nose of my plane ahead of his and get the lead. I fired. The Zero exploded.

I figured out later that the Zero that had poured all that gunfire into me had blocked the line of sight for the other Zero accompanying him. The other Zero may have been the flight leader. Anyway, the Jap who fired at me did a good job of riddling my Hellcat, but he prevented the other Jap from shooting, and when it was over I was still in the air.

I went down, pulled out at 3,000 feet (9100 meters) or so, and headed back to the rendezvous point.

We escorted the bombers back to the *Essex*. I knew I'd been hit and hit pretty hard, but I had no idea where. Despite the damage, I was able to land. When I got back aboard the *Essex* and checked my Hellcat, I found bullet holes in each wing and on both sides of the fuselage. They went straight through the wing. The Zero had narrowly missed my cockpit. There was not a single hit in my fuselage. I want to thank the Japanese Zero that made that overhead run on me, because if he hadn't hit me when he did, the other Zero flying with him would have gotten me good.

On that mission to Rabaul, we lost one F6F to a Zero and one SBD to ground fire, but we shot down fourteen Zeros. I went on to become the first Hellcat ace and was credited with shooting down twelve Japanese aircraft.

The flight deck of a carrier was like a stage, with every movement choreographed. This F6F-3 Hellcat pilot is awaiting directions on the wooden deck of a carrier in the Pacific during World War II.

[U.S. Navy]

What Happened

At Pearl Harbor, Wake Island, and especially on Guadalcanal, Navy and Marine fighter pilots who faced a hard-driving enemy flush with victory and coming in on overwhelming numbers did some of the toughest flying of the war. To stand against this onslaught, Americans had to struggle not with just one enemy but with many. To the pilot of a Grumman F4F Wildcat taxiing at Guadalcanal's Henderson Field in a torrential downpour, struggling through geysers of water and mud, the list of enemies included bad weather, corrosion, primitive conditions, and tropical disease. Marine fliers sometimes needed a roll of toilet paper or a protective bunker—or a hot meal—as much as anything else. It was hard to stay ready to repel the next wave of Japanese bombers when you had to spend time plucking leeches from your skin with a bayonet, or running to the latrine to disgorge the foul water and poor food. It was no easier for the Navy pilot on a carrier deck, pitching in a violent sea.

Navy and Marine flyers who fought early in the Pacific were well trained and highly experienced but so, too, were their opponents. Though Guadalcanal was billed as an American offensive, the Japanese started out with a position of dominance in the air. It was possible to engage Zeros in a dogfight during the afternoon and limp home, only to find the airfield under attack at night by Japanese bombers.

At sea, as the United States went to war, Wildcats equipped squadrons aboard the carriers USS *Ranger* (CV 4), *Enterprise* (CV 6), *Hornet* (CV 12), and *Saratoga* (CV 3).

But it was the Marines who received early attention. The first Wildcat pilot to win the Medal of Honor belonged to Marine squadron VMF-211, which lost nine F4F-3s on the ground at Pearl Harbor and seven more on the ground at Wake Island the next day. The battered defenders of Wake fought on against overwhelming odds and on December 9, 1941, two VMF-211 pilots teamed up to shoot down a Japanese bomber, the first American Wildcat kill. Before Wake was overrun, Capt. Henry T. Elrod achieved a direct hit on a Japanese destroyer with a bomb dropped from his Wildcat, sinking the ship and losing his life, but winning the Medal of Honor posthumously.

The first American Wildcat aerial victories seem to have been a pair of twin-engine Mitsubishi G3M2 bombers downed by Lt. David S. Kliever and Tech Sgt. William Hamilton of VMF-211, flying from Wake on December 9, 1941.

During the heated defense of Wake Island, Marines kept their Wildcats flying by cannibalizing wrecked aircraft, improvising tools, and hand-making some parts. When the Japanese attempted their first landings on Wake early on the morning of December 11, 1941, four Wildcats attacked the invasion force with 100-lb (45-kg) bombs and .50-caliber (12.7-mm) machine gun fire. During the fighting, the Japanese destroyer *Kisaragi* was sunk and a number of other ships were damaged by the Wildcats, forcing the Japanese invasion fleet to retire.

It was a temporary stay. On December 21, 1941, the Japanese returned, reinforced by carrier aircraft, for the final assault on Wake. The surviving two Wildcats attacked a thirty-nine aircraft raid from the Japanese carriers *Soryu* and *Hiryu*. Escorting Zeros quickly shot down one Wildcat. The second Wildcat shot down two of the raiders before the pilot, Captain Herb Frueler, was wounded. Frueler struggled back to the island, where he crash-landed, wrecking Wake's last Wildcat, and the island fell to the onslaught two days later. Thereafter, the next important Wildcat action was O'Hare's.

In the strategically significant Coral Sea battle of early May 1942, the first Wildcats fought between opposing carrier forces, twenty-two F4F-3s of VF-2 operated from *Yorktown* and twenty of VF-42 flew from the deck of the ill-fated *Lexington*. During an attack on the two U.S. carriers, nine of twenty-seven Japanese aircraft were shot down, against a loss of two F4Fs. The following day, while escorting TBD Devastator torpedo bombers, Wildcats downed a dozen defending Zeros.

Wildcats achieved conspicuous success in the Battle of Midway and in operations at Guadalcanal. The Wildcat really earned its spurs not on pitching, heaving carrier decks but in the heat, stench, and muck at Henderson Field on Guadalcanal, where, slowly, the tide began to turn and Americans mounted the first offensive action of the Pacific conflict.

During the initial landings on Guadalcanal, known as Operation Watchtower, ninety-four F4F-4s were embarked on *Enterprise*, *Saratoga*, and *Wasp* to provide air cover. Early on August 7, 1942, VF-71 pilots destroyed twelve A6M2-N floatplane fighters based at Tulagi, VF-5 pilots struck Japanese facilities on Guadalcanal, and VF-6 Wildcats flew air cover. A series of air battles followed, and one resulted in the loss of nine Wildcats in exchange for five aerial victories. It was the beginning of a long, hard slog.

An early problem in Pacific fighting was the tendency of the Wildcat's .50 caliber (12.7-mm) Browning guns to jam for no visible reason. In early flight-testing and carrier operations, the problem had gone unnoticed, but in the harsh conditions of tropical combat, more than one Zero pilot escaped with his life because the Brownings wouldn't shoot. Navy ordnance men suggested a solution that divided the ammunition trays to keep ammunition belts from shifting. The Navy tested this modest change, and it was adopted.

Maj. John L. Smith's VMF-223, the "Rainbow" squadron, was launched from the USS *Long Island* (CVE-1) on August 20, 1942, and landed at Henderson Field. The next day, the squadron strafed Japanese troops at the Tenaru River. On August 24, 1942, accompanied by five Bell P-400 Airacobras, Smith's aircraft intercepted an enemy flight of fifteen bombers and twelve fighters. VMF-223 pilots shot down ten

Before the magnificent F6F Hellcat came along to wrest the Pacific war away from the Japanese, the fighting was in the hands of F4F Wildcat pilots like Lt. Edward "Butch" O'Hare, who was credited as the Navy's first ace of World War II. O'Hare later lost his life while flying an F6F Hellcat on a night mission.

[U.S. Navy]

bombers and six fighters, Captain Marion Carl scoring three of the kills. Carl became the first Marine ace of the war, and Smith became the third Wildcat flier to rate a Medal of Honor.

At Guadalcanal, Japanese bombers would approach twenty-six at a time in V formations, and Wildcat pilots refined their technique of trying to avoid Zeros and get at the bombers. Wildcats would dive on the bombers and destroy some before the Zeros pounced on them. These hit-and-run tactics forced the Japanese pilots to overuse precious fuel. Once dogfighting began, the Americans learned the importance of teamwork, finding that reliance on one's wingman was crucial and that no "lone wolf" survived for very long.

General Motors–built FM-2 Wildcats came into full service only after Hellcats and Corsairs had eclipsed the Wildcat. FM-2s served in composite squadrons and provided air cover for Marine amphibious forces.

The Wildcat was no Zero. The Japanese fighter was light and fast and

This is a Grumman F6F Hellcat in flight during World War II. It was a robust, fast, and maneuverable fighter that could take punishment and dish it out. Though it didn't arrive in the Pacific as soon as pilots might have liked, once on the scene it decimated the Japanese naval air arm.

[U.S. Navy]

had cannons instead of machine guns. The American fighter was sturdier and gave the pilot a much better chance of surviving if he was hit. As they gained experience, Navy and Marine pilots learned how to coax greater maneuverability from their aircraft. They learned how to make better gunnery compensate for the lesser killing power of their guns. And because their aircraft was tough, they stayed in the fight, day after day. They needed and wanted newer fighters—the F4U Corsair and F6F Hellcat, but for many months they had to "make do" with the Wildcat.

The introduction of the Hellcat may have been the most important event of the Pacific war. The F6F entered combat in August 1943, when planes from several carriers went into action near Marcus Island. Lt. Richard Loesch of squadron VF-6 scored the first aerial victory to be credited to a Hellcat.

Hellcats first flew in combat from USS *Yorktown* (CV 10) during an August 1943 raid on Marcus Island. In the island-hopping Pacific campaign, Hellcats achieved success in the Solomon, Gilbert, and Marshall Islands. In a huge air battle near Kwajalein in December 1943, ninety-

Who's Who

Lt. (later Cdr.) Hamilton "Mac" McWhorter III, F6F-3 Hellcat pilot, squadron VF-9, USS *Essex* (CV 9)

Cdr. (later Capt.) David McCampbell, F6F Hellcat pilot and commander, Carrier Air Group 15

Lt. Edward H. "Butch" O'Hare, F4F-3 Wildcat pilot, squadron VF-3, "Felix Squadron," USS *Lexington* (CV 2)

Lt. Comdr. John "Jimmy" Thach, F4F-3 pilot and squadron commander, VF-3

Lt. (later Adm.) Noel Gayler, F4F-3 pilot, VF-3

Lt. Marion W. "Duff" Dufilho, F4F-3 pilot, VF-3

one Hellcats tangled with fifty Zeros and shot down twenty-eight, with a loss of just two aircraft.

Hellcats are not usually remembered for fighting in Europe, but they did see sharply limited action against Hitler's forces. During Allied landings in southern France in 1944, at least two squadrons from USS *Tulagi* (CVE-72) and USS *Kasaan Bay* (CVE-69) provided air cover, strafed and bombed, and shot down three Heinkel He 111 bombers.

Flying the Hellcat, Cdr. David McCampbell of Carrier Air Group 15 became the Navy's all-time ace of aces, with thirty-four aerial victories. As skipper of Carrier Air Group 15 aboard the *Essex*, McCampbell shot down nine aircraft in a single mission on October 24, 1944. President Franklin D. Roosevelt later presented him with the Medal of Honor.

Grumman F6F Hellcat

The Navy's most famous aircraft of World War II, the F6F Hellcat began with a 1938 proposal by the Navy's favorite builder of fighters, Grumman, at Bethpage, Long Island, New York. After the Navy rejected an improved F4F Wildcat design, engineers created a wholly new fighter with a 1,600-hp Pratt & Whitney R-2600 engine.

A popular myth holds that the F4U Corsair, which was almost as famous and first flew on May 29, 1940, was "backup" insurance against the Hellcat. The opposite was true. The Navy pushed Grumman in case the Corsair, built by Vought-Sikorsky, ran into delays. The Corsair did, in fact, suffer developmental problems, and the F6F went into combat from carrier decks earlier than the F4U.

The Hellcat was a heavyweight, with enormous strength to enable it to survive against Japanese fighters armed with cannons. On June 30, 1941, the Navy awarded Grumman a contract for two prototypes. The first, the all-silver XF6F-1, made its first flight on June 26, 1942, piloted by Seldon A. Converse.

The second Hellcat, initially called the XF6F-2 but known as the XF6F-3 by the time it took to the air, had a supercharger added to the R-2800 engine.

The initial production version of the Hellcat, the F6F-3, first took to the air on October 4, 1942. In an era when American industry per-

---

Grumman F6F-5 Hellcat

Type: single-seat fighter

Powerplant: one 2,000-hp (1492-kW) Pratt & Whitney R-2800-10W Double Wasp 18-cylinder radial piston engine, driving a three-bladed, constant-speed Hamilton Standard Hydromatic propeller with a diameter of 13 feet 1 inch (3.99 m)

Performance: maximum speed 386 mph (621 km/h) at medium altitude; initial rate of climb 3,410 ft (1039 m) per minute; service ceiling 37,300 ft (11369 m); range 1,040 miles (1674 km)

Weights: empty 9,153 to 9,239 lb (4152 to 4191 kg); normal takeoff 12,500 lb (5670 kg); maximum takeoff 15,413 (6991 kg)

Dimensions: wingspan 41 ft 10 in (13.08 m); span with wings folded 16 ft 2 in (4.93 m); length 33 ft 7 in (10.23 m); height 13 ft 1 in (3.99 m); wing area 334 sq ft (31.03 sq m)

Armament: six .50-caliber (12.7-mm) Browning M3 machine guns with 400 rounds per gun, plus provision for two or three bombs, up to maximum total of 2,000 lb (907 kg), and six 5-inch (127-mm) high velocity aircraft rockets

First flight: June 26, 1942 (XF6F-1); July 30, 1942 (XF6F-3); October 4, 1942 (F6F-3)

---

formed miracles churning out the tools of war (nearly 100,000 aircraft in 1944 alone), there were problems. Grumman had inadequate space at its Bethpage factory. The plane maker solved this by buying up thousands of steel girders from New York City's dismantled Second Avenue "el" (elevated railway) and World's Fair pavilion to build a second Bethpage plant.

The F6F-5—the major production Hellcat model—first flew on April 5, 1944. All F6F-5s were powered by R2800-10Ws with water injection and were equipped with bomb racks. Specialized Hellcat models were used as night fighters and for photoreconnaissance.

Chapter Five

Escort Mission to Berlin

What Happened

The first time American bombs fell on the capital of Adolf Hitler's Third Reich, the cost was painful for those dropping the bombs. On March 6, 1944, while fighters flew escort, B-17 Flying Fortresses and B-24 Liberators of the Eighth Air Force carried out the first daylight attack on Berlin—and sixty-nine bombers and eleven fighters fell during a running air-ground battle that raged along hundreds of miles of invisible highway in the sky.

For bomber crews, the mission began with a wake-up call shortly after midnight. Briefing, warm-up, takeoff, form-up, and ingress all entailed work and risks. The fighting began around 11:00 A.M., when the first Focke-Wulf Fw 190s engaged Flying Fortresses over Holland. At least three bombers were rammed by German fighters, one by a twin-engined Messerschmitt Me 410.

For bomber crews, altitude, weather, and aviation itself posed as much danger as the Luftwaffe. The cold clawed at the men inside their narrow steel tubes. At times, there was frost inside the bombers. One B-17 gunner remembers leaving a swath of skin from his penis on the metal relief tube.

Of the three air divisions arrayed in a continuous stream en route to Berlin, two made a minor navigation error and swung farther south than

Major Thomas L. "Tommy" Hayes Jr.
March 6, 1944
North American P-51D Mustang (44-13318)
Frenesi
364th Fighter Squadron, 357th Fighter Group
Royal Air Force Station Leiston, England

In the cockpit of his P-51 Mustang named Frenesi, Major Thomas L. "Tommy" Hayes Jr. holds up five fingers to signify the aerial victories that made him an ace. Hayes fought in the southwest Pacific before becoming a Mustang pilot and participating in the first full-scale bombing raid on Berlin.

[U.S. Air Force]

planned. This confused the fighter defenses mounted with considerable skill by the Luftwaffe, but not for long. It also increased the danger from flak—which bomber crews feared more, even though fighters were more lethal.

In forty-five minutes, Luftwaffe pilots shot down twenty Flying Fortresses. After that, the bombers flew through intense flak at the Berlin outskirts and, after releasing bombs, were struck by fighters again.

It would have been far worse but for the long-range P-51 Mustang fighters escorting the bombers. While still approaching Berlin, the bomber stream came under assault from a second wave of "destroyer" Messerschmitt Bf 110s and Me 410s. P-51 pilots deterred most of the Germans, but some Bf 110s were able to close in and fire air-to-air rocket projectiles. At least eight Fortresses were claimed by this twin-engined Messerschmitt attack.

The American bomber crews ran a gauntlet of over six hundred Luftwaffe fighter sorties, with most German pilots getting airborne at least twice in the course of the day. "I wouldn't be here except for our 'little friends' in Mustangs," one bomber pilot said.

Sgt. Dale VanBlair, a gunner, described his trip to Berlin. "Although

I normally flew in the tail turret, I was drafted to occupy the nose turret with another crew member. When I looked ahead at the flak barrage we were approaching, my main concern was whether the navigator or bombardier on this crew would take the time to let me out of the nose turret if we had to bail out. I always left the doors of my tail turret open, thus didn't have to depend on anyone to let me out. I couldn't do that, of course, in the nose. Fortunately, we made it through, thanks primarily to the P-51s."

One of the P-51 Mustang pilots escorting Fortresses and Liberators over Berlin was Maj. Tommy Hayes, commander of the 364th Fighter Squadron, later to become an ace. Hayes toted up his second aerial victory during the attack on the German capital. "The Germans had their very best in the air against us that day," Hayes said.

Luftwaffe pilots claimed 108 bombers and twenty fighters, in contrast to the actual losses of sixty-nine and eleven. Bomber crews were credited with shooting down ninety-seven German fighters, while the P-51s were credited with a further eighty-two. Although such claims were exaggerated (the Luftwaffe actually lost sixty-six aircraft), it was a terrible day. As a symbol of the horror in that prolonged battle, at Thorpe Abbotts, home of the 100th Bombardment Group, the total number of Flying Fortresses to return safely to home base from Berlin was . . . one. Only three more landed at other bases in England.

The number of Americans killed in the air that day was almost identical to the number of Germans killed on the ground by falling bombs.

TOMMY HAYES. On March 2, 1944, I shot down my first German aircraft. We spotted a flight of four Messerschmitt Bf 109s over Frankfurt at 23,000 feet. When they saw us, two of them broke off, and my element of two P-51 Mustangs engaged them. My wingman, John Carder, and I met the lead pair head-on. It was two on two.

You might think that was a fair fight. But we had a lot of respect for the Germans. Fighter pilots are supposed to be cocky, but we never allowed ourselves to become too confident. Even relatively late in the war, on the eve of the Allied invasion of Europe, the Luftwaffe had very good pilots and very good planes.

In this battle, they were using the best of both. The Germans flew their craft well as we jockeyed for position. But we had an altitude advantage on them. Our engagement with them proved anticlimactic be-

They've called it the most beautiful aircraft ever built. They've called it the solution to the Allied air campaign over Europe. It was the P-51 Mustang and it was a thoroughbred. Hermann Goering said that Allied fighters would never fly over Berlin, but on March 6, 1944, Tommy Hayes and a few of his fellow P-51 pilots reached the capital of the Reich and fought with considerable success.

[Norman Taylor]

cause when they dived for the deck, they played their last card. They could turn, climb, or run. None were viable options. They split and turned. With our greater speed and maneuverability, they quickly "bought the farm" after a short burst from each of our sets of six .50-caliber guns. John and I returned to base, chalked up our victories, and savored the GI ration of whiskey.

It was quick. It was almost a textbook battle. It demonstrated the superiority of the P-51. For me it was fulfilling. It was exhilarating. What an aircraft!

Let me go back a couple of years. On December 7, 1941, I was enjoying my last day with my bride of six months, who was then two months pregnant. The next morning, I was scheduled to board an Army sea transport on a "permanent change of station" move to the Philippines.

Pearl Harbor changed all that. The Army scrounged up fifty-five crated P-40 Tomahawk fighters. They assembled a similar number of pilots, crew chiefs, and armorers, including me. All of us were loaded aboard USS *President Polk* (AP 103), a luxury passenger liner that the Navy had commandeered as a troop ship. Also aboard was an antiaircraft unit from Texas.

We received first-class treatment. The *Polk* had been scheduled to depart on December 8 on a 'round the world cruise. Now, it was taking us to war instead. The plan was to sneak us into Mindanao or some southern Philippine island.

We stopped in Brisbane, Australia, to assemble our P-40s. We worked in shifts around the clock. The crew chiefs were in charge: they told the pilots what to do, like how to use a torque wrench. Most of us knew how to use a crowbar.

Veteran pilots came down to Brisbane from the Philippines to lead those of us who were yet to get our feet wet. They were a gung ho group and were dedicated to getting back to the Philippine Islands and to get even with the Japanese.

They never did. There was no way to get back. The Japanese overwhelmed our forces in the Philippines in a very short time. A secure base in Java was as far north as we were going to get. A lot of Americans don't remember it today, but as soon as the Philippines were overrun, we fought a brief, desperate battle on the island of Java.

As soon as six P-40s were flyable, they headed north through Darwin, Timor, Bali, to Surabaya. The first group left in mid-January 1942. All were assigned to the 17th Pursuit Squadron (Provisional). Major Charles A. Sprague and his colleagues from the Philippines—which had now fallen to the Japanese—were the flight and element leaders.

The Japanese attacking Java flew twin-engine Mitsubishi G4M "Betty" bombers and single-engine Mitsubishi A6M Zero fighters. Without early warning of attack, the air battle was usually joined with them above us. They were experienced, with five years of combat in China. They were cocky and arrogant. They would barrel roll as they commenced their dive while we were hanging by our propellers.

What I said about respecting our German enemy applied equally well to the Japanese fighter pilots.

You were very careful when you went up against the Zero. You did not turn with a Zero. It was hit and run. Deflection shooting. It should be noted, in comparison, that the AVG or American Volunteer Group, the Flying Tigers in China with their P-40Bs, had a great shoot-down ratio because their early warning allowed them to get above the Japanese when the air battle began.

Escape from Java

Some Americans held out on Java until February or March, but the Java campaign effectively came to an end on January 28, 1942. The handwriting was clear when they cut our lifeline from Australia by their occupation of Bali on February 20. No more P-40s. No resupply. An effort was made to bring in P-40s on the old carrier, the USS *Langley* (AV 3), the Navy's first aircraft carrier, converted in 1937 to a seaplane tender with the removal of about 40 percent of its flight deck, by offloading P-40s at the dock and taking them off on an adjacent road. However, the Japanese sank the *Langley* before it could make port. I think the squadron was down to about ten P-40s for its last strike against the Japanese landing on the north coast of Java. The few that returned were given to the Dutch. Evacuation was underway.

Flying personnel were flown out by air. I was in a Dutch hospital recovering from injuries in a crash landing after being shot down by a Zero. I left on a Dutch freighter along with 1,500 ground personnel and British from Malaysia to Singapore.

Back in Australia, I was assigned to the 35th Pursuit Group, being reactivated in Sydney and thence to New Guinea. We flew a British version of the P-39 Airacobra known as a P-400. This was the same aircraft flown by 2nd Lt. Evans G. Stephens (Chapter 3), who caught malaria while flying the Airacobra.

Most pilots who flew the Airacobra doubted that it was particularly useful. It wasn't supercharged and didn't fight well at high altitude. Months after my time in Australia, Java, and New Guinea, I flew the Airacobra in training at Hamilton Field in northern California. I wasn't totally happy about the Airacobra's flying characteristics but loved its wide-track, tricycle landing gear. So instead of thinking about shooting down Messerschmitts or Zeros, I harbored this fantasy of taxiing out the main gate at Hamilton Field, and driving my Airacobra down the highway all the way to Los Angeles. I would follow old U.S. 99 and hold the Airacobra at 120 miles per hour, getting airborne to make those 90-degree turns and setting it back on the pavement for most of the trip. I would also get airborne when I encountered traffic. In my fantasy, the outcome of the trip was to use the nose cannon of the Airacobra to stick up a grocery store in Los Angeles. It was an unforgettable image—a guy in a menacing Airacobra sitting out front, holding up a store. Unfortunately, some people said the Airacobra wasn't much use for anything other than tooling down the highway. That was the only thing the Airacobra could do better than the Tomahawk and the Mustang.

We took the P-400 Airacobra to New Guinea anyway. We were again without a warning network. In ten to fifteen minutes, we usually were climbing through eight or nine thousand feet when the bombs hit and the Japanese were streaking home to their bases on the other side of the island. Here, the line-of-sight radar was blocked by the ten- to twelve-thousand-foot mountain range running down the spine of New Guinea.

The Airacobra may have had flaws, but it was a good gun platform. The Japanese had secretly stockpiled a sizable force of single- and twin-engine aircraft in Buna. They were well camouflaged and hidden under trees. Adjacent grassy areas were used for takeoff and landing.

We made a decision to hit them. We came in under the weather. What followed demonstrated how stable the Airacobra was while we were shooting. The weather was lousy, but we got under a low ceiling and rain. We caught them by surprise, made several runs, and left many burning. I received a Silver Star for this mission. More Airacobras went back in the afternoon. The weather was better, and some of the Japanese got into the air. Again, they had losses on the ground and some in the air.

It's hard to compare an older fighter like the Airacobra with a newer fighter like the P-51 Mustang. It's apples and oranges. To be fair, you really should compare the P-51 with the P-38 Lightning, P-47 Thunderbolt, Messerschmitt Bf 109, and the Focke-Wulf Fw 190.

Homeward Bound

In October 1942, all pilots who'd fought the Japanese in Hawaii, the Philippines, and Java were ordered home. This move was intended to put some experienced guys in Training Command and move away from the blind leading the blind. Though we'd been inadequately trained and poorly equipped, and had learned the hard way, we had knowledge worth passing along. Also, I felt qualified for the big show ahead.

Back in the states, I was assigned to a training unit, the 328th

Fighter Group, at Hamilton Field—our squadron, the 327th, was based at San Francisco airport—with the job of transitioning new graduates from flying school into the P-39 Airacobra. This wasn't the action I'd hoped for. I envied others from the Pacific who were assigned to new groups being activated.

A tragedy gave me my chance to get back into the war. The commander of the 364th Fighter Squadron, Capt. Varian K. White, was killed in a P-39 gunnery crash on May 10, 1943. I was picked to replace him. I became a squadron commander in the 357th Fighter Group. This was the group with which I would fly the immortal P-51 Mustang and make the first escort mission to Berlin.

I could sense immediately that this was a great unit. The guys were professional and dedicated. There was a strong camaraderie. Training was intense. They worked hard and they played hard.

The P-39 Airacobra, its flaws aside, proved to be a good training aircraft. It was unstable and unforgiving of an error. It killed a lot of pilots. But if you survived the P-39, you could fly anything. But overall, and considering logistics, it was better to lose them here than overseas.

By November 1943, we completed our training. We were ready. We were razor sharp. After a Thanksgiving crossing on another luxury liner, the *Queen Elizabeth*—which was by no means as comfortable as the *President Polk*—we disembarked in Scotland and entrained to our base in England. We followed the 354th Fighter Group (Ninth Air Force) in the base-to-base movement of our training. The 354th was already flying missions in the P-51B. They were the first, the pioneer Mustang group. Our 357th was the first P-51 group in the Eighth Air Force.

We had a kind of lend-lease in reverse. The Royal Air Force had Mustangs. The RAF took the birdcage canopy off and put this Malcolm job on it, and it really helped with visibility. In fact, I liked it better than the streamlined D because it bulged out behind you and you could see all around. So, yes, we put Malcolm hood canopies on some of our American Mustangs, and they gave us superb visibility. We also had some Mustangs that were bailed back to us by the British. You could still feel the outline of the British roundel under the paint where the US national insignia had been applied.

The Mustang was easy to check out and easy to fly. The Rolls-Royce Merlin engine gave it tremendous power. And with that huge propeller, one needed a strong leg to hold rudder against torque on takeoff. The

Mustang had great flight characteristics. It was easy to trim and stable on instruments. It gave noticeable warning of a stall. It offered a pilot great speed and acceleration.

Most important was its range and combat radius. Consider this. On the last mission to Schweinfurt in October 1943 (before the P-51 era), over a hundred bombers were lost after the shorter-legged P-47s had to leave their escort and return to base. That's 31 percent losses. The P-51 brought an end to such disasters.

Operation Argument was the effort to destroy the German Luftwaffe or, failing that, to so cripple it that the Allies would enjoy air superiority during the invasion. The bombers were to concentrate on the aircraft industry, aircraft assembly, engines, ball-bearing plants, etc. The German fighters had to engage the bombers. In November 1944, our fighters were given more freedom to move afar from the bombers, to seek and pursue. Argument became more intense in February 1945, with increasing intensity through May.

My hat is off to the 354th Fighter Group. Its P-51Bs were the Mustangs the Germans saw. They set the stage with their aggressiveness. The German pilots became fearful. When the 357th became operational in February, our goal was to be just as aggressive and capable. "Don't let the Germans off the hook," we were thinking.

My second victory was in the first large-scale attack on targets in the Berlin area on March 6, 1944, or four days after my first kill. That was a landmark day. Never before had large numbers of four-engined bombers flown over the German capital.

They launched over eight hundred B-17 Flying Fortresses and B-24 Liberators. As always, the bomber crews expected to face the danger of German flak and fighters on their way to Berlin. The Luftwaffe was ready. The Germans made two large fighter attacks on our aircraft. The first came between Hanover and Brunswick and met our P-47s. The second was between Magdeburg and Berlin. Our Mustangs from the 357th Fighter Group met the second attack. I was latched onto a Bf 109 but lost him when distracted by a flash in my peripheral vision, then another. These were falling bombs.

I looked up. All I could see was bombers. You can't grasp the concept of an entire sky filled with bombers from horizon to horizon, not until you've seen it. And they were all above me, bay doors open. I needed to get out of the spot I was in before they bombed me.

The B-17 Flying Fortress (shown) was the best-known Allied bomber of the European war, but B-24 Liberators went to Berlin, too. American officers believed at first that bombers could defend themselves against Luftwaffe fighters. They were proven wrong, and the P-51 Mustang drew the job of being a "little friend" to the B-17s and B-24s.

[U.S. Air Force]

Fight over Berlin

I made an abrupt split-S maneuver, paralleling the falling bombs, and pulled out just over the rooftops of Berlin. I headed for the closest open area. Soon after that, when I had just barely escaped being hit by falling bombs, a Messerschmitt appeared in the middle of everything that was going on.

The other three of my fellow P-51 pilots joined up to reestablish our four-plane formation, and that's when I spotted a Messerschmitt Bf 109 at low altitude.

Very quickly, I closed on him—closing fast. I fired as he dropped his gear. "Hey! He's landing," I thought, "there's an airfield ahead." Instead, he crashed and burned. Poor fellow, shot down on final approach. I carry no guilt. He was landing to reservice his aircraft and to go back up and try to kill the boys in our bombers.

We had not expected to find ourselves over a Luftwaffe airfield. We strafed the field, and all of us got hits on twin-engine Heinkel bombers,

Junkers Ju 88s, and even some Junkers Ju 52 transports. One pilot got some nice film as he brought his nose up through the control tower, still firing. On our way out of there, we shot up locomotives and a truck convoy. None of this would have been possible but for the huge fuel-carrying capacity, range, and endurance of the P-51 Mustang.

That first mission to Berlin was a milestone, but it was also just the beginning. For my squadron, it was back to Berlin on March 8, 1944.

That day, I engaged a twin-engine Messerschmitt Me 410. The Germans called it a Bomber Destroyer. It was loaded with rockets—large rockets and cannons. It could do a job on our bombers when it went through them head-on. But I'll say it was a dead goose if caught by a Mustang.

When I closed in on the Me 410 from behind, I felt some concern for the gunner.

ROBERT F. DORR. The twin-engine Messerschmitt Me 410 Hornisse (Hornet) was probably underrated by the Allies. It was a big, heavy, tough fighter, powered by two 1,850-hp (1380-kW) Daimler-Benz 603A inverted V-12 in-line piston engines, had a maximum speed of 364 mph (625 km/h) and was heavily armed with forward-firing guns. In addition, and of greatest concern to Hayes, the Me 410 had a gunner who controlled two .51 caliber (13-mm) MG 131 machine guns, with 430 rounds each in remotely-controlled, rearward-firing barbettes. The gunner sat behind the pilot but, somewhat disorientingly, facing to the rear and operating the guns using a remote-control pistol grip. From Hayes' point of view, attacking from the rear, the gunner was likely to be hit directly by any rounds Hayes fired. Ironically, the gunner's body and his seat served, in effect, as armor to protect the pilot from the same rounds. Like many pilots in combat, Hayes had the aggressive spirit to attack and shoot down an enemy aircraft, but felt distaste at killing the man inside the aircraft.

TOMMY HAYES. My only concern was my respect for the tail gunner. From dead astern, I closed gingerly and began firing from a bit beyond range at 400 to 500 yards. I was sure the men in the Me 410 saw me, but they apparently were unable to move out of the way. Rounds from my Mustang's six .50 caliber (12.7-mm) machine guns walked across the rear fuselage of the Me 410 and disintegrated pieces of the right wing root.

I had him when his right engine exploded. The Me 410 threw back fire and smoke, began to break up, and rolled over. It went down.

The Me 410, my third German kill, added to my two aerial victories against the Japanese, made me an ace. My eventual score was 8.5 German, plus two Japanese aircraft.

About my fighter: The Mustang may have been the best fighter of the war, but I didn't like that damned P-51C model (my second plane named Frenesi) because the visibility was so restrictive. Also, the plane was a pain in the neck to get in and out of. Earlier, I had flown a P-51B model (my first Frenesi) with the Malcolm canopy. That canopy bulged out like an electric light bulb and extracted a penalty in air speed, but the aircraft had better visibility to the rear. A pilot had taken my P-51B, rolled over, and dived into the ground, so I was stuck with the P-51C until we got the newer, bubble-canopy P-51Ds.

Over Munich on March 16, 1944, I had a quickie aerial victory over a Messerschmitt Bf 110 twin-engine fighter. We didn't have much respect for it because it was slow and sluggish, so I found myself asking, "You mean I get credit for an Bf 110?"

With my overconfidence, I found myself chasing a Focke-Wulf Fw 190. The pilot obliged with a lesson in how not to do it. It started at 22,000 feet (6705 m). He rolled over for the deck. In the dive, he never flew the plane. He slipped and skidded. Power off. Almost stalling speed. Power on. When he cut the throttle, that large radial engine became one big brake. His attitude changed continuously. Even dead ahead, I led and my fire was on the side.

After the pullout, I spread my flight of four left and right. If he turned, one of us would get him. He didn't turn. He pulled away from us. Yes, it was a lesson. He made a fool out of me. "I'll get the next one," I swore.

On another mission to Munich a few days later, we had to cross the Ruhr where the German flak was heavily concentrated. They had a lot of 88-mm guns there. The German gunfire always frightened me more than German fighter aircraft did. You could see the flak. You could hear it. You could smell it, in the cockpit. This was one situation where the coolant in the Mustang's underbelly was a problem and you wished you were in P-47. It was a God-fearing situation, and I was scared-to-death fanned out to avoid flak. We did all sorts of aerial calisthenics to avoid taking hits, but all four P-51s in my flight came home with battle dam-

Experienced, aggressive pilots were at the controls of the German fighters that defended Berlin on March 6, 1944. The Focke-Wulf Fw 190 (shown) and Messerschmitt Bf 109 were the main adversaries but were joined by twin-engine Messerschmitt Bf 110 and Me 410 fighters. The Americans in their P-51 Mustangs were equally capable.

[U.S. Air Force]

age. After I'd landed, when they inspected the plane and I saw how much metal had hit me, I got down on knees thanking God. My crew chief Bob Krull said he'd do the same; he couldn't believe a P-51 could come back with so much damage.

Sure enough, a few weeks later, the group intercepted a gaggle of Fw 190s. I think we knocked down about eighteen. It was a dogfight at altitude with no dive to the deck. I claimed one 190, but my wingman said it was a 109. We argued. The combat film proved it was a Bf 109. That day, the ground was credited with seventeen Fw 190s and one Bf 109. I never got another chance at a 190.

Usually, Bf 109s were relatively easy. But now and then, the 109 pilot put up a hell of a fight. The difference was either the pilot or the aircraft. Of course, if the pilot had over a hundred kills, he knew what he was doing. Then there were considerations involving the aircraft. Did the 51 have a full fuselage tank (located behind the center of gravity)? Was the 109 low on fuel and ammo?

On this encounter, we were in a rat race at about 28,000 feet (8534 m).

Who's Who

Major (later Brig. Gen.) Thomas L. "Tommy" Hayes Jr., P-51 Mustang fighter pilot and commander, 364th Fighter Squadron

Sgt. Dale VanBlair, aerial gunner aboard a B-24 Liberator bomber over Berlin

Capt. Varian K. White, Hayes' predecessor as commander, 364th Fighter Squadron; killed in training

Sgt. Bob Krull, crew chief of Hayes' P-51 Mustang

We climbed and struggled for position up to over 35,000 (10558 m). It was give and take. Finally, he rolled out for the deck.

"Is he low on fuel?" I wondered. We both hit compressibility at about the same time. This was not new to me. I'd experienced it several times. The airframe and its controls had reached the plane's terminal speed. The plane shook. Stick and rudder got no response. It came out of it when you reached more dense air, around 12,000 feet (3660 m). We never bottomed out together. He had control before me. He rolled 180 degrees and pulled out. Moments later, I had control, but he was gone. Out of sight.

Here's my recollection of another battle that stressed the importance of plane and pilot: One day, we fell into the middle of a classic interception of bombers by fifty to sixty Bf 109s and Fw 190s, with a top cover of thirty Bf 109s, plus or minus. Some continued for the bombers, and the rest turned into the Mustangs.

In minutes, it all broke down to units of one, two pairs, and fours. There were about seven or eight as we engaged.

The ensuing fight got confused. Like an RAF pilot told me during a dogfight in the Battle of Britain, he started with another Hurricane on his wing and ended with himself on the wing of a Bf 109. For me on this day, I was alone and there were five Bf 109s. But only the leader and I were one-on-one. The other four were covering. Probably ordered to.

For what seemed an eternity (maybe twenty minutes), it was a standoff. Each of us struggled and jockeyed for position to close the circle. "What's going on?" I wondered. I knew I was just an average pilot. But, I'm thinking, unlike that German, "I am in a P-51!"

The P-51 Mustang was the only Allied fighter with the range to accompany bombers to Berlin. Tommy Hayes also flew the P-39 Airacobra and P-40 Tomahawk, but he calls the Mustang "my first love." The clean lines and classy appearance of the Mustang belie the fact that it is a very functional machine.

[U.S. Air Force]

"What's the problem?" I'm wondering. Has he given up? Is he tired? Is he low on fuel? "The game has changed," I'm thinking. His cover has joined the fight. They have coordinated their passes from different headings. They are doing all the shooting. There is a cloud cover below, with tops at around 10,000 feet. I do what I did on my checkout: I chopped my throttle, applied full rudder, and pulled the stick back. Snap! I'm spinning. Not flying. When I hit the overcast, I let go of the controls. The spinning stopped. I rolled my P-51 level and broke out in the clear after fifteen minutes on instruments. Back at bomber altitude, I joined up with other friends and returned to base. "Tomorrow will be another day," I thought.

I named my P-51 *Frenesi*. It was a popular piece of music in the early 1940s, sung in Spanish to a south-of-the-border rhythm. It was our song, my wife and me. "Frenesi" translates, "Love me tenderly."

Frenesi really belonged to the ground crew, and they let me fly her. What an airplane! We all loved her tenderly.

I flew my first sortie February 11, 1944, and my last on August 12, 1944, a total of seventy-five missions.

Chapter Six

Mustang vs. Messerschmitt

What Happened

After the Allies invaded Normandy in June 1944, American fighter pilots began operating from small airfields on the European continent.

Former Capt. Clayton Kelly Gross flew P-51 Mustang missions on the continent. Gross, 82, a retired dentist in Vancouver, Washington, was a member of the 354th Fighter Group. "My experiences included shooting at Germans and getting shot down," Gross said. He became an ace.

Fighting on the continent sometimes meant surviving more like a soldier than an airman, living in tents, mud, and the elements, but the experience also enabled fliers like Gross to meet the people of France. Some pilots regarded life in the town of Gael, in the French province of Brittany, as "the lushest days of their career on the continent," as one put it. In 2002, residents of the town dedicated a monument to the American airmen.

Gross considers himself typical of those airmen, "not a hero, that's for certain, but a real fighter pilot." Like so many, Gross was a citizen soldier who donned a uniform when there was a war to be won, and then came home afterward.

"I wanted to fly at a very young age." When he signed up in 1941 for duty in the Army Air Forces, Gross had already accumulated ninety

**Captain Clayton Kelly Gross
April 14, 1945
North American P-51D
  Mustang
355th Fighter Squadron, 354th
  Fighter Group
A-66 Airfield, Gael, France**

Capt. Clayton Kelly Gross (right) poses with "Mary Pat II," a P-51D Mustang that belonged to fellow pilot Maurice Long (not shown). Other Mustang pilots in this posed portrait are Gil Talbot and Dick Kenyon. Gross became an ace and shot down a German Messerschmitt Me 262 Jet fighter.

[U.S. Air Force]

flying hours in a civilian Waco UPF-7 biplane. He was a member of Flying Class 42-H, the first to graduate new pilots after the December 7, 1941, Japanese attack on Pearl Harbor.

Gross, who is five feet, eleven inches in height, pinned on his wings and was handed a set of instructions saying, "If you are five feet eleven or taller, you may not request [duty in] fighters." He made the request anyway, and no one ever came around with a tape measure. For fighter training, the Army assigned him to the 328th Fighter Group at Hamilton Field, California, flying the P-39 Airacobra—apparently months too late to cross paths with 328th veteran Tommy Hayes (Chapter 4). "We lost many pilots in training," Gross recalled. He served in other U.S. locations before going overseas.

Gross flew the P-47 Thunderbolt in combat for two or three months in the 354th Fighter Group. The P-47 was one of the most impressive fighters of the war, but Gross was a critic. Gross said the P-47 was less vulnerable to ground fire, but the P-51 performed better in air-to-air action.

"All of my six aerial victories were with the Mustang. But I got shot down by rifle fire and had to bail out of the Mustang near Metz in the fall of 1944. A rifle bullet wouldn't have done that to me in the Thunderbolt."

Gross was in action for an extended period. He shot down five Messerschmitt Bf 109 propeller-driven fighters—two on May 11, 1944, and one

Kelly Gross battled a German jet, but his main job was to escort Allied bombers over Germany. This photo of B-17 Flying Fortresses en route to their target was taken by Army Air Forces photographer Clark Gable, who was better known as a film actor.

[U.S. Air Force]

each on May 28, June 14, and October 29, 1944. These aerial victories are listed in an Air Force internal document listing of victory credits.

Gross's sixth aerial victory, on April 14, 1945, is not listed in the document but was recognized during the war and is recognized by the American Fighter Aces Association, and by historians today. It was remarkable, because it was a Messerschmitt Me 262 jet fighter, an aircraft that was especially difficult to defeat.

Gross's 354th Fighter Group achieved a number of distinctions. According to the book *Air Force Combat Units of World War II*, the 354th "was instrumental in the development and execution of long-range missions to escort heavy bombers . . . deep into enemy territory." After moving to the Continent, the 354th group "assisted the Allied drive across France by flying fighter-sweep, dive-bombing, strafing, and escort missions." The unit supported Allied ground troops during the Battle of the Bulge in December 1944 and January 1945, according to the book, by "conducting armed reconnaissance operations to destroy enemy troops, tanks, and rail lines."

KELLY GROSS. Before I ever put on a uniform, I completed civil pilot training and had about ninety hours and a private license flying a Porterfield and a Waco UPF-7 biplane. As a youngster growing up in the Pacific Northwest, I bowled with Maj. Gen. John Brooks, commander of the Second Air Force at Geiger Field, Washington, who influenced my choice of the air force.

When I became a pilot trainee in the Army Air Forces, I went to Coleman, Texas, for primary instruction in the PT-19 Cornell, and then to Randolph Field, Texas, for basic training in the BT-14. After that, I went to Kelly Field, Texas, and did advanced training in the AT-6 Texan. I was a member of Flying Class 42-II and graduated at Kelly Field, on September 6, 1942.

After my brief experience with P-39 Airacobras at Hamilton Field (Chapter 3), I was one of twelve pilots assigned to the 354th Fighter Group. In January 1943, we formed the 354th group at Tonopah, Nevada—still, piloting P-39s that were even older than those at Hamilton Field.

We became the original flight leaders of the group's three squadrons. I had the advantage of having five hundred hours of fighter time in the P-39 before our group was sent to the European Theater of Operations in October 1943.

The group became the first to fly the P-51 Mustang and adopted the name "Pioneer Mustang Group." I was one of three pilots sent to a British base to check out the new fighter during the period November 7–16, 1943. We flew the A-36 version (a dive-bomber) and the P-51A for several flights and then headed back to check others out in the P-51B.

I flew two hundred combat hours (considered a combat tour for fighters) and finished on June 28, 1944. I had four confirmed aerial victories at that time. We were flying from airfield A-2 near the Omaha Beach area, having made the move about ten days after D-Day. I was sent home for a thirty-day leave and then returned for a second tour. My first flight back in combat on the second tour took place on October 28, 1944. On my second mission back, on October 29, I destroyed a Bf 109 to become an ace. Three weeks later, on November 18, I was shot down by ground fire while destroying six German motor vehicles. I bailed out east of Metz, which the Germans still held, but was picked up by one of Patton's armored units and returned to my base twenty-four hours later, after spending the night with them. I flew one more mission in a P-51 after returning, and then on December 1, 1944, our fighter group transitioned to P-47s.

We shifted to the P-47 at an odd time. We were fighting on the continent of Europe. My 354th Fighter Group was now at airfield A-66, Gael, France, after the move from England, when my fellow pilots and I were told we must change to the "Jug."

We were told that the Eighth Air Force was converting to P-51s, and wanted our aircraft for Col. Hubert Zemke's 56th Fighter Group, which was the last outfit in the Eighth that hadn't transitioned to Mustangs.

It was like stepping out of a racing car and climbing into a two-and-a-half-ton truck. It had an impact on our morale. It also had an impact on our production as far as aerial victories were concerned.

For generations, veterans have argued about which was the better World War II fighter, the P-47 or the P-51. Maybe my preference for the P-51 started with my first flight in a "Jug," when I learned how much runway it needed. "Jug" was the nickname given to the P-47 because of its portly shape. As we must always do in a single-seat fighter, I spent a few hours in the cockpit memorizing all the instrument and control positions. Then I was ready, and they told me one of those monsters had just finished a 100-hour check and needed a test flight. I decided to take it.

The field at A-66 was the usual for advanced landing strips—carved from the countryside, cleared, somewhat leveled, and covered with a metal mesh mat for its 2,700-foot length. It was adequate for operations with our beloved Mustangs.

The Jug, even with its water-injection feature, took every last foot of runway to get into the air. To make matters worse, the French had a custom of beautifying their roads by planting trees on each side in a geometric pattern, about ten to twelve feet apart. It made for very pretty, shady country lanes, but unfortunately one of those crossed just beyond the end of our runway. When we flew the P-51, we were well airborne by that time. Now, it became a challenge to clear the treetops.

The first day of P-47 flying, one unfortunate young pilot didn't make it. He was about ten feet up when he reached the line of thirty-five-foot trees—quite inadequate. It was hard to tell which fared the worst, tree or Jug. The tree was snapped off where he hit it. The Jug disintegrated, but we gained a measure of admiration for the way Republic had put those monsters together. When the first people reached the scene, they found the egg-shaped frame of the cockpit had rolled a hundred feet from the point of impact but still contained the seat with the pilot still strapped in it. While he was seriously injured, he was still alive and conscious.

My first flight was probably one of the reasons I didn't like the P-47 as much as I did the P-51. "Well, I've got one down here that needs to be test-hopped," they told me. They said it was not like the Mustang. They said I was going to need the whole field to get it off.

On the Continent

That dirt field in France had wire mat superimposed. I had taken P-51s off in half the distance this short runway offered. Now, I used every inch of the runway and still hadn't felt the Jug leave the ground. With trees fast approaching, I almost had to physically lift it off to clear the trees. Once in the air, I couldn't gain altitude and flew only feet above the tree-tops, using all my strength to hold it. Logically, I would hit the trim tab back to help me go up and I tried it, and it wanted to go down. I almost lost my life on that first flight. Later, we learned that a trim tab had been installed backward. So when I almost went into the trees before finally getting control, it wasn't due to any fault in the design of the P-47. But it almost killed me, and I was upset about it.

That was enough to convince me I wanted my P-51 back. We didn't get them back for some time though, flying the P-47 through December, January, and half of February.

The P-47 was nowhere as maneuverable as the P-51. At the time of Bastogne, when the weather finally cleared enough to let us into the air near the besieged 101st Airborne Division, I was dive-bombing in the P-47 and got hit by a cannon shell that hit my forward fuselage and blew two cylinders completely out of the engine. I didn't even know I had been hit.

"When I landed, people were running alongside the aircraft pointing at it. I climbed out and saw that the whole right side of the aircraft was covered with oil. So the P-47 could take great punishment.

The hit that had brought me down in a P-51 near Metz wouldn't have brought down a Thunderbolt, which was built like an anvil. Still, to choose between a plane that could take punishment and one that wasn't likely to be hit as often (the P-51), I would rather not get hit as often.

The P-47 could carry a huge load. We were flying short-range missions, so we did not need the two 185-gallon fuel tanks under each wing. Usually, we would carry two 1,000-lb bombs, one under each wing, plus one 500-lb bomb under the fuselage. We did not have the air-to-ground rockets that Thunderbolts in some units carried.

I had incidents in both aircraft that point to plusses and minuses. My bailing out in a P-51 was caused by rifle fire. Before jumping, I counted eight holes—one through the engine, and that brought me down. In a dive-bombing mission in a P-47 around Bastogne, I took a 20-mm hit in the engine that blew two cylinders out and I didn't even know I had been hit. The eight .50 caliber guns in a P-47 had awesome firepower. I actually tipped over a boxcar while strafing in a Jug! Awesome! I also felt the impact of those eight fifties flying a P-51 when a P-47 mistook me for a Bf 109 like the one I was chasing and hit me with all eight. It blew my canopy off, made a four-inch indentation in the steel plate behind my head, without penetrating but nearly knocking me out. I did an involuntary snap roll and then spun but recovered to find myself alive. The Jugs, two of them, abruptly recognized me and left me. I found one of my squadron to escort me home and then flew up to Boxted to confront the guy that hit me. It was Major Francis S. "Gabby" Gabreski's squadron, and he defended them until finally bringing in a new pilot who had "made a mistake." They had destroyed their gun camera film.

Here are some differences between the P-47 and P-51:

The Mustang was faster, more maneuverable, had less firepower, and was more vulnerable.

The Jug climbed slower, flew slower, was less maneuverable, had more firepower, and could take a lot of punishment. It maybe dove faster, according to P-47 lovers, but I thought the Mustang was as good. At least it dived fast enough to catch an Me 262, which I shot down.

The 354th group shot down more aircraft in aerial combat than any other group in the European Theater of Operations, even though the 4th and 56th groups had a head start on us. Veterans of those groups claim that it's because they had shot down all the "good" German pilots, and we had the poor ones left. But after we arrived, they fought the same Germans we fought, and we did better. Their argument doesn't hold water.

P-47 Critic

Our aerial victory totals dipped when we got the P-47s. We were in the Ninth Air Force, and our commander, Maj. Gen. Elwood "Pete" Que-

Even when taxiing on the ground, the P-51D Mustang looked sleek and fast. This pilot is wearing the oxygen mask that will protect him at high altitude over Germany. Ports for three of the Mustang's six guns are visible at the leading edge of the wing.

[U.S. Air Force]

---

sada, was very proud of our aerial victories. The P-47 was very effective for air-to-ground work, and that became important after the invasion of Normandy. But while many pilots swear by the P-47, I was not an advocate for the airplane.

Fighting a war in Europe from bases on the Continent was an unforgettable experience. I believe the hospitality of the French people made pilots' lives easier.

In February 1945, we got our Mustangs back and finished the war with them. Having flown both, I have a definite preference, and it isn't the P-47. Still, I respect the P-47, having used that tremendous eight-times .50-caliber firepower on the enemy. I also know how much punishment the P-47 can take. It wasn't my favorite, but it was a great aircraft.

I was an ace by virtue of two kills on May 11, 1944, followed by one each on May 28, June 14, and October 29. They were all Messerschmitt Bf 109s. But my most important victory came on April 14, 1945, when I faced a Messerschmitt Me 262 jet fighter.

It was the third time I had seen one of the German "wonder weapons." We were not briefed about these aircraft. When I saw my first one during a bomber escort, I was startled by the speed as one made a pass at the bombers. It seemed that we had zero chance to intercept or chase. We pilots discussed these new aircraft amongst ourselves as more of our group saw or had contact with them. They were recognizable from silhouettes eventually furnished by our intelligence people.

The first time, I saw a thing that looked like a beer barrel with flaps sticking out of it. That was a Messerschmitt Me 163 Komet (Comet) rocket plane. The second time, I was escorting bombers. I was on the right side of a box of B-17 Flying Fortresses. Someone hollered, "Bogie at two o'clock!" I said, "I've got him!" I turned into him. But I didn't have him. He went right by me.

This last time, I was leading a flight of eight P-51s with orders to find anything we could to shoot at. I sent one flight south and kept mine north near the Elbe River. We were cruising at 12,000 feet (3660 meters). I saw movement below me. I recognized it as a 262.

This Me 262 had a big red number "1" painted on it. The Germans identified their planes by ranking number. The Staffel commander's aircraft was number one. His second in command was two, and so on. The bigger the number was, the lower in rank the pilot was.

He was at 2,000 feet (6096 m). I rolled over and went down. I entered compressibility. My control surfaces stopped working. I don't know how fast I was going, but it was very, very fast. I did a little praying. At lower altitude, I finally regained control and, lo and behold, the 262 was right in front of me. I shot at very close range. I opened fire from very close range and saw strikes on his left side. A fairly large piece of his left wingtip came off and the left jet engine began burning. I had to pull off right to avoid collision, and when I rolled back—found him climbing straight up.

I hit him again, and he burst into flames. Then, I shot again, and he burned some more. I had sight of him in his cockpit. He climbed another thousand feet or so and, then, seemed to stop in midair. The canopy came off. The pilot ejected. I was thrilled as hell. His aircraft fell apart, and it went down in flames and smoke.

I tried to make a pass around the parachute, but we were over a German airfield by this time and the antiaircraft was opening up at me. I thought the guy lived. I was told after the war that he was killed that day. Years later, I was at a reunion of German fighter pilots. I met the pilot I'd shot down. Kurt Lobgesong. The big red "1" on the nose of the jet belonged to him, a German commander. He thanked me for saving

One U.S. pilot said that only one word came to his mind when he thought of the German Messerschmitt Me 262 jet fighter. *Dread.* The Me 262, also known as the Stormbird, wasn't perfect, but it was faster than the P-51D Mustang and could carry plenty of armament.

[U.S. Air Force]

his life. He had been wounded in the left side and didn't have to fly any more, which meant he lived through the war—something a lot of his mates did not do.

North American P-51 Mustang

Hermann Goering, one of the more unpleasant figures in Nazi Germany, once boasted that Allied warplanes would never reach his capital.

On March 6, 1944, American bombers struck Berlin, escorted by the magnificent P-51 Mustang, regarded by many as the finest fighter in history.

Other fighters performed well during World War II, but only the sleek, speedy P-51 had the range to routinely fly from England to targets deep inside Germany.

"When I saw Mustangs over Berlin," said Goering in a subsequent remark, "I knew the war was lost."

During the war years, 15,684 Mustangs were built. It all began in

Who's Who

Capt. Clayton Kelly Gross, P-51 Mustang and P-47 Thunderbolt pilot and air ace, 355th Fighter Squadron, 354th Fighter Group

1939, when Sir Henry Self of British Purchasing Commission was posted to New York and approached North American Aviation in Inglewood, California, to seek help with a new fighter. The British approved a preliminary design in May 1940. The legend persists that North American vice president J. Leland Atwood and a design team led by Edgar Schmued and Raymond Rice cooked up the Mustang from scratch, but in fact, Atwood spent months working with the British and had access to material on a Curtiss fighter, the XP-46.

Still, the design work on the new fighter, known at first by the company name NA-73X and rolled out at Mines Field, Los Angeles, in September 1940, was genuinely a work of genius. Powered by a 1,075-hp Allison V-1710-F3R engine, the prototype made its first flight on October 26, 1940, at Mines Field (today's Los Angeles International Airport), with Vance Breese as pilot.

It wasn't obvious, but the all-silver NA-73X was a quantum leap forward. A low-wing, flush-canopy, liquid-cooled aircraft, the NA-73X looked more or less the same as any other fighter in its class, including the Spitfire and Messerschmitt Bf 109. But the plane took good ideas and used them well. Among these was a low, square-cut wing, the laminar-flow airfoil of which reduced drag, and a radiator scoop streamlined into the lower fuselage behind the pilot. Breese was delighted when the NA-73X attained a speed of 382 mph (615 km/h), making it as fast as early Spitfires that carried half as much fuel.

On flight number nine, November 20, 1940, pilot Paul Balfour made an error in switching fuel-feed, and the engine went dead. Balfour had no time to attempt a restart before the NA-73X piled up in an upside-down wreck. Unhurt, Balfour had just introduced a major delay into the Mustang development program, although the NA-73X did resume flying on January 11, 1941.

The NA-73 was ordered into production for the Royal Air Force on September 20, 1940, under terms that specified that two planes would be delivered for testing to the U.S. Army. The first of these XP-51s flew on May 20, 1941, at Inglewood, piloted by Robert Chilton. These two aircraft went to Wright Field, Ohio, for tests. Meanwhile, the U.S. Army ordered five hundred A-36 Apache dive-bombers. These were Mustangs powered by the 1,325-hp Allison V-1710-87 engine and fitted with large wing-dive brakes.

The P-51A designation went to the first U.S. version built in at least modest numbers. Power came from a 1,200-hp Allison V-1710-81 with an improved supercharger. Four .50 caliber (12.7-mm) machine guns were installed in the wings. The P-51A went aloft for the first time on February 3, 1942, piloted by Chilton.

There was nothing wrong with the Allison engine, but the decision to switch to the superb British Merlin was a choice that illustrated the Mustang's growth potential. In April 1942, Ronald W. Harker, a test pilot with Rolls Royce, flew a Mustang I and was favorably impressed with its performance up to medium altitudes. Harker told his superiors the fighter would perform even better with a Merlin 61. Lt. Col. Thomas "Tommy" Hitchcock, air attaché at the American embassy in London, was also reporting to Washington on the merits of the Merlin.

Packard developed an American version of the Merlin, the V-1650, and this became the basis for the next production version of the North American fighter. The first of two XP-51Bs appeared in late 1942. The P-51B went into production immediately.

There remained one final change to create the definitive Mustang: the bubble canopy. As happened with the P-47 Thunderbolt, the flush canopy was discarded and the bubble adopted instead, itself the result of research that had developed the plastic bombardier's nose on Army bombers. The "razorback" aft fuselage was cut down level with the fuselage forward section and the bubble installed.

The P-51D was armed with six .50-caliber (12.7-mm) guns. There was no P-51E model. The P-51F, P-51G, and P-51J were lightweight models, while the P-51H was a postwar version that never saw combat. The P-51K designation went to 1,335 Mustangs from the Dallas plant, identical to the P-51D but for a different propeller.

The first air-to-air victory for the Mustang was racked up in British colors during the star-crossed Dieppe raid on August 19, 1942, when an American in the RAF, Pilot Officer Hollis H. Hills, shot down a Focke-Wulf Fw 190. Hills went on to become the first Mustang ace.

They called it a thoroughbred. The North American P-51D Mustang was the first fighter with the range to routinely escort Allied bombers to targets deep inside the Third Reich. In an un-expected development for which it wasn't as well prepared, the Mustang also became the U.S. fighter that most frequently battled the German's "wonder weapon" jet fighters.

[U.S. Air Force]

The Mustang later became so important as an escort for Allied bombers that it's worth remembering the P-51's best-known mission evolved gradually. As the bombing campaign over Europe grew, the Eighth Air Force in England looked at disturbing losses of four-engine bombers and assigned high priority to a need it had earlier identified, the need for a long-range fighter to escort the bombers and duel with the Germans' superb Messerschmitts and Focke-Wulfs. The need was graphically illustrated by the August 17, 1943, Schweinfurt-Regensburg raid when sixty out of 376 bombers were lost, a disturbing 16 percent of the total force. Soon afterward came "Black Thursday," the October 14, 1943, raid on Schweinfurt, when sixty out of 280 bombers were shot down, 20 percent of the entire force.

Merlin Mustang

The Eighth sent Col. Cass Hough, head of its technical section, to test-fly the P-51B. He reported back on the Mustang's many qualities and its enormous potential, but he also said that directional stability problems needed to be fixed. After the P-51D with teardrop canopy and dorsal fin came along, and in spite of the fact that the Thunderbolt packed eight guns to the Mustang's six, no one worried about these problems any longer.

The first Merlin-powered P-51Bs to become operational in England belonged not to the Eighth Air Force, which needed them for bomber escort, but to the Ninth Air Force, which was charged with air-to-ground combat responsibilities to support the expected invasion of occupied Europe. The 354th Fighter Group at Boxsted under Lt. Col. Kenneth Martin was the first unit in the European theater of operations to receive Mustangs. The group remained under the jurisdiction of Ninth Air Force but was immediately ordered to support bomber operations.

In the Mustang's first combat mission by an American fighter group, on a December 11, 1943, bomber escort to Emden, not much happened. A few days later, Lt. Charles F. Gumm shot down a twin-engined Messerschmitt Bf 110 for the first aerial victory by an American Mustang group. By the end of the month, the 354th group had shot down eight Luftwaffe aircraft, including four more rocket-carrying Bf 110s but had lost eight Mustangs, most due to technical problems. While this was going on, the group's pilots were adjusting to what amounted to a new kind of warfare. Now, Mustang pilots were facing four- to five-hour missions. This kind of flying imposed new demands on the pilot, creating all kinds of discomfort, but it was even worse on the airplane. The Mustang was prone to coolant loss at high altitude, where engines overheated and eventually seized. Coolant, oil, and oxygen problems needed to be resolved.

On January 11, 1944, Major James H. Howard of the 354th repeatedly risked his life to defend bombers from Luftwaffe fighter attack. Separated from his flight, Howard was alone near a B-17 bomber formation, which came under attack from six to eight twin-engined German fighters. There were at least dozens of Luftwaffe fighters not far away. Howard unhesitatingly went into harm's way and shot down, in quick succession, a twin-engine plane, a Focke-Wulf FW 190, and a Messerschmitt Bf 109. Moments later, he shook another Bf 109 off the tail of an American aircraft. Howard continued fighting aggressive and persistent Luftwaffe pilots for a half hour thereafter. His ship during the engagement was nicknamed "Ding Hao." A soft-spoken figure who wrote up a report of the incident without mention of his own heroism, Howard was awarded the Medal of Honor.

The 357th and 363rd fighter groups equipped with Mustangs soon afterward, followed by the 4th Fighter Group under Col. Donald Blakeslee, which also began converting to the P-51B.

Blakeslee was chosen to lead his fighters to Berlin on March 3, 1944, but fate threw a monkey wrench into his prospect of being first over the Reich's capital. Blakeslee's group was recalled en route because of deteriorating weather. P-38 Lightnings of the 55th Fighter Group under Lt. Col. Jack Jenkins failed to receive the recall and continued on to Berlin, becoming the first Allied fighters to do so. A second attempt to take P-51Bs to Berlin was also fouled by the weather, but on March 6, 1944, Blakeslee led his Mustangs into a furious battle over the capital. That, of course, was the battle where Major Tommy Hayes scored an aerial victory. By the spring of 1944, five more fighter groups in the Eighth Air Force were equipping with P-51B/C Mustangs. By then, too, the Mustang began appearing in the Mediterranean theater of operations.

In Europe, the 352nd Fighter Group produced the top-scoring Mustang pilot of all, Major George E. Preddy, who was credited with 26.83 aerial victories and five aircraft destroyed on the ground.

By summer of 1944, rapidly arriving P-51Ds were in command of the air. Although the very top-ranking American aces in Europe flew P-47 Thunderbolts, the Mustang was the aircraft of many air aces whose mastery over the Luftwaffe made their names familiar to a generation of aviation followers—Lt. Col. John C. Meyer, with twenty-four air and thirteen ground victories; Preddy; and Captain Don S. Gentile, with 21.83 air and six ground kills.

On July 18, 1944, Mustang pilots of the 359th Fighter Group on an escort mission to Merseburg ran into the Messerschmitt Me 163 rocket-propelled fighter for the first time. On August 5, Me 163s shot down three Mustangs with their 30-mm cannons.

Germany was first with jet aircraft, and the Messerschmitt Me 262 was the world's first operational jet fighter. Eighth Air Force chief Lt. Gen. James Doolittle was seriously concerned about German jets and said there was very little he could do about the problem, except to increase the number of escort fighters per long-range mission over the continent.

On October 7, 1944, 1st Lt. Urban Drew of the 361st group scored the first Me 262 kills for the Mustang, claiming two Me 262s as they were taking off from Achmer. Capt. Charles E. Yeager of the 357th Fighter Group, who earlier had downed five Luftwaffe aircraft in a single day, toted up a Mustang victory over the Me 262 on November 6, 1944.

In the Pacific theater, the first Mustang to see service was the F-6D reconnaissance aircraft, which began to replace P-40s with the 82nd Tactical Reconnaissance Squadron at Morotai in November 1944. In early 1945, the 35th and 348th Fighter Groups, in the Philippines, began to replace their weary Thunderbolts with P-51Ds.

It was that tiny crag of rock, the island of Iwo Jima, invaded by U.S. Marines on February 19, 1945, which eventually became home for a massive P-51 force. Mustangs of the 15th Fighter Group began arriving at Iwo Jima's South Field on March 6, 1945. The 23rd and 306th groups followed, joined later by the 506th. Soon, P-51 Mustangs, usually carrying two 165-gallon drop tanks, began escorting B-29 Superfortresses in the final campaign against the Japanese home islands.

North American P-51D Mustang

Type: single-seat fighter and fighter-bomber

Power plant: one 1,590-hp (1186-kW) Packard V-1650-7 (Rolls-Royce Merlin) liquid-cooled in-line engine

Performance: maximum speed 437 mph (703 km/h) at 20,000 ft (6096 m); initial rate of climb 3,475 ft (1060 m) per minute; operating radius with maximum fuel 1,300 miles (2092 km)

Weights: empty 7125 lb (3230 kg); loaded 11,600 lb (5262 kg)

Dimensions: wingspan 37 ft 0-½ in (11.29 m); length 32 ft 3 in (9.84 m); height 13 ft 8 in (4.10 m); wing area 235 sq ft (21.83 sq m)

Armament: six .50 caliber (12.7-mm) Browning M3 machine guns, with 400 rounds for each inboard gun and 270 rounds for each outboard gun; provision for two 500-lb (227-kg) bombs, eight rockets, or other underwing ordnance in place of drop tanks

First flight: October 26, 1940 (NA-73X); May 20, 1941 (XP-51); May 29, 1942 (P-51A); November 17, 1943 (XP-51D)

On January 11, 1945, Maj. William A. Shomo was at the controls of a P-51D on a mission over northern Luzon in the Philippines. Attacked by a swarm of Japanese fighters, Shomo pulled off the unprecedented feat of shooting down seven Japanese warplanes in a single mission. For this achievement, he became the second Mustang pilot to be awarded the Medal of Honor.

The Mustang emerged from World War II as the best-known fighter of that conflict. When the Air Force became an independent service branch in 1947 and changed its system for aircraft names the following year, the P-51 became the F-51. With its new appellation, the Mustang guarded the United States early in the Cold War and fought in Korea.

Chapter Seven

Jet Kills over North Korea

What Happened

It was the first time naval aviators fought high above the gnarled brown ridges and soot-filled cities of the Korean peninsula. On July 3, 1950, the target was an airfield near North Korea's capital, and the U.S. Navy was flying its first-ever combat mission using jet aircraft. It was also the first combat for the portly, blue Grumman F9F Panther carrier-based jet fighter.

The air-to-air part of that mission was an anticlimax. Panther pilots were credited with shooting down two North Korean Yakovlev Yak-9 propeller-driven fighters, the Navy's first aerial victories of the Korean War. It happened quickly: The Yaks had only minutes to threaten the carrier-based Panthers.

The Korean War began eight days earlier. In the predawn hours of Sunday, June 25, 1950, in darkness and driving rain, North Korean armed forces crossed the 38th Parallel and invaded South Korea with 90,000 men and hundreds of Russian-made T-34 medium tanks. North Korea also put into the battle its air arm, commanded by Maj. Gen. Wang Yon, a Soviet Air Academy graduate. The North Korean air force had about 150 propeller-driven warplanes, including Lavochkin La-9s, Ilyushin Il-10 Sturmoviks, and Yakovlev Yak-7s, Yak-9s, and Yak-18s.

Early in Korean fighting, American pilots returned from chaotic and

**Ensign Eldon W. Brown Jr.
July 3, 1950
Grumman F9F-3 Panther
   (bureau no. 123026)
Fighter Squadron VF-51
USS *Valley Forge* (CV 45)
The Yellow Sea, near North
   Korea**

Eldon W. Brown Jr., seen here as a new naval aviator in 1948, was credited with shooting down a Yakovlev Yak-9 fighter near Pyongyang, North Korea, on July 3, 1950.

[Margie Brown]

confusing air strikes to report that the North Koreans were flying Bell F-63 Kingcobras, thousands of which (when known as P-63s) had gone to the Soviet Union under Lend Lease during World War II. The reports of P-63 sightings were in error, but the Yaks were very real.

That first day of the war, the nearest aircraft carrier was USS *Valley Forge* (CV 45), which was at anchor near the British colony of Hong Kong. "Happy Valley," the ship was called. Its fighter squadrons included VF-51 and VF-52, with Grumman F9F-3 Panthers; and VF-53 and VF-54, with Vought F4U-4B Corsairs. Its attack squadron was VA-55, with Douglas AD-4 Skyraiders.

ELDON BROWN. It all happened very quickly. We were only over Pyongyang for a short time. After it was over, a lot of attention was focused on the fact that we were credited with shooting down two Yakovlev Yak-9 fighters. But our main purpose was to enable *Valley Forge*'s strike group of F4U-4 Corsairs and AD-4 Skyraiders to strike at the rear of a North Korean offensive that was succeeding in the south. *Valley Forge* was the first U.S. carrier to fight in Korea, and our straight-wing, under-powered F9F Panthers were the first Navy jets to fight. The enemy Yaks, as well as our own Corsairs and Skyraiders, were all propeller-driven aircraft, which were still the mainstay of military aviation.

Before most of us had ever heard of Pyongyang, we were on a routine, peacetime cruise on the *Valley Forge,* which was nicknamed the "Happy Valley." We paused in Hong Kong to give radar operators there a chance to work with jet aircraft for the first time. We expected to be heading for home soon. Everybody was singing the song "Won't You Come Home, Bill Bailey?" It was a happy cruise aboard Happy Valley. But then we learned something was happening in Korea.

What was happening, of course, was war. We scrambled aboard ship and steamed north, with no idea of what would happen next.

As we steamed toward the war zone, there were moments of relaxation. If we didn't have other duties, we would go to a gun tub on the bow of the *Valley Forge*—where a 40-mm Bofors cannon had been removed earlier in the ship's history, and we would sunbathe. We could see huge schools of jellyfish, some four or five feet in diameter. When we got closer to Korea, we occasionally saw a body floating at sea.

I remember a twin-engined Soviet aircraft flying over the fleet. F4U-4B Corsairs of squadron VF-53 intercepted the aircraft and shot it down. This encounter is not covered in any of the histories of the era.

When we drew within range of targets in North Korea, we began preparing for action. A lot of our preparations were unremarkable, even on the morning of July 3. In those early morning hours before *Valley Forge*'s first combat mission, we received sparse briefings on weather, intelligence, and procedures. One pilot said he had never before heard of Pyongyang. My fellow Panther pilots and I were subdued and businesslike as we climbed into our aircraft. *Valley Forge* turned into the wind in the Yellow Sea about two hundred miles (320 km) southwest of the North Korean capital. The weather was clear and bright.

HARLEY THOMPSON. Most of us scheduled for that first strike didn't sleep very soundly. It hardly seemed possible that we had just finished a shooting war five years ago. I doubt if any of us were highly motivated to get into another, except for a few young tigers who, like Gen. George S. Patton, "love the smell of war." I wasn't one of those. I hated the smell of war and thought, and still do think, that it stinks.

Because the Navy was making the transition from props to jets, we had enough challenges without a war.

Before we went aboard *Valley Forge,* eight of us from squadrons VF-41 and VF-52 made the first night carrier landings aboard the USS

Boxer (CV 21). Lt. Don Engen was with us on that venture. It was supposed to convince doubting admirals that a jet fighter could be more than just a toy to be tucked away after the sun went down. I don't know if we really convinced anyone, but we proved experienced naval aviators could do it. After we had completed the landings and were in the ready room, somebody got the idea of looking at our age and experience. I think it turned out that the average age of the eight pilots was something like thirty-four, and the average single engine/fighter-type experience over two thousand hours. That fact would kind of make the demonstration very interesting but of limited practical usefulness. What about the nuggets and less-experienced pilots in Naval Aviation? Could they be expected to operate at night, in those days, with that equipment? Obviously, that would be very risky business. Today, round the clock, any kind of weather, any kind of target is routine for the fighter/attack squadrons. Good thing the doubting admirals didn't succeed in stopping the clock on progress for very long.

In Korea, of course, we flew in daylight.

We got up about 6:00 A.M., showered, dressed, and went to breakfast. I have no idea what I ate, but the officers' mess had stewards who took your order and delivered it to your table. It was probably eggs and bacon or ham, maybe even French toast. Our appetites were not the greatest, not having any idea of what we were about to get into.

The launch was scheduled for 9:30 A.M. We started gathering in the ready room a couple of hours before, at about 7:30 A.M. Each squadron in the air group was assigned its own ready room, which was equipped with lockers and a place to put our flight gear and equipment, and with individual easy chairs with classroom-like desks. The ready room was also equipped with briefing facilities, including an overhead projector, a blackboard, and bulletin boards. It was in the ready room where squadron air intelligence officers conducted briefings for the mission, providing us with target information, likely antiaircraft fire, enemy aircraft information, and so on.

We received weather information from *Valley Forge*'s combat information center, or CIC. Each squadron received its operational assignments from the Flag, thru the ship's operations department to the air group staff and then to the individual squadron. On the basis of the scheduled operations for the day, each squadron's operations officer was responsible for preparing the squadron's flight schedule, in detail. This

When the Korean War began, the U.S. Navy's standard jet fighter was the F9F Panther. The Panther had straight wings rather than the sweptback wings found on other jets, but it was more than a match for enemy propeller-driven Yak fighters encountered in the war's first weeks.

[Grumman History Center]

gave us our mission, time, aircraft assignment, launch time, and estimated recovery time, with as much detail as they were able to provide.

I was ops officer for squadron VF-51. Don Engen was my flight officer, whom I charged with the detailed preparation of the daily flight schedule. Don also assigned a plane, based on its side number, to each pilot. (The side number, or modex, is the three-digit number on the nose of an F9F Panther.) We were organized in four plane divisions, each with a division leader, his wingman, and the second section of two planes. We always flew in those assigned positions unless illness or incapacitation of a pilot required a substitution. That is the way we trained before our deployment aboard *Valley Forge*.

Preparing to Launch

The air intelligence officer based our intelligence briefing on an article about North Korea in *National Geographic* magazine, because that was about all he had to go on. So, as you can imagine, we were not really prepared for enemy opposition we might encounter, be it enemy aircraft, antiaircraft, or targets.

We really went into Pyongyang woefully unprepared.

Pilots remained in the ready room until the air officer gave the order to man aircraft over the ship's MC sound system.

On that signal, we all proceeded to the flight deck on the double. We went out of our ready room, which was just below the flight deck, onto the catwalk, and up a few short stairs to the flight deck. Our parachutes were already in the cockpits of our aircraft, put there by our plane captains, those all-important enlisted men who made certain all was in readiness for launch. We had great love and respect for these sailors who served us so well and did their work so well.

Sometimes a plane captain would even put a candy bar or a snack in the cockpit. They all took such pride in keeping our aircraft ready to go.

Climbing into the F9F-3 was quite easy. I think there were three steps recessed into the side of the fuselage, and with normal flight gear of flight suit, life vest, g-suit, side arm in a shoulder holster, it was quite easy to get into the cockpit.

Once in the cockpit, with help from the plane captain, we wriggled into our shoulder harness, went over the preflight checklist, hooked up the oxygen mask, and prepared to start engines on signal. That signal came from the air officer from his station in the island overlooking the flight deck, where he could observe all that was going on. When we received the "start engines" command, it came from the air officer, whose station was termed "Primary Fly." It was his job to supervise and direct all flight deck operations.

Two Panthers at a time moved to the catapult, ready for the launch signal. Aircraft spotted aft of the catapults would began taxiing under the direction of the flight deck personnel. They all wore colored jerseys depending on their duty assignments—yellow for flight deck handling crew, red for armament personnel, I think brown for the catapult crew, and so on.

As we taxied forward, we were passed by hand signals to the yellow-shirt handler ahead until we arrived just aft of the catapults. When it was our turn to taxi onto the catapult, the "cat" crew took over and taxied us into position. Two men put the "bridle" on the front of the aircraft, attaching the aircraft to the catapult "shuttle." Another sailor put the "hold back" mechanism into place, gave the thumbs up to the catapult launching officer, and got clear of the aircraft and into the catwalk alongside. The cat officer then "tensioned" the bridle by giving a signal to the deck edge catapult personnel. He gave the pilot the signal for brakes off, and the aircraft was ready to go.

The catapult crew made sure the wings were locked in position, flaps were down, and control surfaces were clear and operating. Hand signals between deck crew and Panther pilot made sure all these things happened in proper sequence.

With everything ready, the cat officer gave the signal to the pilot for full power. In the cockpit, the pilot made sure he had 100 percent power, checked exhaust gas temperatures, oil pressure, hydraulic pressure, and no doubt some other stuff I have forgotten.

When the pilot in the cockpit was satisfied that all systems were go, he would put his head firmly against the headrest to prevent it from being slammed there by the force of the launch and lock the throttle by grasping the handle and the throttle quadrant to avoid pulling the throttle back during the launch. It was also standard practice to place your elbow in your gut to avoid pulling the stick back and inducing a high angle of attack and possible stall, and cessation of flying and a dunking in the briny. This happened—although not that day, and not to me, thanks. Oh yes, standard procedure was to launch with the canopy open so that if we ended up in the water we would have a chance to get out. Our ejection seats were quite new in our racket, and we weren't all that convinced that we could eject if the aircraft sank. Having an open cockpit made it noisy, but it was also a confidence builder.

The launch was sort of like pandemonium. All of a sudden this enormous force, a gigantic boot in the rear, so to speak, hits you, and suddenly you realize you're airborne. You fight your way back to take control of the aircraft and fly away.

ELDON BROWN. The first eight aircraft to leave Happy Valley's deck and fly toward Pyongyang were our F9F-3 Panthers of fighter squadron VF-51. We began launching at 9:35 A.M. The target was two hours, twenty minutes away.

Carrier air group commander, or CAG, Comdr. Harvey Lanham led the eight Panthers. He was a very experienced pilot who seemed very confident about how we would perform against the North Koreans.

My division—the Navy's term for a four-aircraft formation—

consisted of Lt. Comdr. Bill Sisley, with me (Ensign Eldon W. Brown Jr.) on his wing, followed by Lt. Mike South, with Lt. (jg) Leonard "Len" Plog as wingman. We were a mix of somewhat older and younger Navy pilots, although all of us had a certain level of maturity and had flown props before moving to jets. In a different division was our VF-51 squadron commander Comdr. A. D. "Dave" Pollock. Not flying that day was a veteran Panther pilot, Lt. Donald D. Engen, who stayed aboard the carrier to handle communications.

Remember, this was a transitional time for aviation and for warfare. Propeller-driven aircraft were mature and were still the backbone of the flying Navy. Jet-propelled warplanes were new, cantankerous, and shamefully underpowered and had yet to demonstrate that they could take over major military missions.

Our F9F-3 was powered by the 4,600-lb (2085-kg) thrust Allison J33-A-8 turbojet, essentially the same power plant as the Air Force's standard fighter in the Far East at the time, the Lockheed F-80C Shooting Star (which by July 3 had already shot down several Il-10s and at least one Yak-9). The choice of engine in the dash-three Panther was a last-minute compromise. We considered the F9F-3 both underpowered and unreliable. Later, we would celebrate when F9F-3s were re-engined with their intended power plant, the 5,750-lb (2608-kg) thrust Pratt & Whitney J42, which was also used on the more numerous Navy's F9F-2 model.

The F9F-3 was armed with four 20-mm cannons but, at this juncture in the war, was not yet fitted with underwing pylons to carry bombs and rocket projectiles. A widely distributed painting that shows Plog and me taking off carrying two 1,000-lb (454-kg) bombs and six 5-inch high velocity aircraft rockets is inaccurate.

The Navy's transition from props to jets was proceeding slowly. At this late date—while the United States was preparing the F-86 Sabre for action in Korea and the Soviet Union was readying the MiG-15—the Navy did not yet have a combat aircraft with swept wings. It lacked a lead-computing gunsight. Routine flight at supersonic speed was still years away. Despite all this, our untested Panther was a giant leap forward. It also offered advantages over the Air Force F-80C: I found that the cockpit was roomier and the canopy had operated hydraulically, while the F-80C (which we Navy pilots flew as the TO-1) used a manual crank. The F-80C was skinny and sleek, while our F9F was kind of a barrel-shaped aircraft with a round fuselage.

As we headed toward Pyongyang, I don't think we had any special thoughts. After all, we were all experienced. I guess I was typical of those who hadn't gotten combat experience in World War II, which ended five years earlier, but who were pretty experienced, nevertheless. I can tell you that we all wanted to fly, and if necessary to fight, and when the time came, we were ready to go.

Aviator Upbringing

It says "Eldon W. Brown Jr." on my logbook, but a lot of people call me Brownie. Briefly, in the squadron, I was called Littlehead, because no one else could fit in my helmet. I was born in 1927 in Little Rock, Arkansas, and grew up there.

I always wanted to fly. At age fifteen, I saved up my money and took flying lessons from Central Flying Service in Little Rock, with an instructor named John Ogden.

Right after World War II ended, I joined the Navy in the aviation cadet V-5 program. They required two years of college, so they sent me to Tulane in New Orleans. After that, I had preflight training in Ottumwa, Iowa, and went to Grand Prairie, Texas, near Dallas, for initial flight training.

After that, I had further training in Corpus Christi, Texas, in the N2S Stearman, a fabric-covered, open-cockpit biplane. That was quite a plane. Someone had to be on the ground to crank the starter.

In 1947, I went to Pensacola, Florida, and flew the SNJ Texan. They also provided twenty-five hours of multi-engine training in the PBY Catalina and SNB Expeditor. Flying big planes was different for me, and today I often talk about it with my older daughter, who is a flight attendant on twin-engined transports for Sky West Airlines.

I went to Jacksonville, Florida, for advanced training in the F4U-4 Corsair. I got my wings in May 1948, and then went back to Pensacola to complete carrier qualification in the Corsair. Then, I went to San Isidro, California, to instruct in SNB Expeditor trainers. I later spent some time in ferry squadron VR-2 flying various airplanes.

Around Christmas 1948, I went to Seattle to join squadron VF-211, flying F6F Hellcats. There, I met Commander Lanham, who later became our carrier air group commander in Korea. I was flying F6Fs in Seattle when Secretary of Defense Louis Johnson cancelled our air group for funding reasons.

When they abolished our air group, I delivered an F6F to El Toro, California, and picked up orders for VF-51. I joined the squadron in San Diego in 1949, in time to see the squadron's last FJ-1 Fury fighters, but not to fly them. My first jet flight was in a TO-1 Shooting Star. It had an Air Force instrument panel, which measured air speed in miles per hour. We used knots in the Navy, so we would look at that panel, see the numbers, and think we were flying really, really fast.

As for VF-51, the squadron had formerly been known as VF-5A and had been the first Navy jet squadron on the west coast. The squadron reequipped with the F9F-3, which I discussed above. Some things didn't change. In those early days in jets, you always landed on the carrier with your canopy open

LEONARD PLOG. I suppose you could say I bridged the gap between props and jets, between experience and experimenting. Long before those jet kills over North Korea, I had flown a clunky, propeller craft mockingly dismissed by critics as the "Beast."

We were all excited about being in the Navy's first jets. Later in my career, I worked with nuclear weapons, but nothing impressed me so much as the transition from props to jets. We were changing the way the Navy does things.

I was flying F9F-3 bureau number 123071 that day. Our eight Panthers approached Pyongyang at 16,000 feet (4876 m). In contrast to the brightness of the day, Pyongyang was cloaked in industrial smoke, soot, and haze. There were no obvious muzzle flashes or tracers, but some of our Panther pilots believed they were fired upon once we were within a few miles of the city.

When we arrived over the North Korean airfield well ahead of the approaching Corsairs and Skyraiders, CAG Lanham went down on the deck and attacked a transport plane on the edge of the airfield. I watched Lanham's cannon shells stir up the area around the transport, which may have been a Tachikawa Ki-54 Army Type 1 "Hickory," inherited by the North Koreans from Japanese forces during World War II. Lanham's hits punctured the transport and kicked up dust but started no fire. I doubt that plane ever flew again.

We made a strafing run. Lanham led the Panthers in circling the airfield and returning for a second strafing run. Some of the World War II veterans in the air that day—Sisley, South, me, and in the other division,

Leonard Plog, seen here as a lieutenant, junior grade, in the postwar period, flew SB2C Hell-diver dive-bombers in World War II and F9F-3 Panther fighters in the Korean War. In the Navy's first jet mission, he shot down a Yakovlev Yak-9 fighter near Pyongyang, North Korea, on July 3, 1950.

[Leonard Plog]

Lt. Harley Thompson—were displeased with the CAG. "Making a second run over the target would have been unthinkable in World War II," Thompson told me later. "They would have blown us to bits."

I returned to a spot right over Pyongyang airport on Mike South's wing. With the exception of the transport shot up by Lanham, I saw no aircraft on the ground. It was a big airport and, initially, it seemed surprising that we didn't see any other airplanes on the ground. Normally, an airport supporting a city the size of the capital of North Korea would be very busy.

We began flying up one of the runways, when my attention was drawn to a hangar to my right. An airplane taxied out of that hangar and took off from a taxiway. That's when I thought, "Something is happening here . . ."

Combat Experience

Like I said, I may have bridged a gap. I was born in 1921 in Oregon. The war was at its height when I entered the Navy in 1943 and pinned on the gold wings of a Navy pilot, and the gold bars of an ensign in June 1944. Soon afterward, I was aboard the aircraft carrier USS *Essex* (CV 9), fighting in the western Pacific.

I flew the SB2C Helldiver, a two-seat dive-bomber some pilots dismissed as the "Beast" and criticized for poor handling qualities. During the 1945 invasion of Okinawa and subsequent carrier operations against mainland Japan, I was happy with the Helldiver.

The old SB2C did "vertical" pretty good, meaning it handled well when you were flying straight down at a target. I differ with pilots who considered it an inadequate replacement for the older but beloved SBD Dauntless. I flew the SBD in training. The SB2C was significantly faster with a bigger power plant, and had a four-bladed prop that was quite efficient.

After the war, the Navy sent me to the University of Washington. When I returned to San Diego for further training, I joined the Navy's first jet class, flying the TO-1 Shooting Star. I was then assigned to squadron VF-51 and flew the FJ-1 Fury and subsequently the F9F-3 Panther.

So that's how I got to Pyongyang and, on my second pass over the North Korean airfield, saw a Yak taking off.

I watched the North Korean aircraft climb out, and saw Eldon Brown turn to get into position behind him. I looked back and did a double take. A second Yak-9 taxied out of the hangar and took off from the taxiway.

My recollection is that the second Yak-9 got three hundred to four hundred feet into the air and tucked in its wheels.

I squeezed off a short burst. My 20-mm cannon rounds blew the Yak's wing off. It spun out of control and went down.

The adversary on July 3, 1950, was the Yakovlev Yak-9. The propeller-driven Yak-9 had been the principal Soviet fighter of World War II. The U.S.S.R. supplied dozens of the planes to North Korea just before the outbreak of war on the Korean peninsula. American forces captured this Yak-9 later in the Korean War.

[U.S. Air Force]

This was later recognized as the U.S. Navy's first aerial victory in Korea. In an official report, I was later quoted as saying that North Korean "planes were taking off toward each other from opposite ends of the runway." After comparing notes with other aviators, I'm sure there were only three enemy aircraft—the transport and the two Yaks. After my Yak went down, a couple of us got together and formed up to head home.

ELDON BROWN. I was in the cockpit of F9F-3 bureau number 123026 that day. I don't remember being concerned about making repeat passes over the airfield—but unlike some of the others, I hadn't seen Japanese antiaircraft fire in World War II.

When Lanham began our second trip over the runway, I saw a Yak-9 coming at me from my right. This was the first of the two Yaks seen by earlier Plog, but the second that we engaged.

I saw him at three o'clock high, coming in. He passed over me and fired bursts at South and Plog—who, by then, had turned for home. I made a 360-degree turn and went after the Yak.

I rolled out on his tail, had the throttle all the way up, and closed on him pretty fast.

I had time only for a short burst. It blew his tail off. The aft section came off and the main fuselage went into a steep dive. I think it was on fire. The tail came flying back at me. I flew between the tail and main fuselage, and then headed for home. I was struggling to conserve fuel.

I remember that the Panther's gun camera only worked when you were holding down the trigger. So I got a picture of a Yak in front of me, but it was very dim and didn't show it going down. That was a difficult day in other ways. My radio didn't work, either.

I landed on *Valley Forge* with just three hundred pounds of fuel. They fussed at me for coming in with a low fuel load.

That, of course, was only our first day. We continued flying and fighting. On a combat mission in September 1950, I touched off a North Korean ammunition dump, creating a blast so huge some people thought it was an atom bomb.

My logbook reflects forty-two combat missions by the time *Valley Forge*, VF-51, and I departed the combat zone on November 19, 1950. I remember with pride that VF-51 skipper Comdr. A. D. "Dave" Pollock called VF-51 "the best damn squadron in the fleet."

I married Margie on June 23, 1951, in Little Rock, and we're well past our fiftieth anniversary now. I served as a flight instructor and flew in an F2H-3 Banshee squadron before leaving the Navy in 1957. For a dozen years after that, I was a test pilot for the plane maker Lockheed and flew all early versions of the F-104 Starfighter. I later worked for the Federal Aviation Administration. Margie and I have two daughters and several grandchildren.

Those of us who were in the air that day have somewhat differing memories of what happened. I understand that Harley Thompson didn't see North Korean aircraft that day. Officially, the Navy credits Plog and me with one aerial victory each, and I inked a red star into his logbook. Virtually all histories of the Korean War refer to the two kills.

There was only one future historian in VF-51. Donald D. Engen later reached the rank of vice admiral and was director of the National Air and Space Museum from 1996 until his death in a glider mishap in 1999. That day in 1950, he was aboard *Valley Forge*, not over Pyongyang.

VF-51 squadron commander Dave Pollock (left) and Lt. Donald Engen were among the Panther aviators who flew the July 3, 1950, mission in Korea. Engen later became director of the National Air and Space Museum.

[Leonard Plog]

LEONARD PLOG. Like everyone else in VF-51, I finished that combat cruise in November 1950. After Korea, I flew the F9F-6 Cougar and worked with nuclear weapons at Albuquerque, New Mexico, before retiring from the Navy in 1963 and taking up a job with airplane maker Vought. To me, flying early jets was always challenging, but I wouldn't trade the experience for anything. All my jet flying happened after I married nurse Dorothy Schell in 1946. We have two sons and six grandchildren.

Grumman F9F-3 Panther

To a generation of naval aviators, the Grumman F9F Panther was the blowtorch that took them to war in Korea. The public learned about the Panther when William Holden flew one in Hollywood's *The Bridges at Toko-ri*, although the book by James Michener featured the lesser-known F2H Banshee.

Who's Who

Ensign Eldon W. Brown Jr., F9F-3 Panther pilot, squadron VF-51, USS *Valley Forge* (CV 45)

Lt. (j.g.) Leonard Plog, F9F-3 pilot

Comdr. Harvey Lanham, Panther pilot and carrier air group commander

Lt. Comdr. Bill Sisley, Panther pilot

Lt. Harley Thompson, Panther pilot

Lt. Mike South, Panther pilot

Comdr. A. D. "Dave" Pollock, Panther pilot and squadron commander

Lt. Donald D. Engen, Panther pilot, VF-51

The Panther was the primary Navy jet fighter of the 1950–53 Korean War. It was practical and sturdy, prompting sailors to dub its Bethpage, Long Island manufacturer the "Grumman Iron Works." In air-to-ground action, the Panther excelled.

On July 3, 1950, Panthers claimed the first-ever aerial victories by Navy jets, when Lt. (j.g.) Leonard Plog and Ensign Eldon W. Brown Jr. each were credited with shooting down a North Korean Yak-9 prop-driven fighter. On November 10, 1950, Panther pilot Lt. Comdr. William Thomas Amen shot down a MiG-15. Panthers bagged two more MiGs, but in air-to-air action, they were usually outclassed. The Navy was slow to capitalize on swept-wing fighters, which did not reach the fleet until after Korea.

The prototype Panther, called the XF9F-2, made its maiden flight on November 24, 1947. Most early models, known as F9F-2s, used a Pratt & Whitney J42 centrifugal-flow turbojet engine, which (like the engine on the Soviet MiG-15, was derived from the British Nene turbojet). But engine fires plagued the J42 early in its career, so the Navy pursued the possibilities for an alternative engine. Thus, the F9F-3 was developed in parallel with the F9F-2. It differed from the F9F-2 in being powered by the Allison J33 turbojet, which was approximately the same size as the J42 but was somewhat less powerful. The J33 had been planned as a second-source power plant for the Panther in case the program to produce the Nene under license in the United States proved unsuccessful. The first flight of the XF9F-3 (bureau number 122476) took place on August 16, 1948, with the J33. The Navy took delivery of fifty-four J33-powered F9F03s between August 1948 and November 1949. They came off the production line in parallel with the J42-powered F9F-2. Because of initially slow deliveries of J42 engines for the F9F-2, the F9F-3 was actually the first Panther version to enter service with the Navy, when F9F-3s replaced the FJ-1 Fury fighters of VF-51 in May of 1949.

As pilots Plog, Brown, and Thompson say, the J33 turned out in service to perform less well than the J42. In October 1949, virtually all F9F-3s were re-engined with J42s and thereby became indistinguishable from the F9F-2. No further F9F-3s would be built, and subsequent Navy contracts were for the F9F-2 version. However, the aircraft assigned to squadron VF-51 at the outbreak of the Korean War had not yet been re-engined, and the squadron completed its first cruise in 1950 with the J33 powered F9F-3 models.

The F9F-4 was an experimental model with water injection for its J33 engine. By the time it made its first flight on July 6, 1950, the Navy had decided to abandon the J33. The F9F-5 became the most numerous of the Panthers, powered by the Pratt & Whitney J48-P-2 derivative of

---

Grumman F9F-3 Panther

Type: single-seat jet fighter

Power plant: one 4,600-lb (2085-kg) thrust Allison J33-A-8 axial-flow turbojet (as F9F-3); one 5,000-lb (2267-kg) thrust Pratt & Whitney J42-P-6; (license-built Rolls-Royce Nene)(after conversion to F9F-2)

Performance: maximum speed 579 mph (932 km/h) at 16,000 ft (4876 m); cruising speed 481 mph (774 km/h); initial climb rate 5,090 ft (1550 m) per minute; service ceiling 39,800 ft (12131 m); range 1300 miles (2092 km)

Weights: empty 10,113 lb (4587 kg); maximum takeoff 17,965 lb (8245 kg)

Dimensions: wingspan 38 ft (11.58 m); length 38 ft 10 in (11.84 m); height 12 ft 3 in (3.73 m); wing area 250 sq ft (23.23 m)

Armament: four 20-mm cannons

First flight: November 24, 1947 (XF9F-2); August 16, 1948 (XF9F-3)

the Rolls-Royce Tay engine. The Navy also operated F9F-5P photoreconnaissance versions.

The F9F Panther remained the standard U.S. Navy fighter throughout the Korean conflict. Most were F9F-2 and F9F-5 models, with more powerful and reliable engines than the F9F-3s used on that first mission. Although the F9F-3s of VF-51 had no capability to carry underwing ordnance, F9F-2 and F9F-5 Panthers fought in Korea with, typically, two 1,000-lb (454-kg) bombs and eight 5-inch high-velocity aircraft rockets. Photoreconnaissance versions of the Panther brought back valuable intelligence throughout the war.

Panthers continued to fly off Navy carrier decks into the late 1950s. After the Korean War, Grumman experts attached the Panther fuselage to a new swept wing and tail to create the F9F-6 Cougar, which enjoyed a brief career and served for many more years in training and reconnaissance duties.

Chapter Eight

History's First Jet-vs.-Jet Battle

What Happened

It was the first air battle in which both sides used jet aircraft. During World War II, the United States never got a jet into combat. The British and Germans had jets, but they never fought each other. The first jet-versus-jet action had to wait for the Soviet MiG-15 to appear in Korea, where the F-80C Shooting Star was the U.S. Air Force's standard fighter. The United States was readying the better-known F-86 Sabre for action against the MiG, but the Sabre had not yet arrived in the combat zone. The MiG-15, F-80C, and F-86 all were jets.

In a quick, short aerial battle, fighter pilot 1st Lt. Russell J. Brown won a permanent place in Air Force lore—before fading from the limelight just as quickly.

After the Korean War began in June 1950, Soviet fighter regiments gathered at Manchurian bases along the Yalu River, facing North Korea. Under U.S. rules, American pilots could not cross the river to attack them. In fact, few even knew that they were Russians. They first appeared in November, the month China entered the war, and many Americans assumed the MiG pilots were Chinese. In fact, they were Russians, many of them very experienced, and they could pick the time and place of every fight. American pilots were permitted to engage the MiGs only when they crossed over to the Korean side of the river.

First Lieutenant Russell J. Brown
November 8, 1950
Lockheed F-80C Shooting Star (49-713)
26th Fighter Interceptor Squadron, 51st Fighter Interceptor Wing
K-14 Kimpo Air Base, South Korea

1st Lt. Russell J. Brown is credited with the first aerial victory in a battle where both sides used jet aircraft. Here, Brown is in Korea posing in an F-80C Shooting Star—although not the one in which he scored the aerial victory. Now deceased, Brown pursued his Air Force career quietly after the battle and, with one exception, never granted an interview.

[U.S. Air Force]

On November 8, 1950, as a first lieutenant, Brown was flying an F-80C of the 16th Fighter-Interceptor Squadron, 51st Fighter-Interceptor Wing, on patrol along the Yalu. Brown actually belonged to the 26th Fighter-Interceptor Squadron, but was on detached assignment to the 16th, which was commanded by Lt. Col. Evans G. Stephens—a seasoned veteran who had begun his fighter career in the P-39 Airacobra (Chapter 2).

A half dozen MiG-15s attacked the flight of F-80s. The American pilots turned aggressively into their attackers and split them up, sending five MiGs scurrying back across the Yalu. The sixth MiG broke in the wrong direction and appeared below Brown's F-80.

Brown's plane was older and slower, but the American felt he had an edge. He threw his stick forward and went into a dive behind his adversary, peering into his gunsight. No one had ever done this before.

In the only quote from Brown that survives, he remembered afterward telling himself, "Damn, I'm going to get him . . ."

EVANS G. STEPHENS. That day, the Air Force assigned seventy B-29 Superfortress heavy bombers on a mass raid against the city of Sinuiju, North Korea, along the Chinese border. They were also to bomb bridges on the Yalu River.

A half hour prior to the arrival of the B-29s, F-51 Mustangs from the 8th Fighter-Bomber Group and F-80C Shooting Stars from the 49th Fighter-Bomber Group attacked antiaircraft gun positions near the target with rockets and machine gun fire.

We were the top cover. We took off from Kimpo and headed north on a day that was remarkably bright and clear, given the bad weather that had become so familiar in Korea. Our top cover consisted of two flights of F-80Cs from the 16th squadron flying at 18,000 feet (5500 m). Capt. Eldon N. "Neil" Colby led one flight. I led the other and was in overall charge of both. When I saw no threat that would interfere, I led my F-80s down to low level and carried out additional air-to-ground attacks on antiaircraft gun emplacements.

We made two such attacks, descending from and returning to 18,000 feet (5500 m). As we were ascending back to altitude after our second strafing run, we received a radio report from members of the 49th group that seven to nine MiG-15 fighters were seen heading our way from the direction of Antung airfield, China.

The approximate altitude of the MiGs was 27,000 feet (8230 m). That gave them an advantage. In a fighter, you always want to begin the battle from higher altitude than your adversary.

I turned my two flights of F-80s to meet them, head-on. We flew into them and broke up their formation. It wasn't a terribly dramatic moment, or at least it didn't seem so at first. Most of the MiG-15s turned tail and headed back over the Yalu River into China.

The MiG-15 flight leader, however, made a high-speed pass on my flight and went right past us without inflicting any damage. I got him in my gun sight and at a distance of approximately a thousand yards, I fired bursts and got some .50 caliber hits along the left wing. Gun-camera footage later confirmed the hits, and I was given credit for damaging a MiG.

There was another MiG that didn't seem to be operating in coordination with the others. This MiG approached my flight at what seemed an unrealistically slow speed, given the circumstances.

I think I could have turned into him and gotten him, but I didn't

Lt. Col. Evans G. Stephens began his Air Force flying career in the little-loved P-39 Airacobra of World War II. In this Korean War photo, he is waving from the cockpit of an F-80C Shooting Star, the fighter in which he was flight leader on November 8, 1950. Still later in his career, before retiring as a colonel, Stephens flew the Vietnam-era F-105 Thunderchief.

[U.S. Air Force]

---

want to release my wingtip tanks to chase the MiG. I had two relatively inexperienced pilots in my flight and did not want them to be hit by my falling tanks.

When this MiG went past my flight, my wingman, 1st Lt. Russell J. Brown, peeled off and followed him. Brown was later quoted as saying that all but one of his .50 caliber machine guns jammed. With just one gun working, as he described it, he uttered that famous quote ("Damn. I'm going to get him . . .") and fired on the MiG while following it in a dive.

CHESTER WAGNER. It was like being in a different world, cocooned in the pilot's perch of an F-80 with most of the world far below and everything happening very quickly. Later, someone told me that Russ Brown's first view of his MiG was a flash of sunlight, almost like a signal mirror reflecting light. He must have reacted very quickly, because at one point the other airplane and Brown's were converging, which meant they were coming together at around twelve hundred miles per hour.

Up there at high altitude, peering across the river through the haze, it all seems unreal. The bad guys have MiG-15s over there at Antung airfield, lined up wingtip-to-wingtip, glinting in the sun on sunny days. The politicians say we can fight them, but only when they come up and cross the river to engage us. But we're not allowed to cross the river, go that extra mile, and bomb the shit out of them.

In the cockpit, you're attached to the F-80 by Koch fasteners, electrical cords, and the oxygen feed. You have the oxygen mask attached to your face with bayonet clamps, the visor over your eyes, the helmet jammed down on your head. Ironically, the sun is baking you beneath your Plexiglas canopy while, a few inches outside your airplane, the temperature is way below zero. It's the coldest Korean winter in 144 years, you're moving through it at six hundred miles per hour, and even if there were no MiGs, no flak, no enemy targets to dive-bomb, you keep your mind very occupied just thinking, "What the hell happens if I have some kind of emergency?"

Can I release my canopy? Will my ejection seat work? Will the parachute open? Will I freeze to death before the Chinese soldiers swarming in those Korean mountains down there grab me and haul my ass to a prisoner of war camp? If not, will I get frostbite, dysentery, and all the other things they warn us to be prepared for, even if the enemy doesn't use physical torture? And what if he does?

I was assigned to 51st wing headquarters and was flying with Lt. Col. Stephens' squadron, the 16th, on the November 8, 1950, missions. He was the best commander I ever had, and a natural stick. He could handle an F-80 better than anybody I ever saw. But I have to say, I'm not familiar with everything that was going on in the squadron or the circumstances under which he took command.

The 16th had been in the fight for two months, since arriving at Kimpo in September, but other squadrons were operating the F-80 from the day the Korean War started on June 25. When they were flying missions directly from Japan to targets in North and South Korea, there was a slightly ridiculous aspect to it. A pilot would eat breakfast with his wife and children in his house, take off from his base in Japan— sometimes with the loyal wife waving from the sidelines—and fly across the straits to bomb and strafe a target in Korea. There was a lot of metal flying around in those early days, and we left a lot of F-80s splashed across the side of some jagged Korean mountain. When he pulled off the

Capt. Chester "Chet" Wagner was stationed at 51st wing headquarters and flew with the 26th squadron on the November 8, 1950, mission into North Korea. He readily acknowledged that the F-80 Shooting Star was better suited for air-to-ground work than for fighting MiGs.

[U.S. Air Force]

target, if he was still alive, he would settle in for the two- to three-hour flight back to Japan. After landing and debriefing—sometimes, again, with wifey waving in greeting upon arrival, he would be at home in time for dinner and a bedtime story with his kids. It was just like commuting to work. It was portrayed in the newspaper as being exactly like commuting to work, never mind the guys who didn't return from those early missions. In those first weeks of the war, our poorly prepared infantry soldiers were being massacred on the ground, and it was terrible public relations for Air Force fighter jocks to be living in Japan with their dependents.

Our wing and squadron was on Okinawa at that time, so we missed that life. When we arrived at Kimpo, we had very few creature comforts and, of course, no dependents.

I eventually flew 121 missions and loved the F-80, but it didn't bother me that on November 8, I was on the air-to-ground phase of the mission and never saw the MiGs. Our intelligence experts didn't know much about the MiG-15, but we held it in respect, even awe. I got hit by gunfire several times on missions, but never fought an air-to-air engagement. You know what? I was just as comfortable not to have to do that in the F-80.

CURT NELSON. We all greatly admired Grant Stephens and were proud to fly and fight with him. But he became the 16th squadron's commander—and the flight leader on November 8—as the result of an unfortunate incident he had nothing to do with.

The former commander was Lt. Col. Converse B. Kelly. He was a very well respected guy who had been one of the early jet pilots, and it was his misfortune to be flight leader on a weather penetration into Okinawa in April 1950, when he lost a man, Lt. Edsel R. Starnes.

As I said, Kelly was flight leader. I was on his wing. Rosie Edinburg was element lead in the number-three slot and Starnes, who we called Ed, was on his wing. This was before the F-80C became the standard in the Far East. We were flying refurbished F-80B models just picked up from Tokyo.

When we left Itazuke Air Base near Fukuoka in western Japan, Rosie raised his nose too high on take-off, stalled out, and slid off the north end of the runway into a rice paddy and came to rest with the left wing embedded in the retainer wall. Ed Starnes continued his takeoff roll and lifted off without incident. When the tower told us, we circled back over the scene and saw Rosie, walking away from the wreck with his new, deep-sea fishing rod in hand—he'd been carrying it in the cockpit. We did not continue our flight at that point. We landed. But Kelly said we had to continue on our way to Okinawa, minus Rosie, so we took off again.

I was on Kelly's right wing. Ed was on the left. The flight was uneventful until we drew close to Okinawa and there were huge areas of dark, black sky everywhere. We started our penetration of a dense, low overcast, descending to land at Naha Air Base, Okinawa. The colonel turned his lights on, and we sought to maintain close formation as everything got darker around us.

That was when the colonel's canopy came flying off of his F-80. We never knew what caused that to happen. The old F-80B model had the old-style mechanical latch instead of the updated, double-latch system on the F-80C, and it apparently just flew loose.

The colonel's canopy flashed between Ed and me, and vanished. It wasn't intuitive to do so—not when you're trying to hold close formation on an instrument descent in almost zero-zero visibility—but instead of looking around me at the other two planes and pilots, I looked straight ahead and down at my gauges. They told me the three of us were in a steep and severe bank to the right. I had to fight vertigo and, at the same time, force my jet to level out.

Ed pitched left and went directly into the sea. He never got out of his airplane. I climbed back on top and made a solo penetration to Naha. The colonel did the same.

Soon after Ed's death, Lt. Col. Converse B. Kelly was transferred to Japan and assigned to inspector duty. It was widely rumored that he was "bumped up" to Japan for losing a pilot, the first the squadron lost in over a year. That's when Maj. Evans G. Stephens took over the squadron. Stephens was promoted to lieutenant colonel soon afterward.

I was still in the squadron on November 8, 1950, but was not in the flights led by Stephens or Colby. My flight of F-80Cs that day reached their initial point at about 10,000 feet (3048 m). As we approached Sinuiju, we hit the antiaircraft emplacement east of the airport runway. We fired all of our rockets in salvoes into that gun emplacement. We were pulling out of there and were heading for home when I heard Russ Brown on the radio, talking about the fight they were having with MiGs.

What Happened

Although only one of his guns was working, 1st Lt. Russell J. Brown's .50 caliber bullets scored numerous hits on the fuselage of the diving MiG-15.

Pieces of the MiG began to come off. The aircraft started emitting a trail of thick black smoke.

If the MiG pilot panicked, it was never apparent. He apparently made no attempt to bank or roll out of the way. Rounds from the F-80C continued to reach out and touch the Soviet jet and the MiG never wavered, never turned.

Brown watched as the MiG continued straight ahead in its dive and, as he described it later, exploded against the ground. Flight leader Stephens later said that eyewitness testimony of Brown's flight mates and gun-camera footage verified Brown's claim of the first jet shot down in aerial combat by another jet. Lieutenant Brown was flying aircraft number 49-713, borrowed from squadron member Jack Smith, and af-

This F-80C Shooting Star is taking off for a mission against targets in North Korea. When the Korean War began, the straight-wing F-80C was the standard U.S. fighter in the Far East. Pilots loved the aircraft and used it well in air-to-ground fighting, but it was never a match for the swept-wing, Soviet-built MiG-15

[U.S. Air Force]

ter he landed back at Kimpo Airfield, Korea, he jumped out on his wing and began hollering, "I got me a MiG! I got me a MiG!"—to the delight of his ground crew.

After his moment of glory as the Air Force's first MiG killer, Russell J. Brown faded almost immediately into obscurity. He reached the rank of colonel and retired. He died in the 1990s. Except for an interview with *Life* magazine during the Korean War era, Brown never spoke about his experience. He simply vanished from the public's eye.

In 2002, Brown's brother, Glenn Brown, was reached for comment and said that the pilot's wife, Gloria, and two children survived him. They could not be located. The brothers were not close, and Glenn had no other details.

In recent years, new access to Soviet records strongly suggests that the other side did not lose a MiG-15 that day. The Soviets claim that a Russian pilot, Senior Lt. Vladimir Kharitonov, was flying a MiG-15 that was shot up by Brown's F-80 that day—but did not crash. Kharitonov supposedly dived to escape and dropped his external fuel tanks, and

Who's Who

Lt. Col. (later Col.) Evans G. Stephens, F-80C Shooting Star flight leader and 16th Fighter-Interceptor Squadron commander, November 1950

1st Lt. (later Col.) Russell J. Brown, F-80C Shooting Star pilot credited with destroying a MiG-15 in history's first jet-vs.-jet battle, November 1950

Capt. Eldon N. "Neil" Colby, F-80C Shooting Star pilot and flight leader of the other flight in the area, November 1950

1st Lt. Curtis C. Nelson, F-80B Shooting Star pilot in the 16th squadron in April 1950; F-80C pilot in the squadron in November 1950

Capt. Chester "Chet" Wagner, F-80 Shooting Star pilot at 51st Fighter-Interceptor Wing headquarters, flying with the 16th squadron on November 8, 1950

---

then pulled up just above ground and scampered back across the Yalu River to his base. Col. Yevgeniy Pepelyayev, leading Russian ace of the Korean War with twenty-three downed American planes, said that when the tanks were jettisoned, normally fuel sprayed out and looked like smoke. When the tanks hit the ground, they exploded and burned. Additionally, Pepelyayev noted that given the MiG-15's self-sealing fuel tanks, bulletproof windscreen, and armored cockpit behind the pilot, a single .50-caliber gun would have "acted on our aircraft like peas. It was routine for our aircraft to return home with forty or fifty hits." The Soviet account is flawed—there was no reason for the MiG to be carrying external fuel tanks, and American veterans say the MiGs never did. Still, by the Soviet version, Brown's claim was an honest mistake.

Two days later, on November 10, 1950, Navy Lt. Comdr. William Amen, flying an F9F Panther from off the carrier USS *Philippine Sea* (CVA 47), hit a MiG with several bursts of 20mm cannon fire. The Russian plane dived and rolled over to an inverted attitude. The dive continued until the MiG crashed into a small hill. Russian records confirm the loss of a MiG-15 in that fight. So Russian historians credit the first jet-versus-jet aerial victory to the U.S. Navy. Perhaps we should, too.

The Air Force, however, continues to credit Brown with the aerial victory.

Lockheed F-80 Shooting Star

The saga of the F-80, originally the P-80, begins with a young engineer whose schoolmates dubbed him "Kelly" because he wore green neckties despite his Swedish ancestry. Clarence L. "Kelly" Johnson was no household name, however, and Lockheed did not yet have a "Skunk Works" on June 18, 1943, when Johnson took stairs two at a time, vaulting up to the office of Robert Gross, the company's president. In the office, Johnson found Gross and Hal Hibbard, Lockheed chief engineer.

"Wright Field wants us to submit a proposal for building a plane around a British jet engine," Johnson told the two corporate leaders. "I think we can promise them 180-day delivery. What do you think?"

Lockheed's leaders knew that "feel good" stories about aircraft being developed overnight almost always embody some fiction. In real life, it was almost impossible to develop a new aircraft, especially when introducing a new kind of power—the turbojet engine—in any period that could be measured in days, weeks, or months.

One hundred eighty days! Incredibly, as Johnson later recalled, there was no actual discussion of this seemingly impossible goal. "Okay, Kelly," Gross concluded. "It's your baby. We'll give you all the help we can." Thus did Lockheed respond to an invitation from the U.S. Army Air Forces to propose a fighter using the de Havilland–built Halford H-1B engine.

The Bell XP-59A Airacomet was already the first American jet aircraft. It first flew at Muroc Dry Lake, California, on October 1, 1942, with Robert M. Stanley at the controls. A mix of American airframe technology and British gas turbine knowledge, the XP-59A was followed by a small production batch of P-59s, tested by U.S. Army and Navy pilots.

Germany's Heinkel He 178, powered by a 750-lb (340-kg) thrust HeS 3b engine, became the world's first turbojet aircraft to fly on August 27, 1939, piloted by Flugkapitan Erich Warsitz. Britain's Gloster E.28/39 flew on May 15, 1941. The Messerschmitt Me 262 took to the sky under jet power on March 25, 1942. These "blowtorches," as jet aircraft were nicknamed at the time, preceded the Airacomet. And the XP-59A, unlike Meteor or Me-262, was merely a test aircraft, never viewed as combat capable.

Johnson put together some twenty-three engineers and 105 assembly

The F-80 Shooting Star was almost in time to fight in World War II. When the Korean War began, it was the standard U.S. fighter in the Far East. This F-80 is protected by sandbags at K-14 Kimpo Air Base, Korea.

[U.S. Air Force]

experts, including designers W. P. Ralston and Don Palmer. Brig. Gen. Franklin O. Carroll, head of Army Air Forces' engineering, arranged for Johnson to receive drawings for the Halford engine.

Johnson's designers drew up an unconventional aircraft. The XP-80 was a clean design with straight wings and tail, and tricycle gear. The "gamble," as Johnson called it, was the wing. Departing from proven airfoil designs, Johnson picked what he called a "wind tunnel wing"—a low aspect ratio, laminar-flow surface never tested on a propeller-driven aircraft.

Air intakes on the lower fuselage ahead of the wing's leading edge fed the Halford H.1B turbojet in the main fuselage section. The aft fuselage, with engine and tail surfaces, was detachable for maintenance. The cockpit was forward and enclosed by a rearward-sliding bubble canopy. The absence of a propeller made it easy to install six forward-firing .50 caliber (12.7-mm) machine guns in the tear-shaped nose. Years later, the last F-80 built looked little different from the first XP-80.

Johnson's team worked a ten-hour, six-day week, but the design team chief refused to allow anyone to enter the new facility—the future "Skunk Works" near plant B-1—on Sunday. "By coming back in here on Sunday, you're hurting the project," Johnson told the group. "You don't get enough rest and you get sick. The next man I catch in here on Sunday goes back to [manufacturing] B-17s."

The XP-80 prototype was built without the team having an actual Halford engine. They had only blueprints. When Guy Bristow, the de Havilland engine expert, finally arrived with the H.1B powerplant seven days before completion of the airframe, minor changes had to be made that put the XP-80 six pounds over the guaranteed contract weight of 8,600 lb (3900 m). The Sunday rule was broken to install the turbojet.

The Halford H.1B was to be produced by Allis-Chalmers as the J36. Before the XP-80's first flight, ground run-up tests inflicted damage, requiring strengthening of the intake ducts, and the prototype eventually flew with the Halford engine. But the General Electric I-40 (later J33) was progressing in late 1943 and was chosen for subsequent planes in the series, designated XP-80A.

The prototype XP-80 (44-83020), nicknamed "Lulu Belle," was powered by a de Havilland–built Goblin turbojet delivering 3,000-lb (1360 kg) thrust. The spinach-green prototype made its first flight January 8, 1944, with Milo Burcham at the controls. By war's end, two P-80s were in Italy readying for combat. P-80 accidents claimed the lives of Burcham on October 20, 1944, and of America's top air ace, Major Richard I. Bong, on August 6, 1945.

The highly successful J33 made the Shooting Star work. An April 4, 1944, a production contract was issued for the P-80A model, when the outcome of World War II was far from decided. In the newly completed Pentagon, planners anticipated a protracted struggle for the Japanese home islands. Nine hundred seventeen P-80As were built, and 2,583 more cancelled on VJ Day.

The P-80B model appeared in 1946. Some 240 were built. Next came the P-80C, which was heavier and more powerful. Some 188 were delivered to the Air Force and fifty to the U.S. Marine Corps (designated TO-1) with the 4,600-lb (2,087-kg) thrust Allison J33-A-23 engine. A further 561 followed with the beefed-up 5,400-lb (2450-kg) thrust J33-A-35 engine.

By the late 1940s, a dozen squadrons throughout the continental United States and Alaska operated the P-80. On September 18, 1947, the Army's air arm became an independent air force. As one consequence, on June 11, 1948, all "pursuit" aircraft in this new branch of the armed forces became "fighters:" all P-80 aircraft acquired the F-80 designation. FP-80 reconnaissance aircraft became RF-80s.

In the formative years of the Cold War, punctuated by the Berlin Airlift and the detonation of the first Soviet atomic bomb in 1949, the F-80 was both the backbone of the new flying service and a symbol of American resolve. F-80s were the first jets to serve prolonged duty in Arctic climes. Three fighter groups operated F-80s in Europe, while another reached the Pacific in 1948.

When North Korea attacked its southern neighbor on June 25, 1950, the Air Force's fighter strength in the region consisted of three squadrons of F-80 Shooting Stars and one of F-82 Twin Mustangs. On June 26, eight North Korean Ilyushin Il-10 attack bombers launched a strike at Seoul's Kimpo airport. F-80s shot down four of them.

In one of the most dramatic surprises in modern warfare, China entered the Korean War in November 1950. Flying from Chinese bases (though flown, at first, solely by Soviet pilots), the MiG-15 made its debut. At the very time Westerners were coining the word *MiG*, the swept-wing Russian fighter was being viewed with awe and some fear. It was almost immediately evident that the MiG was a threat to American B-29

Lockheed F-80C Shooting Star

Type: single-seat fighter

Power plant: one 4,600-lb (2087 kg) thrust Allison J33-A-23 axial flow turbojet engine (early F-80C); 5,400-lb (2450-kg) Allison J33-A-35 (later aircraft)

Performance: maximum speed 601 mph (967 km/h) at sea level; service ceiling 46,800 ft (14265 m); range 825 miles (1328 km)

Weights: empty 8,420 lb (3819 kg); maximum takeoff 16,856 lb (7646 kg)

Dimensions: wingspan 38 ft 9 in (11.81 m); length 34 ft 5 in (10.49 m); height 11 ft 3 in (3.43 m); wing area 237.6 sq ft (22.07 sq m)

Armament: six .50 caliber (12.7-mm) fixed forward-firing nose machine guns, plus provision for two 1,000-lb (454-kg) bombs and eight underwing rockets

First flight: January 8, 1944 (XP-80A)

---

bomber formations. First Lieutenant Russell Brown's aerial victory over the MiG-15 came on November 8, 1950. But the straight-wing F-80 was clearly outclassed by the MiG. Only the arrival of the F-86 Sabre gave the Allies much prospect in the air-to-air realm.

On air-to-ground missions, the F-80 acquired a reputation for sustaining heavy battle damage and getting its pilot home. Col. Levi Chase called the F-80 a "flying tank."

Those who placed trust in such numbers reported that F-80s in Korea flew 98,515 combat sorties, shot down thirty-seven enemy aircraft, including six MiG-15s, dropped 33,266 tons of bombs, and launched 80,935 air-to-ground rockets. Total F-80 losses from enemy action were 143, including fourteen destroyed by MiG-15s, 113 claimed by ground fire, and sixteen to unknown causes.

Chapter Nine

Thunderjet over Korea

What Happened

The F-84 Thunderjet began its combat assignment in Korea with a vengeance.

On January 23, 1951, while B-29 Superfortresses were bombing the North Korean capital of Pyongyang, Col. Ashley B. Packard, commander of the 27th Fighter Escort Wing, persuaded higher-ups to "frag" (assign) his F-84s to hit the airfield at Sinuiju, just south of the Yalu River. Thirty-three Thunderjets took off from the pierced-steel runway at K-2 Taegu Air Base in South Korea, flew north, and hit the airfield by surprise. The first eight F-84s, assigned a strafing role, began working the place. Only then, after Packard's force descended over Sinuiju like a tidal wave, did MiGs begin scrambling from Antung, their airfield on the Chinese side of the Yalu.

A furious battle ensued between F-84s and MiG-15s. First Lieutenant Jacob Kratt shot down two MiG-15s and captains. Allen McGuire and William W. Slaughter each bagged one MiG. All F-84s returned home safely. For pilot Kratt, who shot down a Yak three days later to rack up his third aerial victory, it was time to wallow in sweet triumph: in gunnery training back in the States, Kratt had "messed up," as he put it, and flown into a tow target. Only intervention by Packard

First Lieutenant Thomas C. Gill
October 4, 1952
Republic F-84E Thunderjet
(51-625)
428th Fighter Bomber
Squadron
474th Fighter Bomber Group
K-8 Kunsan Air Base, South
Korea

1st Lt. Thomas C. Gill waves a
gloved hand from the cockpit of his
F-84E Thunderjet fighter at K-8
Kunsan air base, Korea, in 1952.
Gill found the Thunderjet to be a
stable gun platform with a roomy
cockpit and excellent visibility.

[Thomas C. Gill]

with a skeptical Gen. Curtis E. LeMay had prevented the young lieutenant from being grounded.

LeMay, of course, didn't want his 27th wing in Korea. The wing was part of LeMay's Strategic Air Command, and he wanted it back. He'd never liked fighters. He'd begrudgingly accepted the F-84 as an escort-fighter in SAC, almost certainly while biting into his famous cigar and twisting his face into a scowl. But as long as the planes were his, LeMay wanted them back and out of Korea. He was one of the architects of a policy that atomic war with the Soviet Union took priority over Korea: Time and again, SAC and the Air Defense Command received factory-fresh equipment denied to those doing the real shooting.

As for the F-84, it was the U.S. Air Force's final jet fighter to have straight wings, developed in the closing months of World War II. The Thunderjet had been built in part as "insurance" against failure of the more advanced Sabre, and pilots knew it.

Packard's 27th wing flew 2,076 combat sorties in January 1951. At the end of the month, the wing moved from Taegu back to Itazuke. The F-84 offered somewhat more respectable range than the F-80, so the wing was able to continue flying combat missions against Communist ground targets. By July 30, 1951, the F-84E Thunderjet-equipped 136th Fighter

Bomber Wing was in action with all three of its squadrons (111th, 154th, 182nd), made up largely of activated Air National Guardsmen. Soon, other F-84 squadrons, groups, and wings came to Korea—not from SAC but from Tactical Air Command, which LeMay didn't own. The F-84 became a fixture in Korean fighting. One F-84 pilot was dubbed the "Junior Commando" by his squadron mates—not charitably—because he had a Thompson submachine gun strapped to his parachute harness and had to be shoved up the ladder to his airplane because of the weight of the .45-caliber ammunition in his survival pack.

The F-84 flew mostly air-to-ground missions, but there were times when air-to-air action was unavoidable. Six MiGs ambushed the F-84Es of the 8th Fighter-Bomber Squadron, 49th Fighter-Bomber Wing, intent on an air-to-ground mission near Sukchon, North Korea, on September 10, 1951. The Thunderjets' flight leader was 1st Lt. William Skliar.

WILLIAM SKLIAR. We were on a rail-cutting mission. After our bomb runs, we were rejoining when the MiGs dove down on us. I called a break into the lead MiG, and when he saw us turn, he reversed his turn. At that moment, another MiG came across my path in a rapid turn . . . about twelve hundred feet (371 m) in front of me. I laid my "Hog," as the F-84 was nicknamed, into as tight a turn as possible and managed to draw a lead. We were at near max range for our .50s but I got some good long bursts in. After a quick glance around to check where the other MiGs were, my MiG just disappeared. Knowing that the enemy pilots often tried to decoy us into chasing them, I backed off in favor of getting everyone together again. At least I had the satisfaction of knowing that some of their decoys had almost bought the farm. I was credited with a "probable" kill.

Out of Oxygen

On November 16, 1951, Thunderjet pilots lived through one of the most publicized occurrences of the conflict. F-84s of the 154th Fighter-Bomber Squadron, 136th Fighter-Bomber Wing, were slashing at railway targets in North Korea, led by Capt. John L. Paladino. The sky was free of MiGs, and the bombs seemed to be on target. Heading home to Taegu at 33,000 feet (10216 m), Paladino's oxygen equipment malfunctioned. Flying nearby, 1st Lt. Wood McArthur and Capt. Jack Miller realized their flight leader was in trouble.

The Republic F-84 Thunderjet occasionally battled MiGs high in the sky of North Korea, but more often F-84 pilots performed the less glamorous job of hauling bombs to the target. This F-84E Thunderjet is operating from K-2 Taegu Air Base in South Korea.

[U.S. Air Force]

JACK MILLER. We were headed south at altitude, when all of a sudden John's aircraft started to turn and then went into a steep dive to the left. I thought maybe he was practicing evasive action or something. After he had dropped down a few thousand feet, his ship did a "pitch up" that was characteristic of the F-84 when it goes through the speed of sound. After a few simple dives and sudden climbs, he was still on course, so we figured he was okay.

When I pulled alongside, I noticed that John was tugging at his oxygen mask. He said he was all right, so I told him to throttle back for the descent home. As we pulled closer, I saw that John's head was resting against the canopy. Before I could call to him, he slumped forward.

The F-84 flight leader had passed out from oxygen deprivation and could survive only if he could be gotten down to lower altitude, where he could breathe. I told McArthur to "put your wingtip under his wingtip on your side, and I'll do the same on my side."

Using the flow of air over our wingtips to keep Paladino's aircraft level between us, without any of the three aircraft touching each other,

McArthur and I began the ticklish job of descending. After a hundred miles (161km) and about fifteen minutes, we used this unusual feat of aerodynamics to lower the unconscious Paladino down to 15,000 feet (4644 m). At 13,000 feet (4024 m), Paladino became fully conscious and was able, now, to fly his Thunderjet home and land safely. Flight leader Paladino had a skull-grinding headache but no memory of the quarter-hour when his plane had been held aloft while he was out cold.

TOM GILL. The most difficult part of a mission is the anticipation. Once you're in the cockpit, you're too busy to think about it.

I wanted jets. I didn't really have a preference as to what kind of jet, but I didn't want a reciprocating-engine airplane. I wanted to fly F-80s. At that time, I didn't even know an F-84 existed.

But once I completed pilot training and got into the F-84 Thunderjet, I was very glad to be flying that airplane. In the F-84, you were not in the glamour business. You were into reality.

The F-84 Thunderjet was a very good air-to-ground airplane. It was a very stable aircraft. It was an excellent gun platform. It had good fuel capacity, although at first it did not have the capability to receive air-to-air refueling. It was a good aircraft on instruments. On the negative side, I would have to say that both the F-84E and the F-84G were underpowered. We flew the F-84E and F-84G in Korea, and neither really had quite enough power. The Air Force didn't really have a fighter aircraft with sufficient power until the F-100 Super Sabre came along.

I was born in 1929 in Canton, Ohio. I started as a student at Ohio State University in 1947, and was studying there when the Korean War began. I was interested in flying. Dad's boss had a private aircraft, and I flew on it several times. I went to the recruiter in Canton in June or July 1950—the Korean War started on June 25—and the recruiter said, "Go home and graduate first." But I couldn't wait for graduation because I was about to drafted.

I joined the Air Force on January 28, 1951. I joined at the same time as Dick Kempler, who was an all-American football player at the University of Michigan in Ann Arbor. Dick was in Flying Class 52-B, and I was in class 52-C. At the time I joined up, enlistments were frozen because the draft was being used to induct people, but my recruiter sent me a telegram that got me in.

I went first to Greenville, Mississippi, where I did primary training in the T-6 Texan from April to November 1951. From there, I went to Bryan Air Force Base near College Station, Texas, where I trained in the T-28A and the T-33A Shooting Star, as well as the single-seat fighter, the F-80 Shooting Star. I pinned on my silver wings and became a second lieutenant on May 10, 1952.

I didn't have an aircraft preference, but I wanted fighters and I wanted jets, not reciprocating-engine aircraft. I went to Nellis Air Force Base near Las Vegas, Nevada, for F-84 transition and gunnery training. They had F-84B and F-84C models at Nellis. I also remember flying an F-84G. Later in Korea, I flew mostly F-84E models but also flew the F-84G about 10 percent of the time.

Thunderjet in Korea

I was assigned to the 428th Fighter Bomber Squadron, part of the 474th Fighter Bomber Group, at K-8 Kunsan Air Base in South Korea. We lived in Quonset huts that had been constructed by the Japanese. You had a cot, an air mattress, and three blankets.

I flew my first combat mission on October 4, 1952, from Kunsan. Like I said, the most difficult part of a mission is the anticipation. Once you're in the cockpit, you're too busy to think about it.

Before each mission, we had a briefing. In the briefing, they sometimes showed us photos of the target that had been taken just twenty-four hours earlier.

We frequently had large numbers of airplanes taking off on a mission. If you were in a 28-plane gaggle, you'd have to begin at your parking slow figuring out whom to follow when you taxi out. The runway ran from east to west. It was 10,000 feet long, with both ends over water. We took off two at a time, climbed out in a 270-degree turn, went back over the airfield, and turned to 90 degrees to fly north.

We flew north together, but it was a fairly loose arrangement. We maintained formation in pairs, but our two-ship formations didn't attempt to fit into larger formations. The number-one aircraft was the lead, of course, and it was his job to take us where we were going. The number-two aircraft would look to the right and clear the right as we proceeded north.

We flew toward the target at 35,000 feet (10668 m). I experienced air-to-air action on three occasions during my hundred missions. The F-86 Sabre boys who flew farther north were responsible for keeping the MiGs off of us, so we were not supposed to take them on. The MiGs flew through us, head-on, and we saw their 37 mm cannons blinking.

They didn't worry us much. You can't hit a guy shooting at him from head-on. They didn't have a lot of fuel and couldn't stick around to mix it up with us.

On a mission, we typically carried two 500-lb (227-kg) or two 1,000-lb (454-kg) bombs, one under each wing, plus six 5-inch high-velocity aircraft rockets, or HVARs, three under each wing, and of course we had six .50 caliber M3 machine guns, with 300 rounds per gun. The airplane had eight hard points for ordnance under the wings. All of that stuff weighs a lot, so the F-84 was a real heavyweight.

BOB JAMES. We went in at low level to bomb and strafe, so we never intended to try to turn with the MiGs or maneuver against them. Once we'd dropped our bombs and pulled off the target, we were fighters, but by then the MiGs would be gone because they wanted to get us when we were vulnerable, going in with our bombs attached. The MiGs did get close enough to fire at me several times. The cannon in the nose of the MiG made smoke rings, so you could see it coming.

I got into the F-84 Thunderjet after being interested in flying as a kid. I was born in 1924 in Danville, Virginia, and went to Georgia Tech, where I was in Reserve Officer Training Corps, or ROTC. The training was an infantry-type deal, and I didn't like those rifles and marching. When I was a kid, my dad got me a ride in a Ford Tri-Motor. I built models. I wanted to fly planes, not carry a rifle.

I learned about the December 7, 1941, Japanese attack on Pearl Harbor that Sunday afternoon while in college. I had no idea what place the words *Pearl Harbor* referred to. We probably didn't know where Hawaii was.

Everybody was getting into the service. I wanted to fly. I went to the Navy recruiter and was close to being accepted for pilot training with the Navy. But I'm a pretty small guy, and they told me that at 119 pounds I didn't weigh enough to become a Navy pilot. I went to the Air Corps recruiter, and they said: (1) if you want to come with us, you'll have to get yourself drafted in the next ninety days; and (2) once you're drafted, we'll make sure you get pilot training. They later dropped the

Wearing the handlebar mustache popular with F-84 Thunderjet pilots and standing on pierced steel planking at K-2 Taegu Air Base, South Korea, 1st Lt. E.R. "Bob" James of the 311th Fighter-Bomber Squadron prepares for a combat mission

[Bob James]

requirement to sixty days, and I got drafted on the fifty-ninth day. I was accepted into flying class 45-A, but they had too many pilots. So they sent me to become a bombardier and later to become a navigator. I was in A-26 Invaders in Valdosta, Georgia, when World War II ended.

I stayed in the Reserve and finished at Georgia Tech. Then they recalled me to active duty. This time I really was able to get pilot training, in flying class 51-G. I got my pilot's wings in November 1951, and went to Nellis Air Force Base, Nevada, for gunnery training in F-80 Shooting Stars. Then, I went to Japan, and from there to Korea to join the 182nd Fighter-Bomber Squadron of the 136th Fighter-Bomber Group, which was an activated Texas Air National Guard outfit. In July 1952, they changed the unit designations, and we became the 311th Fighter-Bomber Squadron of the 58th Fighter-Bomber Group. I had never seen an F-84 until I arrived in Korea and they said, "Fly that."

Thunderjet Impressions

In the F-84, we were the grunts, so to speak. Compared to other fighters, the F-84 was very stable. For a little guy with not much strength, it was a bit of a job, even though it had "boost" for the controls. It was very roomy, the cockpit being much less of a squeeze for me than the F-80, where my helmet was always hitting the top of the bubble canopy.

At Taegu airfield, we had about 7,500 feet of runway, so on hot days and when carrying heavy loads we used jet-assisted takeoff, or JATO. That consisted of two bottles of compressed gas, one on each side of the fuselage. It gave you an extra push and created what looked like giant clouds of smoke. It was electrically operated from the cockpit. When it was working right, you could feel something, but it was not exactly like being pushed by a powerful rocket. If one of the bottles didn't work, your F-84 got into an asymmetrical situation and you'd lose control.

We never seemed to have enough aircraft in service. Most of the Thunderjets in Korea were F-84E models, and they were joined eventually by some F-84Gs. We had the F-84D for a while, and they were not satisfactory. The Air Force pulled them out of training command units and sent them to Norton Air Force Base, California, for "disassemble, inspect, and repair," or DIR. When they arrived in Korea they were supposed to be in good condition—but they weren't. They went kaput. They shed their wings in flight. If you overstressed an F-84D, the wings came off in flight.

This happened to Lt. Col. Sidney Weatherford, the newly arrived commander of the 182nd squadron. He was in the middle of a combat run, and his wings folded. He was killed. Not long after that, the same thing happened to our operations officer. He lost a wing during a run on the Naktong firing range. After that, they removed the F-84D from service in Korea. The disruption from that change probably reduced the number of missions I got to fly. I flew eighty-three missions, rather than reaching the goal of a hundred.

I liked the F-84E model 50 percent more than the F-84G. The F-84G was heavier on the controls and was not quite as agile.

I got hit on a mission in July 1952. I was in a two-ship formation that took off at daybreak to catch the North Koreans who'd been hiding out at night.

We strafed trucks and pretty well beat them up.

An F-84 Thunderjet taxies toward the camera, with typical 1950s tents and vehicle in the background. The F-84 was big and robust, ideally designed for air-to-ground combat, and able to survive when hit by gunfire.

[U.S. Air Force]

The F-84 had a rather sophisticated gunsight for bombing and strafing. The truth is, I don't think we ever really learned how to use it. And we were getting so much battle damage on our low-level runs that General Barcus, the head of Fifth Air Force, ordered us to stay above 3,000 feet. Before that, some guys were getting damaged from their own bomb detonations. Afterward, when we followed Barcus's rule, we were a lot less effective.

I think my truck-strafing mission took place while we still had no restrictions on our altitude over the target. I know we were pretty low. When we were pulling off, I took a rifle round in my right tip tank. The tip tank exploded. It pulled the aircraft down. I brought it through the roll and got level, but it didn't want to fly with the damage. We had a T-handle to jettison the wing tanks. Normally, you didn't want to get rid of them, which is why you hardly ever see a photo of an F-84 flying without tip tanks. And you can't get rid of one tip tank at a time. In this situation, I had to get rid of mine, so I jettisoned them, even though this made me low on fuel.

To my surprise, and contrary to everything they'd told us, my airplane handled perfectly well without tip tanks. In fact, it handled better. I discovered, however, that I didn't have radio contact. Apparently, my departing tip tank hit the fin and damaged the antenna.

After some difficulty regaining control, I was able to head south with no radio and land safely at K-14 Kimpo Air Base near Seoul.

KENNETH L. SKEEN. My encounter with a MiG came on September 19, 1951, after I was forced to jettison my bombs and abandon an air-to-ground sortie.

The entire 49th Fighter-Bomber Group, including my squadron, the 9th Fighter-Bomber Squadron, was going on this strike against a mail/rail complex located between Sinanju and Pyongyang. Each squadron used sixteen aircraft, and total ordnance was ninety-six 500-lb (227 kg) general-purpose bombs. Since I was one of the new pilots, I would be flying the number-four position in the last flight. My call sign was Purple 4.

As we passed east of Pyongyang, I heard the group leader call in MiGs at one o'clock high. For the past few minutes we'd been listening to the controller calling out "MiG trains heading south." We assumed the F-86s would be in a position to intercept them, but unknown to us, the Sabres were still on the ground at Kimpo and we were on our own. There was a lot of radio chatter, with calls of, "MiGs at three o'clock high! They're coming in! Salvo your bombs! Get up some speed!" Then came the dreaded, "Break right, Purple flight!"

Being the last man in the flight, I was just hanging on as we went to full throttle. The MiGs overshot their attacking turn, and I pulled up high to our left, as Purple leader reversed the turn hard to the left into the MiGs. Since I was on the outside of the turn, I started falling behind. As I cut across to the inside to catch up with Maj. Jim Sprinkle, my element leader, who was far ahead of me, a blue MiG-15 dropped down in front of me and locked onto Sprinkle's tail. The enemy pilot evidently never saw me, as he was busy lining up the F-84 in his sights. He was decelerating to get a better shot, while I was at full throttle to catch up. I lined the gunsight on him, took my feet off the rudder pedals to make sure the aircraft was flying true . . . and squeezed the trigger.

I gave him a long burst of .50 caliber (12.7mm) armor piercing incendiary. Immediately, pieces started flying off of the MiG, accompanied by smoke and flames. As he slowed, I saw he was on fire, and I pulled to his left to keep from running into him. He went into the thin undercast as I glanced to my left and saw another blue MiG right on the tail of another F-84. I yelled, "F-84! Break! Break! MiG on your tail! Break right!" I was hoping to bring the MiG into my sights. As the F-84 broke, the MiG pulled up high to the left. I looked back to my right as I entered the thin undercast.

I saw a parachute descending, but not a single aircraft in sight. I climbed back on top, finding the sky deserted, where just moments before, aircraft had been twisting and turning all over the sky. With my fuel showing well below bingo level, I headed south for the base at K-2. The rail-cutting mission had been unsuccessful, as we jettisoned our bomb loads, but all aircraft returned with only one damaged. Most important, the 9th Fighter-Bomber Squadron had gotten its first kill.

TOM GILL. Approaching the target, we let down to 20,000 feet (6096 m) while following the number-one aircraft in the lead position. Exactly when we rolled in on the target was determined by where the enemy's antiaircraft guns were. The leader found the target and began the run-in. When you're ready to roll in, you push over the airplane to get it into trajectory to aim the bombs. We were supposed to pull out at 1,500 feet.

On my seventh or eighth night mission, going up to the bridges on the Yalu River, I got lost, became low on fuel, and couldn't use my radio transmitter, although I could receive. We went on these night missions by ourselves, so you were pretty much on your own except for the controller at Cho-do Island. The object was to harass the North Koreans and Chinese at night so they couldn't move stuff during the hours of darkness.

That was probably my most difficult mission. I couldn't transmit, but I used my "identification, friend or foe," or IFF equipment to transmit—squawk—a signal to Cho-do. I squawked four on the IFF, which meant, "Mayday. This is an emergency." He came back to me with something like: "Aircraft squawking on IFF, if you can read me, turn to a heading of 090 degrees." I did that, and now we had communication of a sort. He said things like, "If your tip tanks are dry, turn to 180 degrees. Okay, got that, sir. Now, if you have your ordnance, turn to 170 degrees. Okay, thank you, sir." Using that kind of communication, he guided me, and I eventually landed safely at K-55 Osan Air Base, which was a little farther north than my base at Kunsan. It was the only time I ever went in there.

A crew chief peers over the shoulder of a white-helmeted pilot (barely visible) into the cockpit of an F-84 Thunderjet in Korea. This aircraft had air-refueling probes extending forward from its wingtip fuel tanks—the first ever used on a combat mission by any U.S. aircraft. The pierced steel planking on the ground is typical.

[U.S. Air Force]

Landing the F-84 was a piece of cake. At Kunsan, we had 10,000 feet of runway, so there was plenty of space. There was water at both ends, so they didn't need to install Navy-style arresting gear, as they'd done at Taegu: If you got in trouble, you went into the water. For a period of time, we were told to practice landing with a brake on one side of the airplane only. Returning from one mission, my flight leader got shot up, lost one brake, skidded, went off the runway, and piled up. So he said, "We've got to practice that." So we got used to landing with one brake, almost as if we were being punished for what he did. When you landed with one brake, you would compensate with rudder and aileron: If you used the stick properly to compensate, you could keep the airplane straight on the runway.

To summarize my experience in the F-84, in a fast aircraft you had to think ahead of the airplane. It helped if your only training was in jets. There were some guys who switched regularly from props to jets and back again. Some of them weren't thinking ahead, and they were getting killed.

I flew a hundred missions. I got out of the Air Force after leaving Korea, mostly because I didn't want to fly a hundred more.

Who's Who

Republic F-84E/G Thunderjet

The Republic F-84 Thunderjet was what many pilots saw as their second choice. It wasn't pretty. It wasn't glamorous. It didn't achieve much in air-to-air action. In Korea, Thunderjet pilots shot down only a handful of MiGs—including the one downed by Navy exchange pilot Lt. Walter "Wally" Schirra, later a Mercury astronaut—but they spent much of the war in the unglorious, unglamorous business of hauling bombs to the target. The F-84 was sturdy, which was why its maker, located at Farmingdale, Long Island, in New York, was sometimes dubbed the Republic Iron Works—and it could sometimes be sprightly, but many pilots found their way into F-84 cockpits only after not qualifying in the slimmer, prettier F-86 Sabre.

On November 11, 1944, the Army Air Forces authorized Republic to build three prototypes of a new jet fighter called the XP-84. Republic completed the first plane at Farmingdale and shipped it to Muroc,

California—site of the future Edwards Air Force Base—where the XP-84 made its initial flight on February 28, 1946. By then, the swept-wing XP-86 Sabre was flying faster in its initial flight trials, and the P-84 remained on the U.S. Air Force's shopping list only as "insurance" against the catastrophic failure of the Sabre, which many believed was too advanced to have any practical use.

The XP-84's original engine was a 3,750-lb (1700-kg) thrust Allison TG-180 axial-flow turbojet, later redesignated J35-GE-7. The first production models of the new fighter, P-84Bs, began to reach squadrons in 1947. That year, the Air Force became an independent service branch. The following year, the "p" for "pursuit" nomenclature was dropped. The P-84 became the F-84. By then, the Air Force was receiving F-84D and F-84E models.

F-84s went into combat in Korea in 1951. They proved tough, able to absorb gunfire and return safely to base. By now, of course, the Sabre was making its mark as one of the great warplanes of all time and an "insurance policy" was no longer needed. At this late juncture, the F-84

Republic F-84E/G Thunderjet

Type: single-seat fighter-bomber

Power plant: one 5,000-lb (2267-kg) thrust Allison J35-A-17D axial-flow turbojet engine (F-84E); one 5,000-lb (2267-kg) thrust Allison J35-A-29 axial-flow turbojet engine (F-84G)

Performance: maximum speed 622 mph (1001 km/h) at sea level, 590 mph (944 km/h) at 35,000 ft (10668 m); cruising speed 483 mph (777 km/h) at sea level; climb to 35,000 ft (10668 m) in 9 minutes, 10 seconds; service ceiling 40,500 ft (12344 m); range, 2,000 miles (3218 m)

Weights: empty 11,095 lb (5032 kg); maximum takeoff 19,689 lb (8930 kg) (F-84D), 23,525 lb (10656 kg) (F-84G)

Dimensions: wingspan 36 ft 5 in (11.12 m); length 37 ft 5 in (11.43 m); height 12 ft 10 in (3.90 m); wing area 260 sq ft

Armament: six Browning M3 machine guns, four in nose and two in wing roots with 300 rounds per gun; up to twelve 5-inch high-velocity aircraft rockets (HVAR); up to 4,000 lb (1814 kg) of bombs and rockets

First flight: February 28, 1946 (XP-84); February 3, 1949 (F-84E)

Thunderjet was a fine fighting machine and was beloved by pilots, but it was no longer on the cutting edge.

The idea of passing fuel from one aircraft to another in flight dated to at least the early 1920s, but two world wars had been fought without it being accomplished in battle. On May 29, 1952, the U.S. Air Force's 116th Fighter-Bomber Wing flew a mission as part of Operation Hi-Tide, in which F-84E Thunderjets were refueled in flight by KB-29M Superfortresses of the 43rd Air Refueling Squadron. Twelve F-84E Thunderjets, each carrying two 227-kg bombs departed Itazuke Air Base, Japan, refueled aloft, bombed the North Korean city of Sariwon, and recovered at Johnson Air Base, Japan. Each F-84 carried a stiff probe that pointed forward from its wingtip fuel tank—plugging into a kind of funnel lowered by the KB-29M. This was called the "probe and drogue" refueling system. Except for a few missions flown by RF-80 photo planes, this was the first use of air-to-air refueling in combat: It pointed the way to a future in which all warplanes would be capable of taking on fuel in flight.

Straight-wing F-84D, F-84F, and F-84G fighters flew thousands of less dramatic missions in Korea and shot down a few MiG-15s. Others served as escort fighters with the Strategic Air Command. The United States exported F-84s to many of its allies.

Chapter Ten

Sabres over MiG Alley

What Happened

In November 1950, Americans were celebrating victory in Korea. The troops would be home for Christmas. After four months of battle, American soldiers stood on the bank of the Yalu River. Having seized most of North Korea, they now peered into the part of China still known, in those days, as Manchuria. North Korea's invasion of South Korea had failed.

On November 1, F-51 Mustangs were engaged by six swept-wing jet fighters from the far side of the Yalu.

American intelligence experts knew of huge airfields at Antung, Tatangkou, and Fen Cheng, on the Manchurian side of the Yalu. Now, they learned that the Soviet-built MiG-15 was operating from those airfields. On November 8, F-80 Shooting Star pilot 1st Lt. Russell J. Brown was credited with shooting down a MiG-15 in the first air battle ever waged between jet aircraft. Brown's flight leader that day, Lt. Col. Evans G. Stephens, had begun his career in the P-39 Airacobra (Chapter 3).

Soviet pilots were flying the MiGs, but Americans did not know that yet. The Americans were too busy registering shock and surprise at China's decision to enter the Korean War. It meant the troops wouldn't be home for Christmas, after all.

**Captain Marty Bambrick
September 4, 1952
North American F-86A Sabre
(49-1272)
335th Fighter Interceptor
Squadron, 4th Fighter
Interceptor Wing
K-14 Kimpo Air Base, Seoul,
Korea**

Martin J. Bambrick Jr., who flew
the F-86 Sabre in Korea, snapped
this self-portrait while still in
training at Williams Air Force Base,
Arizona, in 1951. The aircraft is an
F-80 Shooting Star that was the first
jet fighter Bambrick flew before
moving up to the F-86.

[Marty Bambrick]

Chinese soldiers swarmed down on the 2nd Infantry Division at Kunu-ri and the First Marine Division at the Chosin Reservoir, deep inside North Korea, near the west coast. Along some parts of the front, U.S troops were outnumbered fifty-to-one.

Long before the significance of the new war was understood, on November 8, 1950, the U.S. Air Force ordered the 4th Fighter Interceptor Wing to Korea. Thus began a thirty-month campaign fought between the F-86 Sabre and the MiG-15. In the first contest between the adversaries on December 17, 1950, Lt. Col. Bruce Hinton, commander of the wing's 336th Fighter Interceptor Squadron battled several MiGs, eluded one, and got behind another. Hinton fired a long burst that sent .50 caliber bullets into the MiG's engine. Hinton stayed in a left turn behind his opponent and had a spectacular view of the MiG. He closed in and fired again. In fact, Hinton kept firing. Flames consumed the rear section of the MiG and the enemy fighter rolled on its back and went plummeting to earth. The MiG crashed ten miles (16 km) southeast of the Yalu.

The campaign between the F-86 Sabre and the MiG-15 from December 1950 to July 1953 had a unique purity like nothing before or since. It was a contest between fighters and fighter pilots unaffected by other factors—a pure, air-to-air effort on both sides. When the conflict began, the F-86A Sabre, with a still-unreliable engine, could not fly as high as the MiG and was outperformed in other areas from time to time. By the time it ended, the improved MiG-15bis remained a formidable foe, but the much-improved, hard-wing F-86F (following the F-86E and the slat-wing F-86F) was the better fighter.

Two days after the war ended, the Air Force reported 818 MiGs downed, in exchange for a loss of fifty-eight Sabres, a 13.79-to-1 kill ratio. Sabre pilots, who began with huge disadvantages, carved out the best air-to-air combat record of all time—better than Royal Air Force pilots in the Battle of Britain, better than the Flying Tigers. In the history of air warfare, no other fighter pilots ever achieved such a record.

MARTY BAMBRICK. They called it a fighter sweep. They sent us to the mouth of the Yalu, and we flew up and down along the North Korean side of the river, looking across at those airfields in Manchuria. They called it a fighter sweep but, hell, they should have called it bait.

That's what we were. We weren't supposed to cross the river. So our job was to provoke the MiGs into crossing it in the other direction and attacking us. If we weren't there, functioning as a screen, the MiGs would have been free to cross over and attack our B-29 Superfortress bombers and our fighter-bombers, like the F-84 Thunderjet.

It was a dangerous game, and it could have dangerous consequences. One of our top World War II aces, Col. Walker "Bud" Mahurin went up there masquerading as an F-84 fighter-bomber, trying to lure the MiGs into attacking him. They did. He was shot down and became a prisoner of war. The MiG-15 was capable of flying higher than the Sabre, and when the MiGs came, they were always above us. Since they could choose the time and place of the engagement, they came only when they believed they had pulled off a successful ambush.

My experience was not unusual for men who were just a little too young for World War II and who flew the magnificent F-86 Sabre in Korea. Most of my fellow Sabre pilots had an edge, and I did, too. Most of my fellow Sabre pilots drank from time to time, and I did, too.

I was born in 1928, grew up in Pennsylvania, and lived at various times in Pennsylvania, West Virginia, and Maryland. I was a reckless kid at times, and I suppose I could have easily turned bad. On June 5, 1946, I signed a statement for the police in the borough of Bellefonte, Pennsylvania, acknowledging "disorderly conduct . . . by removing a restricted

The F-86 Sabres assigned to Marty Bambrick (foreground) and air ace Capt. Robert J. Love sit on the alert ramp at K-14 Kimpo Air Base, Korea, in April 1952 while another Sabre takes off above them.

[Marty Bambrick]

parking sign, and destroying the same, and otherwise [conducting] myself in a manner whereby the public peace was broken and disturbed." In order for the cops to let me go, I had to promise to "refrain from the excessive use of alcohol, and . . . never [again] become intoxicated in Bellefonte." Today, I can't swear that I never took another drink in the borough. In fact, I never lost my wild streak, but it didn't matter because soon afterward I was in the Army.

In the late 1940s, I was a reserve officer in the Army and served with the 304th Signal Battalion in Japan. I saw some of the Orient before I saw a fighter cockpit. I was in postwar Japan when the exchange rate was 360 yen to the dollar and a carton of cigarettes from the Post Exchange would buy you almost anything you needed.

Pilot Training

I qualified for flight training and became a member of Flying Class 51-D in the Air Force, which was now a newly independent service branch. I spent six months at Goodfellow Air Force Base, Texas, and six at Williams Air Force Base, Arizona, flying prop and jet trainers. I graduated and pinned on pilot wings in June 1951. By then, the campaign between the Sabre and the MiG-15 was well underway. We flew the F-80 Shooting Star in training, and I was tapped to fly the Sabre.

I'd like to stop for a moment and describe the Sabre. People who are much less biased than I am will tell you that it was the most beautiful fighter plane ever built. It has certain features in common with its nemesis, the MiG-15. Those include an engine air intake in the nose, wings swept back at an angle of about 40 degrees, tricycle landing gear, and a Plexiglas bubble canopy. But the MiG ended up looking like exactly what it was, a Stalinist machine. The Sabre has many of the same features, but its lines are different, and they make for an aerodynamic shape that is really pleasing to the eye.

The Sabre's wing and horizontal stabilizer were mounted lower than those on the MiG-15. The Sabre was armed with machine guns, which have greater reach, while the MiG used cannons, which fire explosive shells. Once I started flying the Sabre, on occasion I would simply walk around it, not for the purpose of doing a routine walk-around check— contrary to what they teach student pilots, we usually relied on our crew chief for that—but simply to admire it. It was a graceful and beautiful machine that, incidentally, happened also to be functional.

They sent me to Korea. By the time I arrived in Korea in 1952, the battle lines had stabilized. The fighting on the ground was still horrific, but very little real estate was changing hands. The Americans and Chinese were battling over hills, ridgelines, and trenches. We flew over their heads and went north looking for MiGs and setting ourselves up so the MiGs would look for us.

According to an intelligence report they showed us, the Soviets had 445 MiG-15s, while FEAF's Fifth Air Force had eighty-nine F-86 Sabres in theater inventory, of which forty-four belonged to the 4th Wing's two squadrons then committed to Korea.

Although our numbers were increasing steadily in 1952, we Sabre pilots remained the most outnumbered band of fighter jocks in history— more than the Flying Tigers in China, more than the Royal Air Force in the Battle of Britain. And some of the MiG pilots were very, very good. Those who led the formations we called "bandit trains," crossing the Yalu to hit us, were as good as they came. "Casey Jones" became our radio shorthand for the Soviet leader of the bandit trains. My roommate and fellow Sabre pilot, Capt. James Horowitz, wrote a novel about a duel between the MiGs' aggressive fighter wing commander, Casey

Jones, and an American Sabre pilot. After his memoir *The Hunters* was published, Horowitz got out of the Air Force, changed his name to James Salter, and became a figure in American letters. He described the Sabre-versus-MiG campaign better than anybody.

It was remarkable how we went against them—traveling far from our base at Kimpo so they could fight close to home near their base at Antung, going up there to meet them on their terms, confronting good pilots in good airplanes, and still defeating them the way we did.

We flew north in some of the most extraordinary aerial formations the world had ever seen. When we were supporting fighter-bombers and the other side was out in force, there could be hundreds of airplanes up there. The world hasn't seen any air battles on that scale since the Korean War ended.

The day I got my MiG, September 4, 1952, we had what I recall as a middle-sized mix-up with the guys on the other side.

Into the Mission

We take off, climb out, join on the lead flight, and throttle back to 95 percent power for the trip north to MiG Alley. That's what we call the slice of North Korea that borders on the Yalu. We carry wing tanks. They are long, slim, silvery things that hold an extra two hundred gallons (755 liters) of jet fuel. The MiGs like to come up and have us drop those external tanks early because that limits our time in MiG Alley.

Every time we drop those tanks, it plucks at my heartstrings because one of the things I want at this time is a 1952 Chevrolet convertible. A Chevrolet convertible costs $2,000, and every time we punch those tanks off, it's $2,000. People in North Korea love these tanks because they made them into water reservoirs, and you see all kinds of pictures of very ingenious utilization of those tanks. When we have a lot of Sabres in the air, like today, and we punch off those tanks, it looks like some of the chaff dropped in World War II, particularly when the sun is in the right position. It's an eerie and beautiful sight.

Our flight leader is in contact with Shorthound, which is today's radio call sign for the radar site on Cho-do Island, off the west coast of North Korea. The guys on that island are tracking the MiG bases on radar. They also have radio-intercept operators who are monitoring the MiG force. While we cruise to the mouth of the Yalu at 38,000 feet (11582 m), Shorthound is looking for bandit trains taking off from An-

Marty Bambrick's F-86 Sabre in its sandbagged revetment at Kimpo. Bambrick, in the center with his head down, appears to be leaning on an access door while his crew chief and armorer look over the aircraft. Because an access panel to the ammunition bay is open, we cannot quite see the plane's name, Wham Bam, or the likeness of Bugs Bunny painted on its center fuselage.

[Marty Bambrick]

tung and Tatangkou. When we draw closer to the Yalu, we can look across the river and see for ourselves. One of the main runways at Antung is unpaved. We see dust clouds rising from that location. That means bandit trains. It means MiGs, coming up to get us.

"They're up," somebody calls. That's when the traffic begins on the radio. We're supposed to observe flight discipline and keep our mouths shut until the fight begins, but nobody ever does.

"I have two bandit trains at Tatangkou," another pilot says. "Three more coming up from Antung."

"I've got more," somebody says. "There's more, more."

Apparently, a Sabre flight about forty miles in front of us has already been drawn into a fight. Now, the voices are coming fast and the words are chopped. Things like, "Break right!" And, "Break! Break now!"

Now we can see vapor trails above us. And then, the vapor trails stop. The MiGs are peeling away to come down at us.

We always try to stay together. We want to maintain flight integrity with four aircraft—two down, two high. We work very hard on tactics. Although we get carried away on the radio sometimes, we have excellent air discipline. That's probably a reason we do well: The pilots who get shot down are invariably the ones who invariably get separated from their wingman. In this game, at this time, you cannot clear yourself. You cannot work a gunnery solution by yourself. You must have that wingman clearing you all the time.

My wingman today is 1st Lt. Raymond A. Kinsey. He is one of the few Americans to have seen and shot down a Tupolev Tu-2 twin-engine, propeller-driven bomber. First lieutenants Coy Austin and Bob Straub are somewhere in the sky around us, but our four-ship discipline is now degrading into two-ship discipline. I can see Kinsey to my right and behind me. Several blurred aircraft in motion seem to be diving at us from the left.

MiG Kill

The MiG-15 is a little smaller, a little portlier, than the Sabre. That is not something you see in the heat of battle, but I can tell from the way they're acting that these are the bad guys. There is a fracas going on in the distance ahead to my right and a couple of them are heading that way, but at least two MiGs are now crossing paths with Kinsey and me. I get a quick glimpse of some red-hot golf balls, the cannon shells from the lethal 37-mm gun carried by the MiG.

"Break right, Ray," I say slowly, thinking there is plenty of time. They have missed us with some wild bursts, fired from too far out, but they're still boring straight at us. Almost like a flight-demonstration team performing a planned maneuver, Kinsey and I roll our Sabres to starboard and lose a little altitude. Four MiGs—more than I thought— pass through our flight path where we were just a couple of seconds ago. Now they are maneuvering to reengage.

Everything happens at split-second speed in these engagements. That's part of the irony of it: We spend hours preparing and at least an hour flying to the scene, and then it happens in seconds. I'm now in a position to cut off two of the MiGs, and suddenly the American pilot closest to me is not somebody from my four-ship but 1st Lt. Al Smiley from "D" Flight. Kinsey says something on the radio suggesting that I caused us to become separated. "For Christ's sake, find me!" I respond, not us-

To Sabre pilots in Korea, the dreaded MiG-15 often was only a blur, arriving from higher altitude and at high speed and tearing through F-86 formations. Early in the Korean War, western intelligence experts still did not know much about the MiG-15. That made it seem especially threatening.

[U.S. Air Force]

---

ing very good judgment. I'm maneuvering into a right turn that will put me behind a MiG and allow me to shoot up his tailpipe. The voice of another pilot from a different four-ship, 1st Lt. Karl Dittmer, says that there are now twenty MiGs swarming around two scattered groups totaling eight Sabres. That's when I realize that there's a bigger problem.

One MiG has pulled above all this and drifted back behind us, like a slow-motion object in a movie. I'm guessing this is a honcho, one of their leaders. Maybe it's not Casey Jones himself. But he's definitely acting like a smart guy, and he's almost in position to bag me. A quick thought crosses my mind, something about those red golf balls and fire. Nothing is scarier than the ideas that cannon shells might set my Sabre on fire. Suddenly, my small, cramped cockpit feels very confining and I can hear my breathing in my earphones.

I pull my stick, hard, drop back on my throttle, begin another break to the right, and interrupt the break before I've moved very far. There's a dull, brittle sound as a 37-mm shell tears into my wing root. Suddenly, my cockpit is depressurizing and water vapor is forming on the canopy, clogging my vision.

But the MiG is going by, and for a split-second, before the water vapor blocks it, he's a big, fat target flying into my gunsight and my thumb is on the trigger. The machine guns in the nose of the Sabre sound a little like a sewing machine when they're going off.

My gun-camera film shows a direct, ass-end view of the MiG-15, taking hits and shedding pieces of metal. There is no fire. There is no smoke. The MiG appears to tremble, just once. It noses over. Kinsey, Smiley, and Austin all confirm the kill. They see the MiG go in. No one sees a parachute.

One of our wing commanders compared this kind of fighting with medieval jousting. He even called us F-86 pilots "young Sir Galahads." The comparison with King Arthur was well intended, but it overlooked the raw truth. The war along the Yalu was grim and dirty. It was no fun to be high over the Yalu on a freezing day. MiG cannon shells slamming into your aircraft, then trying to handle a parachute with a broken arm, then scrambling on the cold, wet ground, pursued by Communist soldiers with burp guns and grenades. Pilots who ejected were cornered and caught, beaten, humiliated, and starved by their communist captors. In the entire war, only one man was captured and escaped. More frequently, a pilot was trapped inside a crippled Sabre as it spun out of control, pinned by G forces or a frozen canopy, unable to get out at all while the world came rushing upward.

We didn't know it in those days, but most of those MiG pilots on the far side of the Yalu were Russians. They parked their airplanes wingtip-to-wingtip and thumbed their noses at us. Prohibited from crossing the border to attack their bases, we had one hand tied behind our backs. They had the advantage of ground-controlled intercept, with radar operators guiding them up to fight. What they didn't know was, our radio intercept guys on Cho-do Island monitored their every word—and most of those words were in the Russian language.

Today, it's easy to forget the breathtaking size of those battles. There were times when three hundred fighters were grappling with each other over just a few square miles. One day, we watched a dozen bandit

Who's Who

Capt. Marty Bambrick, F-86A Sabre pilot, 335th Fighter Interceptor Squadron

Capt. Philip "Casey" Colman, World War II ace and F-86A Sabre pilot, 335th Fighter Interceptor Squadron

1st Lt. (later Col.) James Kasler, F-86A Sabre pilot, 335th Fighter Interceptor Squadron and Korean War air ace

2nd Lt. (later Maj.) James F. "Dad" Low, F-86A Sabre pilot, 335th Fighter Interceptor Squadron and Korean War air ace

---

trains lift off from Antung, each with twenty-four MiGs. They did not always put their best pilots aloft, but when their top pilots led them into the fight, they were as good as any men who ever strapped into a combat. I truly believe that in Korea, the best pilots who ever lived faced each other in one of history's extraordinary tests of skill.

I flew with some of the best. Horowitz, who changed his name to Salter after he wrote *The Hunters* was one of them. First Lieutenant James Kasler, who became an ace in Korea and was a prisoner of war in Vietnam, was another. Second Lieutenant James F. "Dad" Low also became an ace in Korea and a prisoner in Vietnam, but Low (Chapter 11) was more controversial. He was the real-life model for the bad guy, the fictional Pell, in *The Hunters*.

I also flew with Capt. Philip "Casey" Colman, who shot down five Zeros in World War II and four MiGs in Korea. All of these were great officers and superb pilots.

North American F-86A Sabre

At the end of World War II, the U.S. Air Force (which became an independent service branch in September 1947) was making the transition from propellers to jets, and from straight wings to swept wings. On October 1, 1947, test pilot George Welch made the first flight of a new fighter, the North American XP-86, at Muroc, California. It was cream-colored and had no guns, but it was otherwise identical in appearance to the American fighters that battled MiGs in Korea. The P-86 became the F-86 and acquired the popular name Sabre in 1948.

It is not true, as some have suggested, that Welch—first encountered in this narrative at Pearl Harbor (Chapter 1) and later a World War II air ace, flew faster than sound before another test pilot, Capt. Charles E. Yeager, made humankind's first documented supersonic flight on October 14, 1947, in the Bell XS-1 rocket plane. Yeager's flight also occurred at Muroc, site of today's Edwards Air Force Base.

Welch's XP-86, with a better engine and guns, became the F-86 Sabre, a beautiful and beloved combat aircraft that proved to be the right solution at the right moment, when Soviet-built MiG-15 filled the skies over Korea. Had it not been for the foresight behind the F-86, everything might have gone differently. No other fighter was capable of standing up to the swift, swept-wing, cannon-armed MiG when it appeared in December 1950.

The F-86 did almost everything right. Its General Electric J47 turbojet was effective at a time when early jet engines were notorious for being unreliable and even dangerous. Most Air Force and Navy fighters still had straight wings (the F-84 Thunderjet and F9F Panther were Korean War examples), but the Sabre, like its MiG nemesis, benefited from German wing-sweep technology.

With six .50 caliber machine guns, the Sabre was less heavily armed than the cannon-equipped MiG, but the Sabre was also testimony to the simple truth that the American fighter pilot of 1950 was the best the world had ever seen. The older ones were World War II veterans. The younger pilots, like Marty Bambrick, were graduates of advanced jet gunnery training at Nellis Air Force Base, Nevada.

Beginning on December 17, 1950, when Lt. Col. Bruce Hinton shot down the first MiG-15 to be claimed by an F-86, the Americans overcame disadvantages—most models of the MiG could fly higher, an important asset in combat—and maintained the edge.

Though it was not well known at the time, experienced Russian pilots were flying MiGs in Korea. Yet even after exaggerated wartime claims were revised downward, Sabres achieved a 13.79-to-1 victory edge over the MiG-15, the grandest achievement in any fighter campaign in history.

The Korean War versions of the Sabre were the F-86A, F-86E, and F-86F. Only the F-86A model was available in the beginning. It lacked

To Marty Bambrick, the F-86 Sabre was "the most beautiful fighter plane ever built." This lineup of early F-86A models at the North American plant in Inglewood, California, in 1950, shows how pristine the Sabre looked when it came off the production line.

[U.S. Air Force]

some of the features that eventually made the Sabre indisputably superior to the MiG. As it turned out, the Sabre evolved faster, and was improved more than the MiG.

George Welch made the first flight of the F-86A on May 20, 1948. The early production F-86A models had an increased empty weight of 10,077 pounds (4571 kg), or some 347 pounds (157 kg) more than the XP-86 prototype. With its more powerful engine, the F-86A challenged the world air speed record, 650.796 mph (1047.352 km/h), set by the straight-wing Douglas D-558 Skystreak on August 25, 1947. The Skystreak was a specialized aircraft optimized for the high-speed effort. The F-86A, in contrast, was very close to a fully operational warplane.

Maj. Robert L. Johnson made the speed record attempt September 5, 1948, in an early F-86A-1. With an audience of no fewer than 80,000, the only time a vast public gathering observed such an effort, Johnson flew his fully loaded F-86A on six passes over the measured course. The audience saw the new fighter fly faster than ever before, reaching an average speed of 669.480 mph (1077.420 km/h). Unfortunately, technical glitches prevented the effort from being properly recorded and registered. Another attempt was mounted in the privacy of Muroc Air Base, and on September 15, 1948, Johnson achieved a record of 670.981 mph (1079.836 km/h). This time, the achievement was fully sanctioned.

Also in late 1948, North American began to turn out the F-86A-5 version, with slightly more powerful J47-GE-7 and J47-GE-13 engines.

The armament of six .50 caliber machine guns was to be standard on nearly all F-86 day fighters built for the U.S. Air Force (six M-3 guns with a rate of fire of 1,100 rounds per minute and ammunition supply of 1,802 rounds or 267 rounds per gun).

In the 1949 Thompson Trophy Race, Capt. Bruce Cunningham won the Jet Division of the contest, flying a F-86A-5 in ten laps of a 15-mile (25-km) circular course around seven pylons for 150 miles (241 km). Cunningham was credited with an elapsed time of 15:21.23 minutes, or an average speed of 586.173 mph (943.352 km/h).

The F-86A-5 model introduced a V-shaped, bulletproof windscreen and heated gun compartments. The F-86A-5 could carry 200-gallon drop tanks, rockets, and bombs. One F-86A-5 was tested with an aerial refueling receptacle. As it turned out, though, the F-86 became the last major U.S. combat plane that never received in-flight refueling on operational missions.

In early Sabres, the A-1CM gunsight was coupled with an AN/APG-30 radar installed in the upper lip of the nose intake. Although almost useless at low altitude because of ground clutter, the radar could be slaved to the sight for effective tracking of an aerial target. F-86A-5 airplanes retrofitted with A-1CM sight were redesignated F-86A-6 when they retained AN/APG-5C radar, and F-86A-7 when retrofitted with AN/APG-30.

After the 554th and last F-86A model was delivered in December 1950, a number of F-86A Sabres were converted to RF-86A reconnaissance aircraft. These photo-taking Sabres flew clandestine missions not only during the Korean War but against targets in the Soviet Union during the Cold War.

The F-86A was a contemporary of the MiG-15 and was just about its equal in air combat. The F-86B was a design that was never built. The F-86C evolved into an entirely different aircraft and was redesignated YF-93A as a service-test, long-range fighter. The F-86D was an all-weather interceptor.

When it came to improving the basic Sabre day fighter that fought the MiG-15 in Korea, the story leaps from the F-86A directly to the F-86E.

The first flight of the F-86E-1 Sabre, or company NA-170, was made by the ubiquitous George Welch on September 23, 1950. The "all-flying tail" and the irreversible hydraulic systems introduced in the F-86E are considered one of the most important advances of the era. At Wright Field, Ohio, World War II ace and test pilot Maj. Clarence E. "Bud" Anderson flew the early version of the "all-flying tail" and discovered that it didn't feel right. The maneuverability and artificial "feel" were sluggish, awkward, and perhaps dangerous. North American and the Air Force worked together on changing and improving the F-86E's key features until the problems were resolved and the F-86E became, in Anderson's words, "a world-beater."

Sixty F-86E-1 models were followed by fifty-one F-86E-5s, which differed only in minor panel switches. The designation F-86E-6 went to a batch of sixty Canadair-built CL-13 Sabre Mark 2 fighters built in

---

North American F-86A Sabre

Type: single-seat fighter

Power plant: one 5,200-lb (2358-kg) thrust General Electric J47-GE-13 axial-flow turbojet engine

Performance: maximum speed 667 mph (1067 km/h) at 38,000 ft (11582 m); initial climb rate in clean configuration, 9,300 ft (2835 m) per minute; service ceiling 48,000 ft (14630 m); range with tanks 1,270 miles (2044 km), combat radius 680 miles (1086 km)

Weights: empty 10,077 lb (4571 kg); loaded 15,876 lb (7201 kg)

Dimensions: wingspan 37 ft 1½ in (11.31 m); length 37 ft 6½ in (11.44 m); height 14 ft 8¾ in (4.47 m); wing area 288 sq ft (26.76 sq m)

Armament: six .50 caliber (12.7-mm) M-3 machine guns, with a rate of fire of 1,100 rounds per minute and an ammunition supply of 1,802 rounds or 267 rounds per gun; provision for two 1,000-lb (454-kg) bombs or many other weapons loads, plus two 200-gallon (755 liter) jettisonable fuel tanks

First flight: October 1, 1947 (XP-86); May 20, 1948 (F-86A)

Canada for the USAF. The designation F-86E-10 went to 132 Sabres that were powered by the J47-GE-13 only because planned -27 models of the engine were not yet available—in short, the aircraft was an F-86F with an F-86E engine. The F-86E-10 also introduced a new flat windscreen and modified instrument panel. The total for the F-86E series, then, is 336 aircraft, or 396 when the Canadian-built Sabres are included in the count.

Subsequently, out of this order, ninety-three aircraft, which were to have been delivered as F-86F-15s, reverted to the -27 engine because of further power plant delays and were given the out-of-order designation F-86E-15. These brought the total of American-built fighters in the F-86E series to 340 aircraft.

The next improvement—the one that would make the Sabre not the equal of the MiG-15 but superior to it—was the definitive production model, the F-86F. As air ace 2nd Lt. James F. Low said it, "Once we got the F-86F model, we were no longer competing for the sky. Now, we commanded the sky."

Chapter Eleven

Sabres Over MiG Alley (II)

What Happened

Retired Maj. James F. Low and those who know him agree on one point: Just about everything happened to Low that could happen to a fighter pilot.

Low, 80, of Davenport, Florida, fought in three wars, became an air ace, was portrayed in a movie by Robert Wagner, and was a prisoner of war.

Apart from these basic facts, there is little agreement about Low, a controversial figure who has his detractors.

Col. Harrison Thyng, who commanded Low's fighter wing in the Korean War, called him "a real fighter jockey" and "a great pilot." Col. Robert D. "Doug" Carter, who served with Low as a young lieutenant, said in an interview that, "A lot of us didn't like him and didn't want to fly with him."

Low has been called a hero and a turncoat. "I'm a competitive person," he said. "They love me or they hate me. That's the way it is."

Low joined the Navy in 1943 and served in the South Pacific until his discharge in 1946. After four years at the University of California at Berkeley ("but just short of a degree," he said), he became an aviation cadet in Flying Class 51-H and earned Air Force pilot wings and second lieutenant's bars in 1951.

Second Lieutenant James F. Low
December 1952
North American F-86F Sabre
335th Fighter Interceptor Squadron, 4th Fighter Interceptor Wing
K-14 Kimpo Air Base, Seoul, Korea

James F. Low (left) was the lowest-ranking air ace of the Korean War (as a second lieutenant) and the second youngest. He acknowledges that some pilots viewed him as a maverick and a loose cannon, and disliked him. That apparently did not include Col. Harrison W. Thyng (right), Low's wing commander and an ace in both World War II and Korea.

(U.S. Air Force)

A flight school classmate, retired Lt. Gen. William E. "Earl" Brown, said that Low showed extraordinary flying skill while still a student. "Jim was the best gunner in our class," Brown said. "When we got to Nellis [Air Force Base, Nevada for gunnery training], his weapons scores frequently were as good as, if not better than, some of the instructors who were supposedly teaching us how to use the guns and bombs we carried on the F-80 Shooting Star and the F-86 Sabre."

In the Korean War, only forty Americans earned the title of air ace, given to a pilot who shoots down five enemy planes. Rather old for a second lieutenant and nicknamed "Dad," Low quickly established a reputation for having sharp eyes, quick reflexes, and a unique knack for the F-86's lead-computing gunsight. Low shot down his first enemy MiG-15 fighter on May 8, 1952, and his fifth on June 15, in what *Air Force* magazine called "the hottest streak in jet fighting history." Low was also nicknamed the "Doctor" in testimony to his flying talents.

Low scored a sixth aerial victory before going to the United States on a tour to encourage new pilots. He returned to Korea at the end of 1952 to shoot down three more MiGs, bringing his total to nine. He was not the youngest ace of the Korean War but, still a second lieutenant, he was the most junior.

Some of his fellow F-86 pilots accused Low of irresponsible tactics. Carter said Low would abandon flight discipline if it would improve his chances of getting a MiG. Another of his fellow pilots, Capt. James Horowitz, published the novel *The Hunters* in 1956, featuring a fictitious version of Low, a reckless pilot named Pell who took risks and exposed wingmen to danger. Low said *The Hunters* was "a hate book toward me. [The author] needed a bad guy, and I was elected."

When the film version of *The Hunters* appeared in 1958, directed by Dick Powell, with Robert Mitchum at top billing, Robert Wagner's portrayal changed Pell from "a bad guy into a good guy," said Low.

Author Horowitz left the Air Force soon after the book appeared, changed his name legally to the byline on the book, James Salter, and has since become a figure in American letters. "Pell was Low," Salter said.

Low said the Wagner good-guy version was "the real me." Critics slammed the movie, and Salter repudiated it. Salter said the film "had no connection with the book I wrote."

Low acknowledged that on one mission, "after return to base, I was in hot water for losing my leader. But I shot down a MiG, and wing commander Thyng stepped in and congratulated me.

"There were some who thought I was a hot pilot, and some who thought I was a reckless kid," said Low. "But I was no kid in the Korean War. I was almost thirty then."

Low continued his Air Force career and flew the F-4 Phantom supersonic fighter. He went to Vietnam as an F-4 pilot.

On December 16, 1967, Low's F-4 Phantom was blasted out of the sky by an Atoll air-to-air missile fired by a North Vietnamese MiG-21. Low and his backseater 1st Lt. Howard Hill ejected. Low later criticized his flight leader for remaining in the battle until they were low on fuel.

After months as a prisoner of war, Low became one of three men selected by the North Vietnamese for early release to a group of peace activists. The men accepted release without permission of the American POW camp commander. "They are not eligible to participate in the association of Vietnam-era prisoners of war," said Col. Kenneth W. Cordier, 67, of Dallas, Texas, who was a POW from 1966 to 1973 and is a past president of the association.

These are North American F-86F Sabres of the 335th Fighter-Interceptor Squadron, 4th Fighter-Interceptor Wing, heading north to patrol the region along the Yalu River known as MiG Alley. Pilots believed the F-86F model was the finest fighter in the world, capable of defeating the dreaded MiG 15 under most combat conditions.

[Karl Dittmer]

According to Cordier, Low "is a traitor to the other prisoners of war" for accepting premature release on July 18, 1968. In the book *Vietnam Air Losses,* author Chris Hobson writes that, "This early release caused a great deal of controversy and concern amongst those prisoners left behind." According to Cordier, Viet Cong and North Vietnamese forces held 661 U.S. military prisoners, of whom twelve were released prematurely "for propaganda purposes" in batches of three. Low's backseater Hill stayed the full time and, like most of the POWs, was released at war's end in March 1973.

Low retired from the Air Force in January 1973. After many years of ignoring veterans' reunions, he has begun to participate in a few. He is currently battling prostate cancer. "I'm going to fight it," he said. "I've always been a fighter."

JAMES F. LOW. I went to Perrin Air Force Base, Texas, in November 1950, for primary flight training. I had some measure of success. I was the only one in the class who flew a perfect stage—that's six takeoffs and landings, landing on a spot. After that, I went to F-51 Mustangs. I did great in the F-51.

From Perrin, I was sent to Williams Air Force Base, Arizona, for jet upgrade and to Nellis Air Force Base, Nevada, for gunnery. An instructor named Andrew Ritchie wanted to put me into F-80s to penalize me for the failings of several other trainees, but I was given a checkout in the F-86 and a chance to be assigned to the F-86.

On my first flight out to the gunnery range, I shot 40 percent, which meant I outshot my gunnery instructor. I was lucky, but I knew I could fly and that was the name of the game.

I graduated in F-86s. They sent me overseas; first to Tachikawa Air Base, Japan, and then onward. It was kind of like the first scenes in the movie *The Hunters*. I was Pell in the book. Dick Powell made a movie of it, and he did a pretty good job. Robert Wagner played my part.

I got to Tachikawa in April 1952. Again, I was fortunate. I was assigned to the 4th Fighter-Interceptor Wing instead of the 51st. We paraded in, we second lieutenants, my classmates. Again, I was lucky. I was assigned to the 335th Fighter-Interceptor Squadron and, not only that, I was chosen by D Flight. Capt. Philip E. "Casey" Colman was the flight commander. He had shot down five Japanese airplanes in China, and he eventually got four in Korea. Captain Horowitz was in there, too, also known as James Salter. He didn't particularly like me, obviously. You can tell he didn't like me by reading *The Hunters*.

After I was assigned to Dog Flight, they checked me out and gave me some good information. The 335th was getting more MiGs than any of the other squadrons. The reason was, they were spending more time in the combat area. The other squadrons would race up there, fly around, and come right back at Mach 0.92 and log a mission. That's all they were interested in. Well, Dog Flight was interested in getting MiGs. I wanted to be aggressive, and they wanted me to be aggressive. It was a perfect fit.

My first mission was what they called a bomb-line mission. We took off and went just north of Seoul, on the bomb line, just to look around. The next time I went up, I was flying with Capt. Jim Kasler and we were hosing around Pyongyang. I was just flying his wing and, all of a sudden, four MiGs jumped us. They'd never been that far south before.

From any angle, the Korean War era F-86F Sabre was one of the most beautiful aircraft ever built. Boys dreamed of flying it. Young men struggled to excel in pilot training in order to be assigned to it. Pilots like 2nd Lt. James F. Low went to war in it and believed that they were on top of the world, at the controls of an extraordinary machine.

[Bill Ginn]

MiG Ambush

Kasler says, "Break!" I broke. He says, "Break right!"

There's a lot of this: "Break right!" "Break left!" And I never see a thing. I follow him. He says, "Break right!" and I'm breaking away from him. He says "Break left!" and I look back and I don't even see him. I don't see where he was. And here's three MiGs coming right down my ass, firing their 37-milimeter cannons. I've never seen anything that big before. Man!

I drop my tanks. I jacked up my throttle, to full power. And I pull up into them.

I almost stall. They're going a lot faster than I am, and they shoot right by me.

I drop my nose, pick up airspeed, and turn back toward the ground.

One of these MiGs shoots under me, and I go after his ass. Well, I get up on him, and I shoot and hit him in the engine section. There's a big explosion. I hit him in the wing roots. He's out of power, so I come up behind him—this is my second mission, remember—and as I'm over-taking him, I do a barrel roll to kind of lose a little bit of headway. I'm right over the top of his canopy looking down on him. He's an Oriental. He's got one of these brown leather helmets. He's looking side to side. I guess he's looking for me, and I'm right above him. So I roll back behind him again and hit him again, and he bails out.

I've done a bad thing. I've lost my leader. This is what critics will later say about me, that I'm "MiG happy," that I don't respect flight discipline, that I abandon my leader. So I get a little counseling on that. I say, "I tell you, I was fine, but after the fourth break I lost you, and I'm sorry." But, see, I got a MiG. So the wing commander, Col. Harrison "Harry" Thyng, who was an ace also, came to bat for me. I didn't know this, but I found out later. Thyng believed in me.

We were getting MiGs. That was what mattered. We were always going up to the Yalu River and—hanging. We were getting up to 40,000 feet (12384 meters) and—hanging. Throttling back. Everybody else was racing around. Hell, they're all back at the base and we're still up there. So we were getting more contact with the enemy, and we were getting more MiGs.

On another mission, I'm flying and Kasler gets a MiG, and I get tunnel vision. I see this MiG going straight up in the air with the smoke piling on it. I'm looking at it. I look around. Here, I've lost everybody. I can't find anybody. Well, I just head home. I'm right behind them, but it's about four or five miles behind. So now my ass is really in a jam.

Kasler says, "Look, you lost us again. And you lost us on your second mission. What the hell's wrong with you? What's happening?" I say, "Well, I was watching that airplane, and you guys turned around and you were gone." And Kasler says, "Well, did you learn something?" And I say, "Yeah." So I didn't lose anybody after that. I stuck to them like glue. They didn't realize that I made that change, and that's why my reputation remained tenuous.

Before Casey Colman finished his tour of duty and left, he took me across the river, over into China. I hung on to him. We were racing down there into the traffic pattern at Antung. And I'm just a balloon—a new second lieutenant—you know, I'm just flying along, hanging in there, and he shoots at this airplane. There's another one trying to get into him. I'm in constant contact. I say, "You've got a MiG right on your tail, but he's high. He can't pull any lead on you and he can't hit you." Colman says, "You watch him." I say, "Well, I won't go after him, because if I do, I'll lose you, so I'll just hang on to you." I was now being a good wingman and observing flight discipline even if others thought I was a maverick.

So we went around Antung, and he shot his airplane. He says, "Okay, well, I got that one." Now we're on the deck. These MiGs pulled out. They were right on the pattern. They must have been out of fuel. We got guns firing at us from Sinuiju and from Antung, and we're S'ing down the Yalu River on the Mach.

When we got back to Kimpo, in the briefing room, Casey gets on the podium and lauds me as the "greatest wingman he's ever had." It embarrassed me. But he kind of knew I needed it, with some of the rumors that had been going around. He really took care of me. If anyone was complaining about me after that, I never heard it.

Bob Love, another ace, was in that flight. He was an ace. He left. Casey Colman left. And I'm flying on Bob Ronca's wing. Bob talks to me. He says, "Look, you know, there's some scuttlebutt around, about you leaving your leader." I say, "I understand." I say, "Don't worry. I will not leave you. You'll be right in my sights. But I've got pretty good eyes, and I'll look around." He says, "Do that." Good eyesight was probably the single most important factor that separated the good pilots from the great pilots over MiG Alley.

So we're flying up along the Yalu, just the two of us, we're an element. I spotted two MiGs coming across the river on the deck. I called to Bob. I said, "Bob, I've got two MiGs coming due east on the deck." He says, "Okay, you take the bounce." I said, "Wait a minute! Say that again." I knew I didn't want to catch any shit back at the base for not maintaining proper flight discipline. He says again, "*You* take the bounce." I say, "Okay, drop tanks. Here we go."

We were at about 30,000 feet (9288 m). I dove down, right on the deck. I came up behind this guy. I fired a series of short bursts that seemed to arc out in front of me. I hit him all over. I was closing. I kept firing. I was so close I could see bullets puncturing metal. Debris started flying off, came back, hit my airplane and broke my windshield. He bailed out. I took pictures of him in the chute. He had a red beard.

I was looking at the fight through a shattered windshield and there was a wall of noise rushing into my ears, but apparently the windshield was holding against the blast of the slipstream. I looked around, trying to orient myself, trying to understand how the fight was going. My airplane seemed to be handling just fine in spite of the impact of the piece

Ground crews who supported the F-86F Sabre performed nearly all of their work, including major maintenance, out of doors in South Korea, which has all the extremes of summer and winter weather. By the time Jim Low was fighting MiGs in Korea, others were beginning to use the F-86F as a fighter-bomber, carrying bombs like those shown here. In Korea, pierced steel planking often substituted for paved runway.

[U.S. Air Force]

from the MiG, but apparently I had gone out and gotten myself all alone once again.

I thought Ronca, who was my flight leader, had moved to the wing position. It didn't seem possible that Ronca would abandon me, or that, by mistake, I might abandon him. But for a moment, as I looked around, I thought Ronca had vanished. And then, there was this giant gleam of silvery metal as Ronca's jet went right past me. It was a blurred apparition at first, but when I became oriented I could see every rivet on the side of that Sabre. Now, Ronca went and got the other MiG. I could see the "disruption" from the gun ports on his Sabre as he hosed the MiG with .50 caliber. He shot the MiG down, joined up, and matter-of-factly said, "Well, he was trying to get on your tail, so I shot him down." I said, "Well, we both got one." He was happy. I was happy. I had lost that stigma of being a maverick who ignores flight discipline and abandons his fellow pilots. There had been a moment of confusion in the fight, but I had not left my leader and he had not left me. Ronca explained it to everybody, and that made it real nice. But if you want to know the truth, some people continued calling me an upstart or a renegade, even long after that.

Eye of the Storm

After that fight, for a time, there was a complete stand-down. Even in the middle of a very real shooting war, there are long periods when you hurry up and wait. You sit around and gripe. You begin to wonder why the mail from home is so slow. You get on each other's nerves. Real warriors were never meant to sit around and wait.

The MiGs stopped flying. Nothing was happening. I volunteered for alert. Nobody wanted to be on alert. Being on alert was a real pain when nothing was going on. Nobody else liked it, but I had a feeling that somehow there might be an opportunity. Now that I'd gotten a couple of MiGs, I was a flight leader, so if anything did happen while we were on alert, I would be at the head of the pack.

So we went down there, four of us on alert. We were always in contact with the radar site, Dentist. This time, Dentist called us, they said, "We've got some action up there, we don't know what it is yet. But it's kind of circling around the Yalu River. You guys want to go up?" We said, "You want us to go up, you've got to scramble us." They said, "Okay, you're scrambled." So we all jumped into our jets, taxied out, took off, and flew on up to the area along the Yalu River.

I was flying with Al Smiley and Dan Druen. Dan Druen was my wingman. Smiley was from another flight in our squadron, but I knew him well, and we had a fourth guy, I forget who. We were flying a foursome and Dentist said to us: "Well, they're there. The MiGs are smack in front of you." Smiley says, "I don't think they're right in front. I'll go down to the mouth of the Yalu and look for them." I say, "Okay, I'm going to stay here." Each of us was referring to our own two-ship element. I believed the radar guys. If I couldn't see the MiGs and they could, why should I go down there to the mouth of the Yalu to search?

All of a sudden, we saw these short cons—contrails. We were at 45,000 feet (13720 m). The MiGs are at 55,000 feet (16765 m). By this point in the war, we truly believed the F-86F Sabre, which had been so painstakingly developed from the F-86A and F-86E models, was the all-around best fighter in the world. But what an airplane that MiG was for flying high. There was no other aircraft in the world that could routinely carry out a military mission at 55,000 feet.

I say, "Tally ho. I got 'em. They're in the cons." But I made a mistake by not making it clear that I meant short cons. Fighters normally produced *long* contrails: Hell, on some days we'd be up in a huge formation, and the sky would be full of them. You'd have a certain contrail level, depending on temperature, and you'd stay below it for concealment. But we almost never saw *short* contrails, and Smiley didn't get it. So Smiley asks, "Where are they?" I said, "They're in the cons up here!" But Smiley is confused and is asking, "Where are they?" He had gotten quite a distance away from us at this point. Possibly, he believed the MiGs couldn't be so close to us and couldn't be so high. So he started coming back, but we were right in the middle of them.

So one MiG comes diving down, I get him in my sights, he goes into a spin and bails out. I may have fired a short burst at him. I may not have. He simply appeared in front of me and ejected. It wasn't much of a hit.

The next guy comes down. I get on his tail and hit him in the engine section. I can see my bullets chipping away little fragments around the engine exhaust. I roll around him and hit him again. Dan Druen comes down and makes a pass at him, too. Later, Dan got credit for a MiG "damaged," even though I got credit for the kill. This meant I had four. Later, people were saying that there was "ace fever" in the 335th squadron, and maybe that was true, but in any event I was just one MiG away from becoming an air ace.

Aerial Victory

The next time was my fifth. That was a biggie. I was flying with Bob Goodrich. We were flying along the Yalu. I caught this MiG who was right underneath us. He was about 10,000 feet (3096 m) below us. I said, "We've got one right below us, Bob." He says, "Okay, I gotcha." I said, "Okay, let's go down." I'm not sure what was going on with the MiG pilots during this period, because up until then they had been very aggressive and very good. But now I came down and hit him with one burst, and he bailed out. Just like that.

Bob said, "He bailed." I said, "I saw him." So I made ace. That was a big deal. They made a lot of it in the squadron. There were still guys saying things like, "Low is the maverick who doesn't stay with his wingman," but most of the guys weren't thinking anything like that any longer. I was especially glad that I'd made ace on June 15, which was Father's Day. I was very close to my father.

I had some measure of success with the gunsight. That's the initial model we used, the A1C lead-computing gunsight. Gabreski and all these other guys (that's Col. Francis S. Gabreski, a World War II ace who became an ace again in Korea and commanded a fighter wing), they wanted to get rid of that gunsight. It wasn't worth a shit, they said. They had trouble with it. I had some success when it worked. These other guys, they would just lock up the gunsight and pretend it wasn't there. They would stick a piece of gum on the windshield and use that for a sight, or they would aim simply by watching their own tracers. A tracer is something that you can use, and it's a good thing to have in part as an aiming tool, but it is not a substitute for a properly adjusted, lead-computing gunsight. The gunsight was great if it worked.

I went to Japan on R and R. That's "rest and recuperation" leave, although some troops called it "I and I," for "intoxication and intercourse." I came back and immediately got into the middle of the toughest fight I ever had. I got on this MiG who was way, way far away from me. I was at max range. I fired a couple of times, and I must have hit him, because he slowed down a little bit. I finally caught him. Remember that even though the F-86F was our standard fighter by now, we were still flying the earlier models as well. I was flying an F-86A that day.

This guy was going across the river. I pulled up a little bit and lobbed my shots into him, and I hit him. Our gun didn't have as much striking power as theirs, but it could reach out a lot farther. He pulled back around. For a moment I saw him broadside—a top view of the MiG filling the sky. I caught him, cut him off, and got a couple more shots into him. He turned over, and he never got out of the airplane. He went right into the slope of a mountain on the Korean side of the river. That was my sixth.

After that, they pulled me out of combat. I was invited to tour seventeen Air Training Command bases in the United States to lecture on the gunsight.

I went back to Korea. It's three months later. All of my people are gone. I'm treated like a new guy. I had forty-four missions when I left. Now, it's like I'm an FNG, which means a fucking new guy. I flew forty more missions on their wing without leading a flight—and I was already an ace. I flew on the wing with these inexperienced captains and majors. But they forgot about my eyes. I could see at twenty feet what a normal person could see at ten. So I'd go up on a mission with these guys and I'd say, "Well, we got one ahead of us there. He's at twelve o'clock, going to one." And they're straining, straining, and they can't see him. I say, "We're going to lose him." They'd say, "Ah, you take the bounce." This happened when I was flying with Murray Winslow on my seventh kill. I cut him off and knocked him down. There was nothing really great about it.

My eighth MiG was a real doozy. Now I was back to leading occasionally. This guy and I were flying. He got tunnel vision. I was going in to make a pass on this MiG, and he goes ahead of me. He starts firing. I say, "Stop firing!" The guy's pulling about four or five Gs and he just isn't making any lead. I watched him. He had his finger locked on the trigger.

Finally, he's out of ammunition. So he says, "Yellow Three, you'd better come down. I'm out of ammunition." I said, "Well, fine, you're talking to me now." So I went after the same MiG. And he was really a honcho, meaning he was one of their top pilots. He was pulling Gs and racking it around. He knew how to fly. He was a good pilot.

Frenzied Fight

We raced around. I fired one little burst, and I knew I couldn't get him, right then. So I waited until I could get a bead on him. So I finally pulled a little lead and fired another very short burst. I finally nailed him. I got him in the engine. He's S'ing below us. We've got power. I'm flying, trying stay behind him, watching to see what he's going to do, whether he's going to bail. And son of a gun! All of a sudden, that guy pulls straight up. He fires at me with a dead engine. These 37-millimeter balls of fire are out ahead of me. I'm saying, "My God, I flew over this." So I roll

Who's Who

over on him, I finish him off, and he goes into the mountain. He was really tenacious, a honcho.

For my last kill, the ninth, I was flying Colonel Royal N. Baker's airplane. He was the group commander. He had an airplane, number 936, I'll never forget the number. (Author's Note: Maybe so. But Baker's aircraft was actually F-86F Sabre no. 51-2822, with nose art identifying it as "Angel Face and the Babes/the King"). He had a gunsight in there, the new A-4 gunsight that replaced the A-1C. It was just a piece of work—of course, being a colonel's airplane.

So I'm up in MiG Alley in Baker's plane. I'm flying somebody's wing again, and I see a MiG and the other guys can't see the damn airplane. I said, "I got one! He's out at about two o'clock, there, and he's coming across." The other guys are straining, they have binoculars, and they can't see him. They hated to say it but, finally, "Well, you take the bounce."

So I say, "Okay." So the MiG pulled back to the right a little bit. And I'm out at almost max range, at about 4,000 feet (1220 m). And this little gunsight went right down like it was just locked on, and it went right down. I put it right on him, I fired, and I hit him with the first shot. When that A-4 gunsight worked, it really worked. Everybody pissed and moaned about it. Gabreski and the guys in the other Sabre wing, the

Even when sitting on the ramp, the F-86F looked as if it were flying ten miles per minute. This example, seen stateside, wears the large U.S. AIR FORCE lettering that was introduced to fighters in late 1952, while the Korean War was going on.

[U.S. Air Force]

51st, they were trying to go back to the old World War II–style gunsight and do this and do that. They didn't like it. My squadron commander made a trip down to the 51st, and they said, "Who's that balloon you've got up there? He got some MiGs." That was me, not the youngest air ace of the Korean War (I was only the second-youngest) but the lowest-ranking. So I had some measure of success. Again, I could shoot well and I could see well. That's the reason I got so many, because I could see them before everybody else. We had captains and majors who wanted to go shoot them, but they couldn't *see* them.

Chapter Twelve

Fighter Pilot in Two Wars

What Happened

A glint comes to Earl Brown's eyes when he talks about prowling the Yalu River in his F-86F Sabre, peering into the haze at hundreds of MiG-15s, parked wingtip-to-wingtip at the Manchurian airfields of Antung, Fen Cheng, and Tatangkou. His facial expression is that of a man who has been face-to-face with mortal danger.

Those airfields on the forbidden side of the Yalu were "off limits" to Brown and his fellow Sabre pilots. They were home to a formidable enemy force that held all the advantages in the one-sided arithmetic of the Korean War—about 450 MiGs altogether, arrayed against a U.S. force that could rarely put more than about ninety F-86 Sabres into the air. "We would look at the other side of that river, and when dust trails formed against the ground we knew the MiGs were coming," said Brown. "They could pick the time and place of battle. We could not cross the river from North Korea into Manchuria to attack their bases, but we were still over hostile territory on the North Korean side. We traveled far to fight them, over their turf, at the time of their choosing. They were close to home and in a position to ambush us with an airplane—the MiG-15—that could fly higher than we could."

Brown was a wingman in the 334th Fighter Interceptor Squadron, known variously as the "Eagles," or, to some in the unit, the "Angry

First Lieutenant William E. "Earl" Brown Jr.
December 1952
North American F-86F Sabre
335th Fighter Interceptor
**   Squadron, 4th Fighter**
**   Interceptor Wing**
K-14 Kimpo Air Base, Seoul,
**   Korea**

Flying as a very young first lieutenant in a war where the top aces made the news, William "Earl" Brown climbs into his F-86 Sabre jet fighter at K-14 Kimpo Air Base near Seoul, South Korea, in December 1952. Brown was one of the first black jet pilots to complete flight training after the Air Force was integrated in 1948.

[U.S. Air Force]

Pigeons." Being a wingman in the Korean War was a good way to see plenty of action, but it was not a way to have much influence on events, nor was it a way to achieve every fighter pilot's goal—to shoot down an enemy aircraft. "Being a mere second lieutenant, which is the lowliest animal in the officer corps, and being a wingman to some of the top aces, you found yourself pretty much at the bottom of the food chain."

In due course, retired Lt. Gen. William E. "Earl" Brown, 75, of Alexandria, Virginia, fought in Korea and Vietnam, battled discrimination on the home front, and reached three-star rank in the United States Air Force—"a real constellation of stars for a black American who grew up in an era when being black was viewed a handicap," in the words of an airman who flew with him.

Brown was a relatively inexperienced F-86F Sabre pilot when he arrived at Kimpo Air Base, Korea, in 1952.

EARL BROWN. When I arrived in Korea, I had 103 jet flying hours, including forty [hours] of Sabre time.

I left Korea a year later in April 1953, with 372 jet hours, 125 missions, and one MiG-15 damaged. My friends ask me, "How many planes did you shoot down?" I have to say, "I didn't shoot any down. I got one damaged."

The reasons for this are found in the teamwork strategy. In our basic, four-ship flight, the two shooters were experienced captains and majors and the two wingmen were inexperienced lieutenants.

I was a wingman for almost my entire tour. I did get to see six MiGs go down while flying with three of the leading air aces, Major Frederick "Boots" Blesse, Major James Jabara, and Capt. Manuel "Pete" Fernandez.

I believe that the forty Americans who achieved air ace status in Korea—another was 2nd Lt. James Low (Chapter 11)—had special qualities. One thing our top fighter pilots had in common was superhuman eyesight. They also could shoot well.

Pete Fernandez, a former instructor at Nellis Air Force Base, Nevada, had the eyesight and was a very experienced gunner. Looking at his gun-camera film, it is difficult to see the MiG at such extreme range. But then you see the sparkle of machine gun strikes on the distant MiG. In the next frame, the MiG's wings are past the side of the picture, as Pete has closed to killing range right behind the plane.

This pattern was repeated often enough that the fighter pilots stopped talking about how lucky Pete was to get hits at those ranges. He knew what he was doing. He became the third ranking ace with 14.5 kills. A pilot was credited with half a kill when he shared an aerial victory with a fellow airman.

I was a few years behind these great aces. I was born in 1927 in the Bronx, New York. As a northern big-city boy, I missed the discrimination that was aimed at Negroes (as African Americans were then called) in the South and in rural areas. Still, I never would have been able to fly but for the Tuskegee Airmen, the black flyers who came before me during the World War II era. They fought the enemy, and they fought racism at the same time.

I went to pre-medical school at Pennsylvania State University. In 1950, I was an ambulance attendant at Harlem Hospital in New York City, when the Korean War began. Two years earlier—thanks to the Tuskegee Airmen—President Harry S Truman had ordered the U.S. armed forces to be racially integrated. I was accepted into the aviation cadet program and went to Randolph Air Force Base, Texas, to learn how to fly.

We flew in the North American T-6 Texan (designated AT-6 prior to

Earl Brown (standing, second from right) stands with F-86 Sabre pilots of the 334th Fighter Interceptor Squadron at K-14 Kimpo Air Base, Korea. Beside Brown (third from right) is Major (later Col.) James Jabara, who was the first American air ace of the Korean War. Jabara also later became the second-ranking ace of the conflict.

[U.S. Air Force]

1948), a single-engine, propeller-driven, two-place trainer. A 550-horse-power engine powered the T-6 and gave it a top speed of about 210 miles per hour (336 kilometers per hour).

After looking forward to my first flight for so long, I was devastated when I got airsick. Fortunately, we had been warned by the upper classmen, so I had an empty plastic potato chip bag in my pocket into which I deposited my breakfast. After the second time I got sick, my instructor pilot said, "Brown, it's that damn bag you carry. You expect to get sick and so you do. Leave that bag behind and you won't get sick."

Puking Pilot

So I left the bag behind, and on my next flight I had to throw up in my hat. This was my first lesson that my superiors might always be supe-

An F-86F Sabre of Earl Brown's 334th Fighter Interceptor Squadron heads for MiG Alley in Korea, circa. December 1952. As a wingman to great aces, Brown had the same admiration for the Sabre they did: It was the fighter every would-be pilot of Brown's generation wanted to fly.

[Eugene Sommerich]

rior, but they are not always right. I learned to prevent airsickness by staying oriented.

The T-6 gave me another memory that has lasted through the years: the GUMP check. The term was used to remind the pilot to perform certain procedures in sequence as he prepares to land. They are:

GAS: to the fullest tank

UNDERCARRIAGE: down

MIXTURE: full rich

PROP: full forward

This check is normally performed as the aircraft enters the traffic pattern. It's been fifty-plus years and I'll never forget the GUMP check.

My next stop in training was Craig Field, Texas, for training in the F-51D Mustang (designated P-51D until 1948). When I pinned on my silver pilot wings in 1951 as a member of Flying Class 51-H, I had logged 208 hours in the T-6 and fifty-five hours in the F-51D.

After flying school, I went to Williams Air Force Base, Arizona, to train in the T-33A Shooting Star. To me, the ubiquitous jet trainer was not easy to learn. Some problems required almost constant pilot attention. The J33 jet engine had very slow acceleration throughout the range of throttle movement. In the F-51D, you could move the throttle rapidly from idle to full power and get an instant response, but this engine had to be carefully and *slowly* coaxed to its full power level. I had numerous other complaints about the T-33A and was glad to move on to soloing the F-80A Shooting Star, which was very similar but counted as a real jet fighter.

I flew forty-three hours in the T-33 and F-80. And then our class was split. Some of us went to F-86 Sabre training. Others stayed in the F-80. The F-86 group eventually joined the 4th Fighter Interceptor Wing in Korea and flew essentially air-to-air missions. The ones who stayed in the F-80s joined the 8th Fighter Bomber Wing and flew mostly air-to-ground missions.

Nellis was a continuation of a series of remarkable experiences, primarily because now we were past the technical details of how to fly the airplane and we were actually concerned with how to use the airplane as a combat weapon. We learned to shoot our machine guns, we learned to fire rockets, and we learned to drop bombs. Now, when I say we learned how to do it, we were introduced to it. It took quite a while before we gained any real proficiency, but there were standards that we had to meet in each weapon. You had to qualify in each weapon before you could move on.

When I got to combat at 4th Wing, before you could fly combat at the 334th Squadron, we had a ten-sortie program called Clobber College. The idea was principally to make sure that you understood the basics of combat maneuvering, but more important—since we were all going to be wingmen in my flying school class—the people who were going to be our leaders wanted to be assured that we could keep up with them regardless of what maneuvers they would pull on us.

I eventually flew wing for all of those leaders. I always felt like an observer. You observe the enemy coming in, and then the battle is joined. You have to observe every part of the bubble in which the battle takes place. I have to make the point repeatedly that the wingman's job is to provide a pair of sharp eyes and to keep his leader clear.

None of those leaders influenced me more than Maj. (later Maj. Gen.) Frederick C. "Boots" Blesse, who was a respected air combat tactician even at a relatively early juncture in his long career.

I was also influenced by Capt. Joseph McConnell, who became the top-ranking U.S. ace of the Korean War (with sixteen victories). Jabara was second with fifteen aerial victories, and Fernandez was third with 14.5. McConnell was in a different unit, but I flew with Jabara, Fernandez, and Boots Blesse.

Aloft with Aces

Among these almost superhuman fighter pilots, Blesse had fewer MiGs—he had ten kills (nine MIG-15s and a Lavochkin La-9), but in my mind he was the best of the aces.

Not only could Blesse fly outstanding aerial combat maneuvers, but he could tell other people how to do it. Pete Fernandez was a great instinctive pilot, and he was an instructor at Nellis when I went through my combat crew training. So he could get into the details of firing the weapons. But Boots Blesse was great at describing the maneuvering of the aircraft to put the weapons in place to make the kill. Indeed, for our squadron, Boots came up with a single legal-size sheet of paper with eight or ten rules on it that became the genesis of our fighter pilots' bible.

One of Blesse's famous rules became well known throughout the Air Force, and later it was the title of the first really universal tactics book for fighter pilots, called *No Guts, No Glory*. Previous to this, fighter tactics were passed on almost like from father to son. You had to first be humiliated by a superior pilot who then would give you some idea of what he was doing, and then you had your turn to humiliate some other newcomer when he came along. The tactics were passed on this way. Boots wrote them down in a manner or fashion that could be understood easily by any intelligent pilot.

Two of the rules I remember. The first, of course, was: no guts, no glory—which meant you had to be aggressive in your pursuit of the enemy. There were pilots who were very good pilots, who flew only reluctantly to the sound of the guns. Then there were other pilots who flew uncommanded to the sound of the guns. The aces invariably were in the latter group. They not only looked for a fight, they wanted to be in the fight, and that was exceedingly important. So "no guts, no glory" was the prime rule.

Unlike the Korean War air aces with whom he flew, Earl Brown rose to the rank of lieutenant general and functioned as one of the Air Force's top leaders. Here, Brown serves as the U.S. air commander for forces in southern Europe in 1982.

[U.S. Air Force]

Now, there was a corollary to that rule, which has not gained very much exposure and few people know it. The corollary Boots wrote was, "Guts will do for brains, but not consistently." This was his warning not to exceed your abilities; not to exceed common sense when you're in the combat area. Be aggressive but keep a realistic view of your situation.

This experience of flying with these fellows on almost a daily basis gave me an excellent start to my Air Force career. I was with Boots Blesse on September 4, 1952, when he shot down his fifth MIG, and this made him an ace. Being an ace was, of course, a very important thing. It gave the Air Force something to write about in their recruiting documents and to brag about with the other services. For the individual pilot it was recognition of his ability, both as a pilot and as a warrior, because it certainly took skill, but it also took courage and aggressiveness.

Then I was with Boots Blesse when he shot down two MiGs in one mission. This was very extraordinary. Not many pilots were able to do this, even among the aces. For that mission, Boots received a Silver Star, and as his wingman, I also received an award.

During my tenure, two fighter wings were equipped with about 180 F-86 Sabres and were flying 3,000 sorties per month. During one month, there were 5,100 sorties. Soviet, Chinese, and North Korean pilots were flying the MiG-15s. At the time, the role of the Soviet pilots, including many who had been aces in World War II, was not well known.

MiGs enjoyed certain advantages, including superior numbers, sanctuary in China, better performance above 35,000 feet (9150 meters), higher combat ceilings, better climb capability and acceleration . . . and heavier firepower. In the F-86 Sabre, we countered with superior training and leadership, better controllability at nearly the speed of sound, a faster rate of fire with our six .50-caliber guns, and other advantages. The bottom line was a 10-to 1 kill ratio, with 792 MiGs shot down in air-to-air combat as compared with seventy-eight Sabres. That official tally has been subject to much discussion in recent years, but the superior performance of us F-86 pilots is not in question. One theory is that the other side rotated MiG pilots too rapidly, giving a little experience to many, but not a lot of experience to anyone.

Home from War

When I got Korea behind me, I married my wife, Gloria, in 1954. We have two sons and a daughter. I served at McGuire Air Force Base, New Jersey, and George Air Force Base, California, flying the F-100 Super Sabre. The F-100 was the first American fighter routinely able to fly faster than sound in level flight. It was a stable platform and had a really comfortable cockpit.

Before I could contend for a wing commander slot, I drew an assignment to the Pentagon in a non-flying job.

As a major, I went in August 1965 to Ubon, Thailand, as part of the 431st Tactical Fighter Squadron, 479th Tactical Fighter Wing. I flew fifty missions against North Vietnam in the F-4C Phantom II. We also bombed Laos, but weren't permitted to say so at that time.

The frustration we felt was related to the insignificance of the targets they gave us. Military men who'd spent our lives studying the art of war, we were being brushed off as being unable to think. The targets were chosen in Washington. Fighter pilots were risking their lives to hit trivial targets.

I returned to George Air Force Base, attended Armed Forces Staff college, then went to Ramstein, Germany, to join the staff of Maj. Gen. John Lavelle, with whom I had served at McGuire, and who was now commander of the 17th Air Force. Lavelle later lost his career for allegedly bombing illegal targets in Vietnam, but I remember him as a superb officer and a good guy.

Lavelle and I were together at a social event in 1967 when we chatted with an assignments officer. "When are you going to send me a candidate to command the 53rd Tactical Fighter Squadron?" Lavelle asked the officer. The assignments expert shrugged and said, "You have a candidate standing next to you."

Lavelle hadn't thought of it before, but it was radical and courageous of him to send the only black face to the squadron as its commander. That was 1967, and it was still difficult to be black in the Air Force. There was still a lot of resentment toward what were still being called Negroes, and I was still aware of it, every day. The assignment was also an unusual step because there was a tradition of a handful of "good old boys" assigning each other from one outfit to another as commander. I have never been considered a "good old boy."

I commanded the 53rd squadron at Bitburg, Germany, from 1967 to 1969, flying the F-4D Phantom. The 53rd didn't have any accidents in those two years, one of the few squadrons with that kind of record.

As a lieutenant colonel, I returned to the Vietnam war theater in July 1969. Naturally, you had mixed feelings about going back. This was my third combat tour and I felt I had plenty to offer, but it was never easy.

Now, I was flying with the 13th Tactical Fighter Squadron, part of the 432nd Tactical Reconnaissance Wing, at Udorn, Thailand. The title was misleading for political reasons: we were flying fighters, not reconnaissance. And it was time, finally, for me to be shot down.

We flew the F-4D Phantom II, escorting RF-4C reconnaissance aircraft. This was during a "bombing halt," and you couldn't bomb unless they shot at you. So the RF-4Cs trolled for antiaircraft fire. When the trolling succeeded and our planes were fired upon, we struck their antiaircraft artillery, or triple-A, batteries. The expression "limited duration, protective reaction air strikes" came into common use to characterize these actions.

The mission was controversial. Both reconnaissance pilots and fighter pilots objected to it. The RF-4C recce pilots flew the fastest missions of the war because they didn't carry anything that would slow them down, whereas our F-4D fighters were loaded with bombs that created aerodynamic drag. The recce pilots resented having to slow down because it subjected them to greater hazard from North Vietnamese gunfire, while the fighter pilots felt they were being misused in these "protective reaction" sorties.

A recce pilot going down the valley taking pictures was certain to bring up North Vietnamese gunfire. Under the rules then in effect, this, in turn, gave us the authority to drop bombs on their gun positions. This was not an effective way to use the RF-4C or the F-4D, and we all argued against it, especially after six pilots were shot down flying this dumb mission.

On March 30, 1970, I was aloft with backseater Lt. Col. Len Melton. We were over Laos near the Mu Ghia Pass, a key North Vietnamese infiltration route. At the controls of an accompanying F-4D was my wingman Lt. Col. Richard "Dick" Myers, who later became a general and chairman of the Joint Chiefs of Staff.

We were high and behind, trying to keep the recce pilot in sight. They shot at him, and they hit me. We didn't even see it coming. Sometimes, even in daylight, you could see muzzle flashes. We saw nothing. But they were shooting at us. The triple-A ripped into my airplane. We heard it and felt it.

It shocked the whole aircraft. All the warning lights came on. One of our two engines—I forget which one—shut down immediately. The other started vibrating.

We turned toward Thailand. We'd completely lost one engine. We were losing systems, and my instruments were indicating, "This airplane is going down."

I kept having more and more difficulty with my controls as I attempted to get us away from territory where any bad guys were located. When the airplane began shaking and all the warning lights came on, it was pretty clear we weren't going to stay in the air much longer.

The point came when we knew we had to get out. We had previously discussed what we would do in a bailout, and it was a problem. Under normal procedure, the backseater would eject first so he wouldn't be affected by the rocket blast from the front-seater's ejection. But combat lessons had shown that when the backseater went out, the windblast would lock down the front-seater's canopy.

So our plan was that the front-seater would voluntarily release his canopy before either of us jumped. But when we hatched this brilliant plan, no one told me what the noise level would be, traveling at 300 to 400 knots.

Once I released my canopy, Len and I could no longer communicate. The noise was so loud we couldn't hear each other. I yelled, "Go, go, go!" But I couldn't talk through the ejection sequence with Len or anybody else, and now Dick Myers had to take over all the radio communications. Without being able to talk to each other, Len and I both pulled the handle.

We didn't realize how far we had traveled from Bad Guy Land. We ejected just three miles from the friendly base at Nakhon Phanom. Melton's chute narrowly missed a part of the airplane that was on fire. I was so low when my chute opened, I could not get rid of my survival kit, which was supposed to be jettisoned before you hit the ground. We were still dangling from our chutes while we watched our plane go in. It made a crunching sound when it impacted. Myers was flying cover overhead.

We landed close to each other and scrambled out of our parachute harnesses. We got together, waiting to be picked up. Thank goodness we had gotten away from any area where there might be enemy troops, but we were not happy.

Melton looked at me.

"Brownie," he said.

"Yes, Len?"

"Brownie, I want to tell you something."

"Yes. Len?

"We're getting too old for this shit."

Home Again

Finished with my third combat tour, I returned to George Air Force Base. Then, I drew the inevitable non-flying assignment to the Pentagon. Now a colonel, I was very upset because I wanted to fly. But I checked in with my superiors, and they said, "Colonels don't fly." By forcing a

Who's Who

1st Lt. (later Lt. Gen.) William E. "Earl" Brown Jr., F-86F Sabre pilot, 334th Fighter Interceptor Squadron, 4th Fighter Interceptor Wing, K-14 Kimpo Air Base, Korea, 1952

F-86 SABRE AIR ACES IN THE 4TH WING:
Major (later Maj. Gen.) Frederick "Boots" Blesse

Capt. Manuel "Pete" Fernandez

Major (later Col.) James Jabara

F-86 SABRE AIR ACE IN THE 51ST FIGHTER INTERCEPTOR WING:
Capt. Joseph McConnell

change in military regulations, I was able to log time in a T-33 belonging to the District of Columbia Air National Guard at Andrews Air Force Base, Maryland.

That wasn't enough for me, so I became one of six officers who each came up with $2,500 to purchase a V-tailed Beech Bonanza 180. Gloria and I enjoy skiing, and the Bonanza was perfect for this lifelong sport. I would put the skis between us in the Bonanza and fly over to the Shenandoah Valley in Virginia. Gloria would look at me and ask, "How much does this plane cost?" ' I would look back at her and reply, "You don't want to know." The secret is revealed here for the first time.

I retired at three-star rank in 1985. Today, I'm a docent at the Smithsonian Institution's National Air and Space Museum in Washington, D.C.

I love that Bonanza. I loved the F-100 and the F-4. But the F-86F Sabre was a really great fighter plane that stood a notch above everything else with wings. And besides, I didn't have to bail out of one of those. And my squadron, the 334th, still with the same emblem, today flies F-15E Strike Eagles (Chapter 20) at Seymour Johnson Air Force Base, North Carolina. They have been very busy in Iraq and Afghanistan.

This is retired Lt. Gen. William E. "Earl" Brown as a docent, or volunteer, at the National Air and Space Museum in Washington, D.C., in September 1992.

[Earl Brown]

North American F-86F Sabre

The Sabre was a classic. From first to last, seven thousand in all, the North American F-86 Sabre was the standard against which every other fighter was measured. But it was far from perfect, and when the Soviet MiG-15 appeared in Korea, the MiG had advantages. The Sabre was more maneuverable and offered better protection to the pilot, but the MiG had heavier-hitting guns and could fly higher. Only after Sabres and MiGs began to fight each other in Korea, was work undertaken to produce the final wartime version of the Sabre, the F-86F. And only when the F-86F reached squadrons in Korea were Americans able to say, finally, and with total confidence, that they had the best all-around fighter in the world.

Creating the F-86F was painstaking for the plane maker, North

American, and for the Air Force. Part of the solution was to redesign the wing of the aircraft, removing the leading-edge flaps that had been used until then and creating a slick surface with new proportions. The new, "hard" wing came to be known as the 6-3 wing because of the ratio of its cross section to its span.

The first F-86F Sabre took to the air on March 19, 1952, with civilian test pilot James Pearce at the controls. The first batch of F-86F models had new systems earmarked for the "F" model but did not yet have the 6-3 wing. The wing was introduced on the production line a few months later. The first F-86Fs with the 6-3 wing began arriving in Korea in 1952.

North American shifted production of the Sabre from the west coast to Columbus, Ohio. The company turned out 1,539 F-86F models in Los Angeles and Columbus.

It was the F-86F that guaranteed success in close-quarter dogfights with the MiG-15. Other factors had an influence, including a sharp drop in the quality of pilots on the other side. When all the factors were

---

North American F-86F Sabre

Type: single-seat fighter

Powerplant: one 5,910-lb (2681-kg) thrust General Electric J47-GE-27 axial-flow turbojet engine

Performance: maximum speed 695 mph (1118 km/h) at 40,000 ft (12192 m); initial climb rate in clean configuration, 9,300 ft (2835 m) per minute; service ceiling 48,000 (14630 m); range with tanks 1,270 miles (2044 km), combat radius 680 miles (1086 km)

Weights: empty 10,890 lb (4940 kg); loaded 20,357 lb (9234 kg)

Dimensions: wingspan 37 ft 1½ in (11.31 m); length 37 ft 6½ in (11.44 m); height 14 ft 8¾ in (4.47 m); wing area 288 sq ft (26.76 sq m)

Armament: six .50 caliber (12.7-mm) M-3 machine guns, with a rate of fire of 1,100 rounds per minute and an ammunition supply of 1,802 rounds or 267 rounds per gun; provision for up to six 500-lb (227-kg) or 1,000-lb (454-kg) bombs or other weapons loads, plus two 200-gallon (755 liter) jettisonable fuel tanks

First flight: September 23, 1950 (F-86E); March 19, 1952 (F-86F)

---

added up, the Sabre was enormously successful against the MiG. But the Air Force also had another job in mind for the F-86F:

It became the first version of the Sabre widely used in the fighter-bomber role. One pilot commented, "The flight characteristics of the F-86F are excellent for the fighter-bomber role. It is a stable bombing platform and permits any dive angle up to vertical, without danger of control difficulties or effects from compressibility. The speed brakes have proved effective and necessary for tactics that are desired. It is believed that use of steeper dive angles and higher entry altitudes will decrease vulnerability to AAA fire." Typically, a fighter-bomber F-86F carried 500-lb (227-kg) and 1,000-lb (454-kg) GP, or general-purpose, bombs with conical fins and fuel tanks.

Chapter Thirteen

The Last Days of the War

What Happened

Lt. Bill Barron rolled in on his target.

His huge, gloss-blue AD-4L Skyraider banked abruptly into the dive and shuddered as its barn-door dive brakes popped out. Barron aimed the plane and its bombs at a swarm of military troops and vehicles gathered beneath a marshalling yard just below a bare, dirt-colored ridge above the 38th Parallel in North Korea.

It was July 1953. Truce talks were concluding. Aboard Barron's carrier, the scuttlebutt was about a pending cease-fire. Somebody was going to be the last man to die in Korea, a gnarled, mountainous peninsula still little known to many Americans. Barron hoped he wouldn't be the one.

Barron's aircraft was a cross between a fighter (it would shoot down MiGs in two wars) and a bomber (it carried a heavier bomb load than the B-17 Flying Fortress of World War II). The AD-4L Skyraider was a single-engine, propeller-driven warplane painted in the Navy's standard glossy sea blue color scheme. The letters in the military name for the aircraft prompted many to call it the "Able Dog," but they really signified "attack" and "Douglas" (the builder), along with an "L" suffix that was the Navy's symbol for a plane that had been "winterized."

The Skyraider was the focus of a love-hate relationship with naval aviators. The thing was, they loved it and hated it at the same time. They

**Lieutenant (j.g.) Bill Barron
July 1953
Douglas AD-4L Skyraider
(bureau no. 123961)
Attack Squadron Nine Five
(VA-95)
USS *Philippine Sea* (CVA 47)
The Sea of Japan, near North
Korea**

Bill Barron points to battle damage to his AD-4L Skyraider (bureau no. 123961) after a combat mission from the USS *Philippine Sea* (CV 47) off Korea in 1953.

[US Navy]

boasted about the Skyraider, and they vilified the Skyraider. When they swapped tall tales about war exploits carried out while strapped inside the Skyraider's spacious cockpit—hearing that the North Koreans were being attacked with "everything but the kitchen sink," one pilot appropriated a galley sink and dropped it as a bomb—they cussed about the plane from noon until Sunday.

The Skyraider's four 20-mm cannons were prone to jamming. With its four-bladed propeller thrashing in the air, the Skyraider wheezed, belched smoke, and dripped oil in torrents. Pilots joked that if the enemy didn't kill you, you would die tripping over the oil slick created by the leaky R-3350 Cyclone engine. In some Skyraiders, the electrical wiring in the wings had been reworked so many times that nobody remembered exactly what was connected to what, so the aircraft flew into combat every day carrying unnecessary wiring that nobody knew how to remove. In the "winterized" version, the cockpit could become toasty when the heater was working, which was rarely. In all other Skyraiders, the bitter Korean cold could penetrate right through the metal skin and into the pilot's lair.

Love it or hate it—again, pilots usually did both—the AD Skyraider was the Navy's standard medium attack aircraft of the Korean War from 1950 to 1953. That war began on the day Barron planned to leave the Navy and start a family. Instead, Barron pulled two "Westpacs"—western Pacific cruises—aboard Navy aircraft carriers flying the big, brutish, lovable, and detestable AD Skyraider.

"Bad news below" was the beginning of the caption written by the Navy for this official photo of a bomb-laden Skyraider heading for a target in North Korea in 1953. The AD-4L Skyraider flown by Lt. (j.g.) Bill Barron and other carrier aviators during the Korean War was able to carry as many bombs as a World War II B-17 Flying Fortress.

[U.S. Navy]

"We were the workhorses," said Barron, who, like so many, joined the Navy wanting to fly pointy jets only to discover that the Skyraider had an "eyeball to eyeball" military mission. "The job was simple," Barron said. "You take off from a carrier deck at sea with a full load of ordnance. You fly to the target. You attack it. If they're shooting at you, you hope they'll miss."

BILL BARRON. The Chinese troops and vehicles below me were assembling with the apparent intention of moving south about forty miles to attack an American battalion that was stretched a little thin. There was a lot of jockeying for terrain going on, because both sides believed they would be able to keep the ground they occupied if the fighting halted.

You roll in. You know they can kill you. A lot of the time, you can't see their shells whipping around you. It's loud, there's a lot of vibration, everything is happening quickly. One of my thoughts, oddly enough, is that on this cruise my squadron hasn't lost a Skyraider yet—although we've had a couple shot up really badly—and I don't want to be the first to auger in. So it's all happening at once, and your focus is on placing the bombs on the target. Every time, you know your sturdy AD will probably bring you through alive, but you also know it may not.

For me personally, this was a time when my future seemed to be at a crossroads. This was the war that had interrupted my wedding. It was an opportunity to try to excel in a group of men who were motivated and dedicated, with one or two exceptions.

I was a twenty-three-year-old naval aviator who'd signed up to fly with the Navy in the final days of World War II and won my wings and ensign's commission in 1949. During flight training, I had been an aviation midshipman—neither officer nor sailor, but part of a unique pilot-training program that existed for just a few years to train pilots who lacked a college degree. We were among the last in the Navy to fly jets and the first to fly props, and when Korea came, they needed us big-time. I had been planning to get out of the Navy and had gotten married on June 25, 1950—the day North Korea attacked its southern neighbor. My planned departure for civilian life and, perhaps, an airline pilot's career, was put on hold and eventually cancelled. I was actually crossing the Golden Gate Bridge and heading for northern California with my bride, ready to become a civilian, when I learned that my date of separation from the Navy no longer meant anything. There was an extension and we were being kept on duty. It was involuntary, so there was no choice, but once I learned they were going to need us, out there on a distant edge of the world, in our smoke-gushing Skyraiders, I said to myself, "I have to do this." I'm very devout. I believe in my country. I believe in my God. The North Koreans were a little too late to prevent me from getting married—we are still married, all these years later—but they did finish off my vision of "Bill Barron, Airline Pilot," and don't forget that airline flying was really glamorous in those days. Later, the Chinese entered the war, and a couple of times they almost finished off "Bill Barron, Naval Aviator."

"I was born in 1927 in Chicago and graduated from high school in 1945. We did not know it at the time, but the war was winding down. I went down to the recruiting officer and started the process of signing up for the Navy. But as I tried to sign up for the Navy, the war ended. I still saw the Navy as being my future—before becoming an airline pilot, that is—so I joined the V5 naval training program and went to Cornell University in Ithaca, New York. During the summer, my training began at

Livermore, California, at the controls of the Stearman N2S-1 (PT-17), that smooth-flying, fabric-covered biplane trainer. While being carried on the Navy's rolls, I did my second year of college as a civilian at Illinois University in Chicago. Under this program, I went to preflight training with the Navy in Pensacola, Florida. In the postwar era, most Americans were getting out of uniform, but the Navy still had plenty of potential aviators and was still fully prepared to flunk anybody who didn't measure up. Of sixty-five of us in the group, twenty-three graduated.

Armed with the experience of flying the N2S-1 biplane, I went off to naval aviator training in the SNJ Texan at Pensacola, Florida. That's the plane known as the T-6 in Army jargon, a very stable, low-wing advanced trainer. We did our carrier qualification on the USS *Wright* (CVL 49). For advanced pilot training, I went to Corpus Christi, Texas, and flew the F6F Hellcat. My group was the last to fly this famous World War II fighter in training. They were converting to the newer F8F Bearcat. I managed to get in just one flight in the F8F during training and remember I had difficulty getting the gear up. The F8F was a real performer, and in some ways it may have represented the ultimate in the propeller age—at least until the Skyraider came along.

While in training, I was an aviation midshipman. The Flying Midshipman program was a special arrangement that brought up three thousand new naval aviators in the postwar years, pilots who initially were neither enlisted sailors nor officers, among them future Apollo 11 astronaut Neil Armstrong. I got my wings and commission in 1949 and immediately jumped from midshipman status to ensign, the lowest officer rank.

Bearcat at Sea

In August 1949, I was assigned to my first squadron, VF-194 in Air Group 19. In January 1950, we departed to the Far East on the USS *Boxer* (CVA 21). We had just switched to the F8F Bearcat, and this was one of the very few cruises in Navy history when the F8F went to sea. During that cruise, I finished getting the last of my twenty-five hours for minimum carrier qualification landings flying in the Field Carrier Landing Pattern (FCLP). During that cruise, we visited Korea during Easter weekend and were invited for tea with the new South Korean president, Syngman Rhee. I spent that weekend in the spring of 1950 with an Army Intelligence officer. He said there was some activity on the 38th

Parallel and wasn't sure what it meant. It wasn't immediately obvious to us that Korea was a potential trouble spot. The Soviet Union had just detonated its first atomic bomb and a lot of heads were turned toward Moscow as the coming threat, not the North Korean capital of Pyongyang. We would find out two months later.

What an adventurous time that was. We called it the "Far East" because it seemed so far away, back in those days before the world was interconnected. I found that I liked life at sea. I found others in the Navy who shared my devout beliefs. It was peacetime—still briefly, then—and we had good camaraderie and a great flying mission. This was the perfect prelude to my coming life of adventure spanning the globe with the airlines.

When our carrier returned from that 1950 western Pacific cruise, I began making my plans for the next step. I was scheduled for discharge on June 26, 1950. President Harry S Truman decided we had to cut back on the military during peacetime. Two years earlier, Truman had campaigned as the last presidential candidate in American history with a platform for reducing the size of the armed forces. That makes his decision to defend South Korea all the more remarkable. Although I had actually been there and had even seen the South Korean president, few Americans had ever heard of the place.

I got married on Sunday, June 25, 1950. We were driving across the Golden Gate Bridge heading for our honeymoon in northern California, when an announcer broke in to tell us that the North Koreans had just attacked the South.

In the early hours of that day, in darkness and driving rain, North Korean armed forces crossed the 38th Parallel at a half dozen locations. Ninety thousand men and hundreds of Russian-made T-34 medium tanks launched the invasion of South Korea. It was completely unexpected. North Korea also put into the battle its modest air arm, commanded by Maj. Gen. Wang Yon, a Soviet Air Academy graduate. The North Korean air force had about 150 propeller-driven combat aircraft, including Lavochkin La-9s, Ilyushin Il-10 Sturmoviks, Yakovlev Yak-7s, Yak-9s, and Yak-18s. I did not know any of this at the time, of course. I also did not know that the aircraft carrier USS *Valley Forge* (CV 45) was hastily pulling anchor in Hong Kong and heading toward the Korea trouble zone. What I did know was that the radio announcer was saying something very important to me: All discharges from the military were being temporarily suspended. I was still "Bill Barron, Naval Aviator." My birthday comes three days after my wedding anniversary, but that year, the month of June definitely produced mixed results.

Instead of being discharged I volunteered to go back to the squadron. They sent me to San Diego to VR-32, a transport squadron in the Ferry Command, because they were expecting to move a lot of aircraft. After two months, I worked my way back to Alameda, California, and was in FASRON 8 (Fleet Air Service Squadron) and volunteered to go as replacement pilot, but only if I could get on a tactical aircraft. They were not using F8F Bearcats in Korea, but they were using AD Skyraiders galore. I went out in August of 1951 and came back in December 1951. I flew twenty-six missions at that time.

During that first combat cruise, I was a replacement pilot in a Reserve squadron from Oakland, California—Attack Squadron, VA-923, in AD Skyraiders on the carrier USS *Bon Homme Richard* (CV 31), alias "Bonny Dick." One of their pilots diverted to a shore-based field because he couldn't drop one of his bombs, but it fell off when he landed. They were short of pilots and requested a replacement. That was my good luck and my bad luck. I was about to fly in battle in what was both a good airplane and a bad airplane.

Learning the Ropes

It was aboard *Bon Homme Richard* that I first became proficient in the AD Skyraider. I flew mostly the AD-4 and AD-4L (winterized) models from the middle of the Skyraider production run. My experience aboard "Bonny Dick" was much like my previous aircraft carrier cruise: It took all kinds to make up a Navy and not everyone was perfect, but we had some superb people and we worked hard to do a good job. When you're taking off from a ship's deck while it's pitching at sea in bad weather, carrying as many bombs as a B-17 Flying Fortress, plus enough fuel to transform your plane into a blazing torch, you need to work together. There were a few times when we didn't do that well, and we paid for it. So you try to fly right, from the very beginning of the mission.

Here's how it starts.

You brief in the ready room. You get a check on the weather. You make your walk-around, a preflight inspection. You make sure the pitot tube cover is off, make sure the bombs are shackled properly. You check

Illustrating the dangers and difficulty of carrier flying, an AD-4L Skyraider takes a "wave off" from the flight deck and pulls up to go around for another landing attempt.

[U.S. Navy]

the tires. You check the oleos for the landing gear. You check to see the tailhook is up and locked. On the AD, the wings fold a few feet from the fuselage. There are six racks on each wing plus three racks on the fuselage, a total of fifteen stations that can carry 8,000 pounds of ordnance. We carried bombs and rockets in many combinations. On the mission that I'm remembering right now, we had a thousand-pounder under the centerline, six 500-pounders under the wings, and of course a full load of ammunition for the cannon. You have to salute the the sailors, the "ordies," who handle the ordnance cannon rounds below decks and on the carrier flight deck. They make it happen.

You get into the aircraft by climbing up on the wing on the port side. You climb into the cockpit and strap in with help from the plane captain. You look down at him and he'll give you the windup signal to start the engine. You hear a loudspeaker when the Air Boss says to start engines.

For takeoff, you use your right hand to hold the stick back and your left hand on the throttle. When I spread the wings, using the lever on the right, I had to let go of the stick to reach for the locking pin, and reached down to manually lock the wing spread. For a deck launch, not using the catapult, you hold the stick fully back into your gut and go to full throttle. The plane captain will give you a circle with one finger as you're preparing, and when you're ready to launch, he will throw his hand down. For a catapult launch, which we sometimes use for the Skyraider, especially if there is not enough wind across the deck, you go to full throttle and salute with your left hand and they'll fire you off. In a jet, you lift your hands so the launch officer can see them, so he'll know you're not going to get him into an accident. You didn't have to do that gesture in the Skyraider.

You take off. You climb out. To describe the rest of a mission in Korea, I'm going to leap ahead to my second opportunity to demonstrate my growing expertise with the Skyraider during my second combat cruise with squadron VA-95 aboard the USS *Philippine Sea* (CV 47). This took me to Korean waters in the final months of the conflict. As on my first cruise, enemy gunfire was always a danger, but at times Korea reduced a pilot to confronting more basic climate and airmanship challenges. It wasn't always the North Koreans, or the Chinese, or the target that was the problem. Carrier flying in the extremes of the Korean climate was a challenge by itself.

I was part of a flight of four AD-4Ls from VA-95 that was returning to the *Philippine Sea* on June 7, 1953, when low clouds, rain, and wind conspired to make flying conditions difficult. Our close air support mission had, in fact, been cancelled because of the weather. Of the four Skyraiders, only one made a successful landing on the flattop's deck.

Trying to return to the ship, Comdr. Samuel B. Berrey, our VA-95 squadron commander, ran into 100-foot (31-m) cloud cover with one-half-mile visibility, and this dropped to zero-zero in the vicinity of the ship. With our fuel being rapidly used up and everything closing in around us, we tried three times to get down. Berrey went into the water, momentarily disappearing in a huge geyser of spray, and was rescued while his plane went to the bottom of the Sea of Japan. Along with a pilot named Ritchie, I joined forces with a lost F4U Corsair and with an AD-4W Skyraider "guppy" (blessed with the radar, which was so sorely needed in this awful weather), and the new quartet set forth to attempt to reach K-18 airfield at Kangnung, on the east coast of South Korea.

The guppy ran out of gas and had to ditch in the water. I watched that airplane get lower and lower until it skidded and bounced off the

Lt. (j.g.) Bill Barron writes a letter home from his billet in the aircraft carrier USS *Philippine Sea* (CV 47).

[Bill Barron]

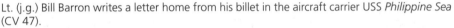

wave tops, came to a halt with its tail pointing upward, and began to sink. I made a pass overhead. The crew of the guppy was climbing out and thrashing around, and after a few minutes it was clear that they would be okay and would be picked up by a fishing boat that was approaching them. Now, darkness was closing in, the fuel situation was bordering on the desperate, and Ritchie and I were looking for some landmark along the Korean east coast that would tell us we were near Kangnung. We sure could have used some of the navigation devices that have been invented since then. There was still a hint of sunlight ahead of us, shimmering on the horizon, when we found Kangnung and landed near a battered F9F Panther that had overshot the runway earlier and crumpled into two pieces. The Corsair landed first, went off the runway, and flipped over, but the pilot walked away. Ritchie and I got our wheels on the ground while the planes were operating on fumes. I was shot at many times in Korea, and hit by enemy gunfire, but there was never such a test as that landing in the fading light without even enough gas for a go-around. After it was over and I could settle down a little, I wrote in a letter that this was the "hairiest hop I've ever flown." On that particular day, I never saw our enemy. The problem was Mother Nature.

Taxpayer Money

Incidentally, I couldn't resist jotting down some numbers when somebody told me what all this was costing. I have an entry entitled "cost of ordnance" in my notebook. A 2,000-pound (907-kilogram) bomb sold to the taxpayer for $436.30. A 1,000-lb (454-kg) bomb was $184.00. A better bargain was the Navy's 260-lb (118-kg) bomb, going for $60.00. I noted that each 20-mm armor-piercing round had a price tag of $1.55, while a high-explosive round sold for a mere seventy-eight cents. The nose fuse for a bomb was $5.45, the tail fuse $5.75.

But let me bring my musings back, full circle, to the be-all and end-all of the Skyraider mission, which is getting over the target, staying alive, and attacking it. On the mission I began with, that memorable mission attacking a railroad marshalling yard surrounded by antiaircraft guns, our formation approached the target and we kept it off to our left. In aviation, you always try to keep everything out there to your left. Traffic patterns are left-handed and you get accustomed to that.

We're at 10,000 feet (3048 m), although we often begin our attacks from higher. After calculating how steep we want to go, we pass more or less directly over the target, looking around constantly for triple-A or MiGs, and once we've passed over it, we roll, peel off, and dive. With the huge, barn-door dive brakes on the Skyraider, you can head straight for the ground at a 70-degree angle. That's steeper than they did dive-bombing in World War II. Once you get the nose point down, you come on top of the target and roll over to the left.

On this particular day, the dropping of the bombs is unremarkable. Boring down on the target, those barn-door dive brakes slow me down dramatically. I'm trying to hold my gunsight on the target while the plane is bouncing around, partly because of normal turbulence and partly because those big barn doors are interrupting the air and giving me drag. It slows me down and gives me enough time to be accurate. I release, pull in the barn doors, and start my pullout. You can pull as much as seven Gs at the bottom of your pullout. That's enough to cause some men to black out. You want to get up and get back to altitude as soon as possible.

This AD-4NL Skyraider, seen during the Korean War era, is similar to the AD-4L flown in Korea by Bill Barron and other naval aviators of squadron VA-95. The searchlight under the left wing of this aircraft is the only feature that makes it appear different from the version that fought in Korea.

[U.S. Navy]

I blasted them pretty good. But my flight leader, who was also the squadron executive officer, had not yet dropped his bombs and wanted to stay around. To enable him to make a bomb run, I decided to go back and work over their antiaircraft artillery positions. I made this decision on my initiative, and he okayed it. So, after I'd pulled up from dropping my bombs, I went for the guns. I was in a much more shallow dive. You just sort of go on in against them, and line them up, and shoot. It's the old-fashioned way, and sometimes you can get close enough to see the bad guys scurrying around, trying to see who's going to kill whom first.

When I took those hits on the rear fuselage and tail of my airplane, it was a bit of an anticlimax. I certainly felt that something was wrong. But I can't honestly say that I saw bullets flashing through the air, or muzzle flashes, or anything like that.

They just hit me. That's all. Well, that's nearly all. My elevator trim tab would go forward but not back. One of the guys said on the radio, "You're full of holes, but you're still flying." He said he could not see

Lt. (j.g.)(later Lt. Comdr.) Bill Barron, AD-4L Skyraider pilot, squadron VA-95, USS *Philippine Sea* (CV 47)

---

anything leaking. The airplane didn't feel right, but it was still in the air, so I wanted to try to get home to the carrier before trying anything drastic. As it turned out, I was able to land safely on the *Philippine Sea*. I got out, and looked at the tail, and there were two hundred holes in the airplane.

The executive officer received a Distinguished Flying Cross for that mission. I was the one who'd taken the initiative, and the one who had gotten hit, but I was just a junior pilot, so I got an ordinary Air Medal.

On July 27, 1953, the day the Korean armistice was signed, I flew my seventy-eighth combat mission. They signed the cease-fire at noon. My mission was from 6:15 A.M. to 7:45 A.M., so I was among the last Americans involved in the Korean War. Our missions were normally three hours long, while the jets flew one and a half hours, but that day was cut short.

I spent much of the remainder of my naval career in accident investigation. I retired from the Navy in February 1967. Then, I went up to Oakland and flew the Boeing 707 for World Airways for a year. My wife Pat and I live today in Bay Point, California, where I'm active in business and church affairs.

Douglas AD Skyraider

The Skyraider was the plane they designed overnight.

The Douglas Aircraft Company engineering team of Edward Heinemann, Leo Devlin, and Gene Root put together the Skyraider design over a 1944 weekend in the Shoreham Hotel in Washington, D.C., after learning that the Navy didn't like another aircraft they were proposing. Their new-but-hastily conceived warplane was originally called the XBT2D-1 and briefly named the Dauntless II. It flew for the first time on March 18, 1945, at Mines Field, California, piloted by LaVerne Brown, a one-time actor who had played "Tailspin Tommy" in the movies.

By 1946, the plane had been renamed the AD-1 Skyraider. Douglas eventually built AD-1 through AD-7 models. The Skyraider was too late for World War II but just in time for Korea.

Skyraiders were on the scene at every juncture as the fortunes of the Korean War shifted in 1950 and 1951—the Inchon landing that sent North Korean forces into retreat, the march to the Yalu River by United Nations forces, and then the chaos and horror of China's entry into the war. Skyraider pilots flew along with their brethren in F4U Corsairs to relieve Marines as they withdrew in the face of the Chinese advance. The Chinese swarmed south to retake Seoul, then were nudged back, and by mid-1951 battle lines stabilized. By that time, Skyraiders were a ubiquitous sight in almost every air-to-ground action.

Lt. Daniel Braugher, who flew AD-3s with squadron CA-35 aboard USS *Leyte* (CVA 32) pointed out that pilots of the big Douglas attack bomber really had three enemies—the weather, the risky tempo of carrier-deck operations, and the enemy. "We lost two pilots during one period on the line without the enemy putting a bullet into them. One of

---

Douglas AD-6 (A-1H) Skyraider

Type: single-seat, carrier-based attack aircraft

Power plant: one 2,700-hp (2013-kW) Wright R-3350-26WA 18-cylinder piston radial engine

Performance: maximum speed 334 mph (540 km/h) at 18,000 ft (5485 m); cruising speed 198 mph (319 km/h); initial rate of climb 2,850 ft (870 m) per minute; service ceiling 28,500 ft (8685 m); range 1,315 miles (2117 km)

Weights: empty 11,968 lb (5429 kg); normal takeoff 18,106 lb (8213 kg); maximum takeoff 25,000 lb (11340 kg)

Dimensions: wingspan 50 ft 0-1.2 in (15.25 m); length 38 ft 10 in (11.84 m); height 15 ft 8½ in (4.78 m); wing area 400.33 sq ft (37.19 sq m)

Armament: four wing-mounted 20mm Mark 12 cannons, with 200 rounds per gun, plus up to 8,700 lb (3629 kg) of external bombs, rockets, and napalm on three under-fuselage and twelve underwing (six per wing) hard-points

First flight: March 18, 1945 (XBT2D-1); circa. February 1946 (AD-1)

---

them simply vanished into weather. One minute his Skyraider was there; the next, it wasn't. We discovered much later that he had gone into a mountainside near Wonsan."

Braugher said that a Skyraider could handily travel more than six hundred miles (965 kilometers) to attack a target. "We attacked troop formations. We went after their railroad infrastructure. We even fired HVAR [high-velocity aircraft rockets] into a railroad tunnel." On a typical mission, an ordnance load was more likely to be in the neighborhood of six thousand pounds (2721 kilograms) and a target not quite as distant.

Skyraider pilots had to worry about antiaircraft fire, but they rarely encountered the dreaded Soviet-built MiG-15 fighters, which stayed close to the border at the Yalu. And above all, they fretted about the weather.

The basic appearance of the Skyraider never changed from that hotel room in 1944 to the final rollout in 1958. When the 3,080th and last AD-7 Skyraider was delivered by Lt. Mark Fowler to squadron VA-215 in 1958, it looked almost identical, externally, do the XBT2D-1 mockup of thirteen years earlier. Aeronautical engineer Devlin was fond of saying that the Skyraider design was "right from the start." That characterization covered all models, including the AD-4L flown in Korea by Bill Barron.

Chapter Fourteen

Skyknight over North Vietnam

What Happened

On March 18, 1966, a North Vietnamese surface-to-air missile shot down an EF-10B Skyknight, killing the two Marines on board—although families didn't learn their fate until years later.

The plane was the first of five Skyknights lost in Vietnam, along with all ten crew members. Their sacrifice points to the contribution made by a little-known electronic warfare aircraft.

During the Korean War, the Skyknight was known as the F3D-2 and shot down enemy planes on nocturnal missions.

The plane was so corpulent that crews called it "Willy the Whale." In the late 1950s, the Marines modified thirty-six Skyknights to become F3D-2Q electronic warfare aircraft. In July 1958, composite reconnaissance squadron VMCJ-3 began flying classified Cold War reconnaissance missions, dubbed "Shark Fin" flights, from Iwakuni, Japan. The flights were carried out near China, North Korea, and the Soviet Union to study adversaries' radar networks.

In April 1965, squadron VMCJ-1 brought six EF-10Bs (as the planes were now called) to Da Nang. They were the first electronic warfare aircraft of any service to operate in Vietnam.

For four years, until replaced by newer, better-equipped EA-6A In-

**First Lieutenant Wayne Whitten
March 18, 1966
Douglas EF-10B Skyknight
Riverboat 1
Marine Composite
   Reconnaissance Squadron
   One, VMCJ-1
Da Nang Air Base, South
   Vietnam**

1st Lt. (later Col.) H. Wayne "Flash" Whitten poses on the starboard side of an EF-10B Skyknight at Da Nang, South Vietnam, in 1966. The plane shown, bureau number 125831, was shot down on June 16, 1968. Skyknights created an electronic pathway to enable other warplanes to attack targets in North Vietnam.

[Wayne Whitten]

truders, Marine EF-10Bs escorted strikes into North Vietnam, jamming enemy radars, and collecting intelligence.

On the March 18, 1966 mission, two EF-10Bs with call signs Riverboat 1 and 2, escorted by Marine F-4B Phantoms, provided jamming support for Air Force F-105 Thunderchiefs attacking Vinh.

"We needed two Skyknights to support a mission," said retired Col. H. Wayne Whitten, who was a first lieutenant and was electronic countermeasures officer aboard Riverboat 1. "That's partly because of the limitations of our two onboard jammers, which were not sophisticated or powerful, so we had to work on tactics to get the most out of them." Because the EF-10B could jam only an enemy radar located in front of the aircraft, Riverboat 1 and Riverboat 2 set up a racetrack pattern that put one plane in the right location at all times.

"We saw one EF-10B turn left, go out a mile, and disappear in a ball of flames," said retired Capt. Eugene "Mule" Holmberg, who was a second lieutenant in the backseat of an escorting F-4B Phantom. "It took just seconds, and he was gone."

A previously unknown SAM installation fired the missile that struck Riverboat 2. Aboard the EF-10B were 1st Lt. Everett "Mac" McPherson, pilot, and 1st Lt. Brent Davis, electronic countermeasures officer. Both men apparently lost their lives when the missile hit their Skyknight. Davis was promoted to major before the Vietnamese government provided information on him in 1988, and he was interred at Arlington National Cemetery in 1997. The Pentagon has issued a presumptive finding of death for McPherson but has not recovered his remains.

WAYNE WHITTEN. The EF-10B Skyknight (known as the F3D-2Q until 1962) was a night fighter during the Korean War and was later modified for electronic warfare duties and assigned to the Marine Corps' composite reconnaissance squadrons, or VMCJ squadrons, in 1956. Because of its portly shape, Marines called the plane "Willy the Whale." It has been written that Marines also called the plane the "Drut," a term that becomes meaningful only when spelled backward, but I never heard any Marine use that name.

From their initial deployment to Japan in 1957 until Vietnam, the EF-10Bs (or F3D-2Qs as they were called until 1962) were used primarily for Cold War peripheral reconnaissance, collecting electronic intelligence or ELINT from over water routes but not penetrating hostile air space. Closer to home, an EF-10B belonging to squadron VMCJ-2 intercepted the first Fan Song radar associated with the Russian SA-2 surface-to-air missile in Cuba before the Cuban Missile crisis in 1962. For years, the EF-10B collected data and provided training to our own radar units, but the plane's radar jammers were never used against an adversary's radar.

Then came Vietnam.

I got to Vietnam November 1, 1965. My squadron, VMCJ-1, had been there since April and had amassed quite a record in the EF-10B. They had been supporting the first strikes against surface-to-air missiles, or SAMs. By the time I got there, the pattern of operations was set. We were supporting the Air Force and the Navy but not the Marine Corps, who had no operations over North Vietnam at that time. We took our tasking from 2nd Air Division in Saigon. We kept one of our electronic countermeasures guys in Saigon to write the daily frags. Our counterparts were the Air Force EB-66 squadrons that were flying out of Thailand.

JERRY O'BRIEN. For part of its career, Willy the Whale used 115/145 aviation gasoline rather than JP-4 jet fuel. That's right—a jet aircraft using aviation gasoline. The aviation gas added a few extra pounds of thrust, but the lead in the gasoline ate up the compressor vanes.

The EF-10B performed well as an electronic countermeasures platform. It was stable and relatively comfortable. The cruising speed was about three hundred knots, and hanging fifty-gallon tanks called for by the manufacturer enhanced range. In cold climates, the increase in drag induced by the fuel tanks didn't matter much, but in the hot air of someplace like Vietnam it made a big difference. Care had to be taken to compute a takeoff roll. Takeoff on a hot day or from a high-altitude airfield could best be described as awe inspiring. An afternoon takeoff on a hot day from a high-altitude airfield was a downright white-knuckle experience.

As ambient temperatures at Da Nang reached 120 degrees, runway surface temperatures soared and cockpit temperatures often approached 140 degrees. You can cook meat at 150 degrees. Sitting there in the cockpit, sweat poured down your face, and your gloves and flight suit were soon soaked.

Typically, we taxied out onto the runway overrun to perform our turn-up. Due to the down-tilting tailpipes of the EF-10B, this procedure tore gaps out of the surface and left gaping holes in the pavement.

When all logical reasons for aborting the mission failed, one pushed the throttles forward and waited until the engines built up to maximum rpm. This allowed engine gas temperatures to build up and added a percentage point to the power. Still, Willy the Whale did not get off the ground easily, and the pilot had to be very careful when to rotate, to avoid increasing drag.

Somewhere down the runway, the pilot gingerly rotated slightly to the takeoff attitude. Then, you sat back and waited for something significant to happen. After a bit, it would rise up on its oleos and the pilot would check the amount of runway remaining. This was always a shock of sorts because on a ten-thousand-foot runway, you were invariably running out of space and ideas simultaneously.

Eventually, it lifted off the ground and the gear came up. You wanted to wait on the flaps for a long moment to make sure the bird was actually flying. Flying along over the bay at the edge of a stall was a common experience and particularly when carrying a fuel tank on one wing and a jamming pod on the other.

A Douglas EF-10B Skyknight of Marine Composite Reconnaissance Squadron One, or VMCJ-1, on a combat mission over North Vietnam, circa. 1965. Built as a night fighter for air-to-air combat, the Skyknight became an electronic warrior with the job of foiling North Vietnamese air defenses.

[U.S. Navy]

WAYNE WHITTEN. When we first deployed to Vietnam, we flew a lot of pure reconnaissance missions trying to identify and locate the North Vietnamese air defense radars. But when Hanoi began deploying Russian-built SAMs, and radar-guided antiaircraft artillery, or AAA, the Air Force and Navy needed all the help it could get from us for electronic countermeasures, or ECM, and real-time threat warning. To put the latter in context, later in the war, all Air Force and Navy aircraft had their own radar warning receivers, but in 1965 and 1966 they did not. We would broadcast code words such as "Red Dog, Bravo Fox 2" over the guard channel to gave the strike force a heads-up that they were being tracked by a SAM radar in their vicinity.

We flew night and day all the way up to the Red River, and out to places like Yen Bai over sixty nautical miles northwest of Hanoi in support of F-105 Thunderchiefs strikes (a round-trip of over eight hundred nautical miles). Our guy in Saigon would study the F-105 targets each day and frag us to support the ones where they were the most vulnerable to SAMs or radar-controlled AAA. We usually used two Skyknights to support a mission, partly because of the limitations of our two onboard jammers, which were not very sophisticated or powerful, so we had to work on tactics and techniques to get the most out of them. They had fixed directional antennas that provided a cone of jamming power from the nose quadrant only. You wanted to align yourself so the aircraft was positioned on the axis of the strike force coming in to provide maximum jamming power against the air defense radars. By using two aircraft we could establish a racetrack pattern where one of the two Skyknights was always coming in toward the target, providing continuous jamming coverage.

In those days the EF-10B crews were very vulnerable themselves to SAMs if they got caught inside the missile's nominal fifteen-nautical-mile engagement envelope, as we didn't have missile-launch warning receivers and our jammers were thought to actually spotlight our radar blips on their scopes. To make matters worse, we typically flew above 20,000 feet straight and level, and old Willie had a three-G defensive maneuver limit. Not to mention that most of our missions over the western regions of North Vietnam were well beyond navigation aid range, so we had to use dead-reckoning techniques and hoped we stayed clear of the SAM rings that looked nice on our maps but unfortunately didn't translate to the real world in the air.

On March 18, 1966, we were fragged [assigned] to support a flight of F-105s going after a target ten miles (16 km) west of Thanh Hoa, inside a known or suspected SAM ring. On that day, we planned to establish a racetrack about twenty miles (32 km) long that took about four minutes to fly. My pilot and flight leader was Capt. Bill Bergman. First lieutenants Mac McPherson and my closest squadron mate Brent Davis crewed the other Skyknight. Our call signs were Riverboat 1 and 2. Our squadron call sign was Cotton Picker, but we didn't use it on Air Force support missions for security reasons.

It was a dawn brief for a 7:30 A.M. launch. The MiG threat had picked up in the spring of 1966, so we were assigned two Marine F-4B Phantoms as fighter escort. They came from the VMFA-314 "Black Knights," who briefed with us. Our route of flight would take us west out of Da Nang a hundred miles (161 km) or so to the Mekong River, where our fighter escorts did their aerial refueling from Marine KC-130F Hercules tankers. After tanking, they would go with us as we headed up over Laos into North Vietnam passing just to the west of Vinh, toward our target area southwest of Thanh Hoa.

This was March, remember, after President Johnson's long Christ-

The wings of the EF-10B Skyknight were designed to fold to enhance storage on aircraft decks, but the EF-10B rarely flew from a carrier. This Skyknight is at Da Nang airfield in South Vietnam in about 1966, during a break between missions over North Vietnam.

[U.S. Marine Corps]

mas bombing halt, which stood down operations over North Vietnam for nearly six weeks. During the period when we weren't flying up there, the North Vietnamese expanded their air defense network and significantly increased the threat. At that time, we knew of no confirmed SAM sites below Thanh Hoa, but one of our EB-66C counterparts had been hit by a missile a couple of weeks earlier along the coast near Vinh, in a location where we'd believed there were no SAMs. In retrospect, given their "shoot and move" tactics, that was probably the same SAM unit that we were about to encounter.

As our flight approached the North Vietnam border, I detected a Fan Song radar with its distinctive rattlesnake-like audio somewhere off our nose. I called Brent in the other EF-10B and asked, "Do you see what I see?" and he replied he did. I broadcast a SAM warning on guard, then we quickly decided to err on the side of safety by changing our flight path to arc out to the west about twenty-five miles (40 km) to bypass this unforeseen threat. This change in our approach route would have us enter our planned racetrack pattern from the west instead of the south. Dealing with a Fan Song radar with our antiquated equipment was most frustrating, as its strong track-while-scan signal tended to overpower our receiver, making it difficult to obtain a good line of bearing, and accurate location was practically impossible. I knew for sure we had a new SAM operating somewhere in the vicinity of Vinh, but that was about it.

Monitoring the Fan Song signal as we continued our approach I noticed it kept coming up and down after a few seconds. This erratic operation was puzzling because normally the SAM radar operator would track a target for several minutes before an engagement, unless it was under attack. Years later, I learned from an Air Force counterpart that there was intelligence indicating the Russians themselves were operating some of the new SAMs instead of just providing training assistance to the North Vietnamese. This could have accounted for this more sophisticated use of the radar.

We had lost time with our route change and the F-105s were coming in. As we approached our initial point for our racetrack, we did a 360 degree separation turn and followed our wingman inbound toward the target at about 26,000 feet. At this time, the target area seemed clear of SAMs, although I was still getting intermittent Fan Song signals from behind us. I now had a Fire Can, the radar associated with heavy caliber AAA, active in the target area and turned my attention to it. The problem with our old manual ECM equipment was it was hard to jam a Fire Can and monitor a Fan Song at the same time. It was okay for a "one-on-one" situation but with two types of enemy radars to work, you had a handful. Their operating frequencies were far enough apart to require retuning the receiver, and you couldn't see the signals through the interference caused by the jammers, a literal Catch 22.

Shortly after we made our turn outbound from the target, Bill and I saw a large explosion out ahead where our wingman would have been coming inbound toward us. My fears were confirmed when our frantic radio calls went unanswered and our fighter escorts reported losing sight of them on radar. We all saw the missile detonate but did not see any chutes or smoking aircraft emerge from the orange cloud. We were all sure that our wingman was incinerated, right there.

Nobody ever said it was pretty. A generation of aviation writers solidified the legend that the Marines referred to the Skyknight as the "Drut," a term that makes sense only when read backward. Marines interviewed for this history could not remember anyone using the term: They called the EF-10B the "Whale" because of its shape.

[U.S. Marine Corps]

MULE HOLMBERG. I was the radar intercept officer in the backseat of the VMFA-314 F-4B Phantom piloted by Lt. Col. John Trotti. We didn't determine the flight path. The EF-10B Skyknights determined the flight path, and they were a little off in their calculations. So as we headed into North Vietnam, we drifted a bit east from the track we were supposed to be on.

We were escorting the EF-10Bs, above them and behind them doing a weave, because the maximum speed on an EF-10B is a little bit slow for an F-4. The EF-10Bs began to set up their separation so they could orbit to jam the North Vietnamese radars. One aircraft turned left and went out a mile and disappeared in a ball of flames. Trotti said, "Shit!"

In the next three seconds, our F-4 was thrown almost vertical. There was a huge explosion at our five o'clock. I looked back over my shoulder, and there was a little ball of gray with smoke coming out.

Trotti said, "What was that?"

I said, "That was an SA-2."

I looked down and there was the bend of the river at Vinh. The lead [Whitten's aircraft] didn't know that the other EF-10B was gone. They were performing their Fire Can suppression—just one EF-10B now—and were ready to go home.

I looked down and saw five puffs erupt in the six o'clock position to the EF-10B. That was antiaircraft fire coming from antiaircraft guns that were guided by Fire Can radar.

I said, "You have Fire Can bursts going off at your six, tracking you." The next two rounds exploded up closer to his tail. Then, he put his jammers on, and the third round exploded right in front of us. I said to Trotti, "Maybe he should turn his jammer off so they hit him instead of us."

We recovered in our F-4B Phantom at Da Nang. They all got Distinguished Flying Crosses. We didn't get anything, but what the hell? We were just doing our job.

WAYNE WHITTEN. This was March, remember, after Lyndon B. Johnson's big long Christmas stand-down. During the period when we weren't flying up there, the North Vietnamese expanded their SAM network and increased the threat. At that time, we knew of no confirmed SAM sites below Thanh Hoa. But one of our counterpart squadrons of EB-66s had been shot at in a location where we'd believed there were no SAMs. In retrospect, that was probably the same SAM site that we encountered on March 18.

No sooner had we turned north, just entering North Vietnam, when both my counterpart Davis and I detected the Fan Song radar associated with the SA-2.

I called him and asked, "Do you see what I see?"

He said, "Yeah."

But dealing with a Fan Song signal was the most frustrating thing I've ever dealt with. It was very difficult to get a bearing on it. It ate up the receiver. It was a track-while-scan radar that was simply too much for our old ECM gear. We knew there was a SAM site off our nose somewhere in an area we did not anticipate. To err on the side of safety, we put out a warning and changed our flight path to arc out at least twenty or twenty-five miles (32 or 38 km) on a path to the west or northwest. We would then come in more from the west than from the south. The signal kept coming up and down. It was erratic. That was puzzling because at that point we didn't think the North Vietnamese were that sophisticated. Our Air Force counterpart was certain that this sophisticated use of the radar was a sign Russians were at the site.

We had lost time. The F-105s were coming in. Our aircraft separated. We did a 360, and our wingman pressed on to the target. At this time, there seemed to be no SAM ahead of us. It was clear up there. But we were still getting indications of Fan Song radar behind us and Fire Can, the radar associated with AAA, was coming up in the target area.

All this happened within five minutes: We were focused on the Fire Can. The problem with our old, antiquated equipment was, it was hard to jam Fire Can and Fan Song at the same time. Our equipment was okay for a "one-on-one" situation, but with two types of enemy radar at work, you had to change frequencies, which could take as much as a minute.

The unknown SAM site that had suddenly appeared on us when we were going up hit our wingman. He fired a missile and hit the other Skyknight. We saw the detonation. We saw no chutes. We'd have bet dollars to donuts that the other EF-10B was incinerated, right there. We saw no chutes, no smoke, nothing.

That caused all kinds of pandemonium and voice calls to our wingman. By that time, the Air Force strike aircraft had pulled off and were out of there. We were on our own, and when we withdrew toward our fighter escort, we fell into a flak trap. We had 85mm stuff exploding all around us. It was the most hectic five to ten minutes of my life. We got no radio responses from our wingman. We went for years with no information about our wingman. We thought he had taken a direct hit and that was the end of the subject.

In any war scenario, you're always playing catch-up in the world of electronic countermeasures. In the first year of operation, we were well trained—no one is perfect—but the equipment had limitations and the SAMs were a serious threat. It was in the nature of war that they could take advantage of watching our operations and put a missile site underneath. We were in outdated equipment out on the cutting edge. This whole thing was new to both sides.

By June 1966, the Air Force had enough EB-66s that we could stop supporting the Air Force and support the Navy instead. There was an F-4 loss later involving Howard Dunn. This was the first and only Marine F-4 lost supporting us. The sad part of what happened in Vietnam was, none of us knew what the other was doing, so, soon afterward, an F-100 Wild Weasel was lost in the same area. I think one SAM unit, possibly with Soviet technicians, shot down four U.S. aircraft in the same general area in a short time.

What Happened

The EF-10B Skyknight being flown by McPherson and Davis, Riverboat 2, was simply blown out of the sky. They were hit by an SA-2 surface-to-air missile and never had a chance to get out of their aircraft. An attempted search-and-rescue mission found no trace of them. After the war, freed U.S. prisoners had no information on their fate.

WAYNE WHITTEN. The search-and-rescue, or SAR, effort proved fruitless. The names of lieutenants Brent Davis and Everett McPherson were added to the growing Missing in Action, or MIA list. Two years later while on the CINCPAC staff in Hawaii, I received a letter from Mac's younger brother Raymond, a Navy chaplain serving with the Marines in Okinawa, searching for any details of his brother's fate. I reluctantly gave him the same information I have related here. He was most grateful. The family had learned next to nothing from official sources. We stayed in contact nearly thirty years, with Ray keeping me informed as his family pressed for some final word of Mac's fate, as did the Davis family, who used the family's foreign service contacts to get some information through the North Vietnamese Paris peace talk negotiators, but without results.

The return of our prisoners of war, without any of them able to provide any information was sobering, and the family turned their quest toward finding some tangible evidence that would bring closure. Finally, in July 1991, an American field team reviewed documentation in a North Vietnamese museum listing McPherson and Davis as being buried in Nge An province, northwest of Vinh. In January 1992, the Vietnamese released a Military Region IV Air Defense Operations Journal from 1964–73. There were entries listing the shoot-down of an EF-10B on March 18, 1966, by the 61st Battalion, 236th Regiment and indicating two crewmen died. Unexplainably, this information was not passed to the families until July 1993. That same month, the field team interviewed several residents of a Vietnamese village that were eyewitnesses to the crash of what was confirmed to be EF-10B bureau number 127041, our missing aircraft. One reported seeing the aircraft flying in smoking and veering wildly with obvious control problems and what appeared to be someone ejecting from the aircraft just before it impacted the mountain above the village. The crash site was some twenty-

Who's Who

1st Lt. (later Col.) H. Wayne "Flash" Whitten, electronic countermeasures officer, EF-10B Skyknight, Riverboat 1, squadron VMCJ-1

Capt. Bill Bergman, pilot, EF-10B Skyknight, Riverboat 1, squadron VMCJ-1

1st Lt. Everett "Mac" McPherson, pilot, EF-10B Skyknight, Riverboat 2, squadron VMCJ-1

1st Lt. Brent Davis, electronic countermeasures officer, EF-10B Skyknight, Riverboat 2, squadron VMCJ-1

Col. John Trotti, F-4B Phantom pilot, squadron VMFA-314

2nd Lt. (later Capt.) Eugene "Mule" Holmberg, F-4B Phantom radar intercept officer, squadron VMFA-314

five miles (40 km) southeast of our officially reported location of the explosion, so it appears Mac survived the hit and made a valiant effort to get the aircraft out over the coast.

A team of villagers went to the crash site and found one body in the wreckage and the other in a tree about a kilometer away. To further add to the speculation as to who was manning this SA-2 system, one of the witnesses from the village reported a visit to the crash site by foreigners whom he believed to be Russians.

The surveyed site was marked for future recovery efforts that ultimately resulted in the retrieval of Davis's remains in May 1997 from the crash site, but nothing on McPherson, who apparently bailed out at a very low altitude. Maj. Brent Davis was buried in Arlington in December 1997 with full honors including a missing-man flyover.

Douglas EF-10B (F3D-2Q) Skyknight

Air combat successes at night in Korea meant vindication for the F3D-2 Skyknight (later the EF-10B), a portly plane developed in response to 1946 Navy requirement for a night fighter and accused by detractors of being ugly, ungainly, and underpowered. During the early 1950s, most of the publicity went to the better-known Marine Air jets like the F2H

Banshee and F9F Panther, but it was the big, fat, slow, twin-engined, two-seat F3D Skyknight that got the kills in Korea.

The first Skyknight, the XF3D-1 prototype, made its initial flight on March 23, 1948, at Muroc, California. The F3D entered service in 1950 with Navy composite squadron VC-3 and Marine Air's VMF (N)-542, "Flying Tigers."

Douglas Aircraft Company built 268 Skyknights at its El Segundo, California, plant between 1948 and 1957, including three XF3D-1, twenty-eight F3D-1, and 237 F3D-2 models.

When the jet era was beginning, the Navy went shopping for a new aircraft that would be an ambitious leap forward—a jet-powered, radar-equipped, carrier-based fighter capable of doing battle in bad weather and during the nocturnal hours. It became the aircraft that was known during the Vietnam era as the EF-10B Skyknight.

The first XF3D-1 Skyknight took to the air on June 23, 1948. It was a blue, whale-shaped airplane with a pair of Westinghouse J34 jet engines. The crew of two sat side by side in a spacious cabin enclosed by a braced cockpit.

In the book *Night Fighters Over Korea*, written with E. T. Wooldridge, the late Capt. Gerald G. O'Rourke described the Skyknight from a pilot's perspective:

"A transport-type cockpit flared into the nose, just above a huge semiglobal radome [radar dome]," O'Rourke wrote. "To get in, you climbed up the engine nacelle onto the high wing, walked forward atop the fuselage, slid back a flat square glass door, and dropped down into a spacious cavern that seemed more like a control room than a cockpit. Once you were in the left seat, the view forward and to port was fine, but astern there was just a metal bulkhead. To starboard there was the space for the [radar operator] and all the radar controls, a distant console, and a high sill. Visibility, then was similar to that of a transport, as was the high wing."

The Navy's use of the Skyknight drew so little notice that a respected reference book, *U.S. Navy Aircraft Since 1911*," by Gordon Swanborough and Peter M. Bowers states—erroneously—that, "Operational use of the F3D-2 was exclusively by Marine squadrons." During the Korean War, Marine Skyknights shot down six enemy aircraft. But the Marines had company. By the end of the war, Navy Composite Squadron 4, or VC-4, also participated in the fighting.

The EF-10B Skyknight was designed to detect enemy aircraft with radar and shoot them down with cannons, but it entered service just as the United States was developing air-to-air missiles. Long before the Skyknight became a collector of electrons in Vietnam, this EF-10B (known at the time as an F3D-2M) was testing Sparrow missiles in California in 1956.

[U.S. Marine Corps]

Douglas F3D-2 Skyknight

Type: two-seat carrier or land-based night and all-weather fighter

Powerplant: two 3,400-lb (1542-kg) thrust Westinghouse J34-W-36/36A turbojet engines

Performance: maximum speed 565 mph (909 km/h) at 20,000 ft (6095 m); cruising speed 390 mph (628 km/h); initial climb rate 4,000 ft (1220 m) per minute; service ceiling 38,200 ft (11645 m); range, 1,200 miles (1931 km)

Weights: empty 18,160 lb (8237 kg); maximum takeoff 26,850 lb (12179 kg)

Dimensions: wingspan 50 ft (15.24 m); length 45 ft 6 in (13.97 m); height 16 ft (4.88 m); wing area 400 sq ft (37.16 sq m)

Armament: four fixed, forward-firing 20-mm cannons, with 200 rounds per gun

Crew: two (pilot and radar operator)

First flight: March 23, 1948 (XF3D-1); February 13, 1950 (F3D-1); February 14, 1951 (F3D-2)

Contrary to plans, the Skyknight operated aboard aircraft carriers only briefly. However, the Navy used specialized versions to test missiles and radar units and to train night-fighter crews. When the F4H-1 Phantom II fighter (later called the F-4) was introduced in 1960, the Navy trained its crews aboard a modified Skyknight model called the F3D-2T2.

When the Pentagon system for naming airplanes was overhauled in 1962, the F3D series became the F-10 series. The Navy retired most of its Skyknights soon afterward, but a Marine Corps version used for electronic countermeasures and intelligence gathering, the EF-10B, flew combat missions in Vietnam.

Today, a Vietnam-era EF-10B Skyknight is part of the National Museum of the Marine Corps at Quantico, Virginia.

Skyknight in the Korean War

Just after midnight on November 2, 1952, an F3D-2 Skyknight flown by Maj. William T. Stratton and M. Sgt. Hans Holind made radar contact high over North Korea with an enemy Yakovlev Yak-15 jet fighter.

When they drew closer, Stratton saw the orange glow of the Yak's jet exhaust. He fired three short bursts of 20mm cannon fire. The Yak went down in flames, leaving the Marine Skyknight crew flying through smoke and debris.

This was history's first jet-versus-jet aerial victory at night. A week later, on November 8, 1952, F3D-2 pilot Captain O. R. Davis repeated the feat by shooting down a MiG-15 northwest of Pyongyang, the North Korean capital.

This night action during the Korean War was vindication for the whale-shaped F3D Skyknight (later called the EF-10B), a portly plane developed in response to 1946 Navy requirement for a night fighter. The first Skyknight flew on March 23, 1948, at Muroc, California. The F3D entered service in 1950 with Navy squadron VC-3 and the Corps' VMF(N)-542, "Flying Tigers."

Enemy fighters were a serious threat to U.S. B-29 Superfortress bombers operating over North Korea. As part of the response, on May 26, 1952, Marines of squadron VMF(N)-513, "Flying Nightmares," commanded by Col. Peter D. Lambrecht began flying at Kunsan, South Korea.

Lambrecht was killed in action in August. Col. Homer G. Hutchinson took the helm.

On December 10, 1952, the VMF(N)-513's crew of 1st Lt. Joseph A. Corvi and Sgt. Dan George shot down a Polikarpov Po-2 night intruder without ever seeing it, using radar only. Another F3D crew, Maj. Jack Dunn and M. Sgt., Lawrence Fortin shot down a MiG-15 on January 12, 1953.

On January 28, Capt. James R. Weaver's F3D claimed another MiG, and three days later, Lt. Col. Robert F. Conley claimed the sixth and final Skyknight aerial victory of the Korean War. Conley had just taken command of VMF(N)-513 from Hutchinson, and his MiG also counted as the tenth and final aerial kill for all Marine night fighters (F4U Corsair, F7F Tigercat, and F3D Skyknight).

The F3D Skyknight went on to a long career. The F3D nomenclature was changed to F-10 in 1962 (the F3D-2Q model then in service became the EF-10B), and the Skyknight went on to serve the Marine Corps as an electronics intelligence platform in Vietnam. The Marine Corps has an EF-10B Skyknight at Quantico, Virginia, ready for display when a new museum opens there in the near future.

Chapter Fifteen

Thud Down in North Vietnam

What Happened

They called it "Thud," the "Sled," and sometimes just the "One Oh Five." When loaded and armed, it may have been the heaviest single-seat warplane ever to go against an enemy. The men who sat in its cockpit, and who stared down at Hanoi, scratch their heads today with the realization that half a century has passed since its debut.

On October 22, 1955, civilian test pilot Russell M. "Rusty" Roth took off from Edwards Air Force Base, California, to begin the 45-minute first flight of the YF-105A, the first example of the plane better known as the Republic F-105 Thunderchief. Fifty years after this historic first flight, the F-105 is remembered as the powerful, robust fighter-bomber that spearheaded Operation Rolling Thunder—the first sustained U.S. air campaign over North Vietnam from 1965 to 1968.

The F-105 was designed for atomic war with the Soviet Union. It had an internal bomb bay capable of carrying Mk. 28, B-43, and B-61 nuclear bombs. On conventional missions, the big, robust F-105 carried about 20,000 pounds (9075 kg) of bombs, or more than a World War II B-17 Flying Fortress bomber.

At one point in 1965–68, it was calculated that an F-105 pilot stood only a 75 percent chance of completing a hundred missions over North Vietnam without being killed or captured. Beginning with its first mis-

Major Charles C. Vasiliadis
May 3, 1967
Republic F-105D Thunderchief
(62-4405)
333rd Tactical Fighter
Squadron, 355th Tactical
Fighter Wing
Takhli Air Base, Thailand

Charles C. "Vas" Vasiliadis was one of the first U.S. Air Force pilots to fly the mighty F-105 Thunderchief, at Eglin Air Force Base, Florida. He was later shot down in one over North Vietnam. Vas's combat tour in the F-105, alias the Thud, came after a stint in Vietnam flying the prop-driven A-1 Skyraider.

[U.S. Air Force]

---

sion on March 2, 1965, when F-105s attacked the Xom Bong ammunition depot north of the 17th Parallel, the actual odds against a pilot surviving may actually have been higher.

The F-105 may have suffered higher loss rates than any other combat aircraft in history—evidence not of any flaw in the aircraft but of the intensity of North Vietnam's defenses. Howard Plunkett, author of *F-105 Thunderchiefs* and a researcher of F-105 statistics, said that of 833 Thunderchiefs built, some 682 F-105D and F-105F models were available for operations in Southeast Asia. Of that number, 333 were lost in combat and sixty-three in accidents, a 58 percent loss rate.

But often, the F-105 came home safely despite battle damage. On June 28, 1966, attacking a highway bridge in North Vietnam, Major William McClelland was hit by an 85mm shell that exploded in his underwing pylon, continued laterally along and through the wing, and tore out everything for about four feet. Despite the great drag generated by this enormous hole and protruding wing sections, McClelland nursed his craft home.

Two Air Force pilots were awarded the Medal of Honor while flying the F-105 in Southeast Asia, colonels Merlyn Dethlefsen and Leo Thorsness. Although the F-105 was not designed as a dogfighter, its pilots shot down twenty-nine MiGs during Vietnam fighting.

This is an F-105 Thunderchief high over North Vietnam, but it's not just any F-105. Aircraft no. 62-4405 is the actual aircraft from which Major Charles C. "Vas" Vasiliadis ejected over North Vietnam on May 3, 1967. In this view, the light-colored shape beneath the fuselage is part of an F-4 Phantom II flying behind the Thunderchief.

[U.S. Air Force]

The Air Force operated F-105A, F-105B, and F-105D single-seaters, and F-105F and F-105G two-seaters, many of the latter used in "wild weasel" missions against North Vietnamese surface-to-air missile sites. The F-105C and F-105E were versions that were designed but never built.

Today, not a single Thud is in airworthy condition in the world, but many are on display in museums, The National Museum of the Air Force in Dayton, Ohio, has an F-105D painted to represent an aircraft of the 357th Tactical Fighter Squadron of the 355th Tactical Fighter Wing based at Takhli Royal Thai Air Base in Thailand. Visitors to the museum frequently speak of how poignantly the display reminds them of what it was like to fly against Hanoi's defenses.

CHARLES VASILIADIS. I was coming off my strafing run. I pulled my nose above the horizon and was making about 560 knots. I jinked hard left, and then jinked hard right. The North Vietnamese antiaircraft artillery, or triple-A, always shot in front of a moving aircraft. A series of jinking maneuvers was intended to throw them off. I never heard or felt anything tearing into my fuselage, but after I jinked, my aircraft felt a little squirrely.

I put my hand down and pushed down on the first of two stability augmentation controls. My first thought was that I was doing something wrong in the cockpit. "Vas, don't manhandle the airplane!" I said aloud to myself. I still didn't realize I'd been hit. Then, I looked down at my number-one utility gauge and it read zero. I had lost my hydraulics and this, in turn, had disabled the stability augmentation.

Even though I was number two in the flight, I was now in front of Tom Leeson. He was pulling off the target. I got on the radio: "Lead, this is Two. Continue pulling off high to your right. I'm passing you low to your left. I've been hit!"

I wanted Tom to do a visual look-over to see whether I could stay in the air. But Tom was already on the radio to CROWN control to start a rescue mission. I was getting ready to tell Tom this was premature. That's when I lost my radio and the master caution light came on. So right after my final transmission, I got rid of everything that might be weighing my plane down. We carried a multiple ejector rack or MER, two 450-gallon tanks, a jamming pod on the left wing, and an AIM-9 Sidewinder on the right wing. I jettisoned all that stuff and put my F-105 on afterburner at about 16,000 feet (4880 m), thinking that I would try to get as far south as possible. Now that we no longer had voice communication, Leeson was looking out at me from his cockpit and giving a thumbs up, meaning: "Get out of there! Get out of that airplane!"

The F-105 was a great aircraft, and I was privileged not only to fly it but also to be one of the early guys on the airplane. My experience with the F-105 actually pre-dates my Vietnam combat tour in the propeller-driven A-1 Skyraider. I flew the F-105 at Eglin Air Force Base, Florida, in the early 1960s.

Getting Assigned

When I came home from my first tour in Vietnam, Tactical Air Command was taking measures to standardize the tactical air force. A one-star, T. D. Robertson, was empowered by TAC commander Gen. Walter G. Sweeney Jr. to stand up a 4450th Stan Eval Group (standards and evaluation). T. D. Robertson says, "How about coming up here to TAC to be my F-105 systems officer? We're going to write manuals on standardization, on how we're going to standardize the takeoff, handling rules, and so on." I say, "Okay." I go up to TAC headquarters at Langley Air Force Base, Virginia. My wife, Joannie, is pregnant with our second son, Doug, so I ship her up to New York to live with her mother because we don't have a house near Langley. I go up to Langley in December or January. Doug is born in February 1962. By then, I've bought a house near the base. Now, I've become the F-105 guy but just as I'm getting settled into the job, Col. Abner Aust wants me to become the A-1 Skyraider flight examiner. They're starting a tactics and techniques group. I promised Joannie I would come back home to America after my tour in the Skyraider in Southeast Asia, but now an opportunity to return to Asia opened up.

I can stay at TAC and be the A-1 flight examiner or go to Okinawa and fly F-105s with the 6002nd Stan Eval Group. Those are the two choices they've given me. My previous tour in A-1s in Southeast Asia qualifies me on the housing list at Kadena. So I say no to the A-1 job. I say, "I'll tell you what. I'm going to go with the F-105 at Kadena."

See, at this point in time, the F-105s are hitting North Vietnam. Earlier, when I was in Vietnam in Skyraiders, we weren't bombing the north, so there was no chance for big-time missions with a robust jet like the F-105. Now, I want to go back to where the big boys are. I say, "Make me the F-105 Stan Eval officer at Kadena," and they do it. I finish my tour at Langley. They send me TDY to some place to bone up on the F-105. And then, we're off to Okinawa. Not long after that, I'm in Thailand flying the Thud against targets in North Vietnam.

On May 3, 1967, they brief us for three targets. The weather is crappy. The primary target is somewhere around Route Package 6, near Hanoi. The first alternate was on the other side of Thud Ridge, that long string of mountain slopes near Hanoi. The second alternate was Dien Bien Phu. We were flying near Son La on Route 6, a main highway into China. I was flying number two on Tom Leeson. Jim Baldwin was number three and Mac Houston was number four. We dropped our bombs on the second alternate and were in a turn near Son La, when we saw truck tracks going from the highway into a clump of trees.

We still have a full load of 20-millimeter. We can strafe them. So Tom Leeson goes in first. And he squirts. I'm behind him, and I'm checking because we're not sure what we might encounter here. I'm checking along the left side, and then the right side, and I think, "Well, hell, I may as well squirt some, too." This was a really easy mission, actually, or at least until I got shot down.

So I strafed. I hosed the trees. I didn't get any secondary explosions, so I couldn't tell whether I was hitting stored petroleum, or munitions, or what. As I'm pulling on out and get my nose above the horizon, I start jinking left and right, and that's when everything goes wrong. That's when I think, "Uh-oh." And that's when Tom Leeson is signaling to me to bail out.

I have to make a decision. I'm heading south, roughly 190 degrees. At least I'm going in the right direction, thank God for that. I see little hills to the southwest with a nice build-up of foliage. I say, "Well, I could slow down to three hundred knots, make a controlled ejection, and hope they can get me." But those welcoming hills are awfully close to North Vietnamese troops.

Crisis Aloft

Then I think, "I'm too far north. I'll end up a prisoner of war. And I don't know when this stupid war is going to be over. So I think I'd better just take my chances and stay with this airplane."

So I plug in the afterburner. I hit the emergency jettison and clean up the airplane, and continue on 190 degrees. After the master caution light, the fire warning light comes on. The light warning that my landing gear isn't safely locked comes on, too, which might mean my wheels could pop out into the airstream. I say to myself, "I don't know how long this airplane is going to stay like this." By now, I know it's a hydraulic fire.

Leeson has moved over to my left side. I have gone up possibly another thousand feet. I'm supersonic at about 17,000 feet (5180 meters), and my F-105's central air data computer is still working, but Leeson is using hand signals to tell me: "Eject now! Get out, now!"

But I'm saying to myself, "I'm moving at eleven or twelve miles per minute." That's how fast I'm moving toward being safe from a lot of people who want to kill me. I'm thinking, "I must be getting close to Laos." I'm flying at 535 knots now, and a safe bailout speed is 300. The F-105's gear-down speed is 275 knots. So if my gear flops down when I don't want it to, who cares? I'll be gone by then." My number-two hydraulic system is still working after number one failed, and I'm still thinking I can keep humming on down and getting farther south.

I think, "I've got a tailhook. I'll try to make it to Udorn [Thailand] and use my hook to catch the mid-field barrier"—because I know I don't have any brakes or anything like that. But Leeson is watching my

A pair of F-105 Thunderchiefs takes off for a mission against targets in North Vietnam. These "Thuds" are each carrying six 750-pound bombs under the fuselage plus a 450-gallon fuel tank under each wing. The F-105 suffered a 58 percent loss rate in Southeast Asia.

[Fairchild Hiller Corp.]

airplane melt around me, because it's a hydraulic fire, not a fuel fire, and he's still gesturing: "Vas, get the hell out, now!" I'm still thinking, "I'm going to fly a little longer," when the airplane pitches down.

It yawed hard to the right and pitched down. I applied full left stick and full left rudder. The stick locked, and that's when I knew I'd lost every system in the airplane, so I went for the ejection handle, put my head back, and bailed out at about 535 knots. You are not supposed to eject from an F-105 when flying that fast. I remembered reading the manual where it cautioned that serious injury could result from bailing out at that speed.

The canopy goes. And I'll tell you something. Things slow down. Everything happens in slow motion. The canopy goes. I've got my hands in the right position and my head tucked, and I'm thinking, "Okay, the seat's going to go in three-tenths of a second." Then, all of a sudden, I'm seeing all this in slow motion. I feel the slipstream hitting me in the face, then on the shoulders, and then lower down, as the seat pushes me straight up out of the airplane.

Everything seems to take an eternity. The seat separates from me and I'm free falling. I lose consciousness.

In the Parachute

I swear to God, while I'm unconscious floating through the air over North Vietnam, my mother talks to me. She says, "Charlie, my boy, please be careful. You know how I worry about you." And I say to her, "Spudsie, don't worry. Everything's going to be all right." And that's when I come back from unconsciousness. This is happening at 8:00 A.M. in North Vietnam, which is 8:00 P.M. on the east coast of the United States. Later, I learn that at that exact moment halfway around the world, my mother is driving along a road in Long Island with my father and she says, "Dad, something has happened to Charlie. I just know it." My father says, "Mama, don't worry about Charlie. He can take care of himself." Later on, I went over this story with my mother and father again and again, and you can believe me, some kind of communication happened at that instant even though we have no human explanation for it.

I'm free-falling into North Vietnam. Or is it Laos? I'm not sure. The aneroid barometer on my parachute is set to open a thousand feet above the highest terrain. So far, my chute hasn't opened. I'm free-falling. And the pain is indescribable. My leg is coming out of my belly button.

When I came out of the airplane, I had my left foot on the rudder. My foot was there because I was trying to hold the airplane steady. When I went for the ejection handle, I expected to be in the correct position when I went out of the airplane, but I wasn't. The ejection seat has nylon rope leg garters that are supposed to pull your legs into the correct position for an ejection, but something went wrong with my left leg and it was battered on the way out of the F-105. Back at the plant where they made the airplane, they later redesign and rebuild the whole design because the leg garters didn't work right during my ejection. After my ejection and their investigation at the plant, they discontinue the use of the leg garters—but that doesn't help me now.

There isn't a nerve, a muscle, or a blood vessel intact in my leg. My left leg is a dead piece of meat. Finally, the parachute opens and I'm hanging there, and I'm in really awful pain. Tom Leeson's F-105 is overhead. He's trying to cover me.

When I'm free-falling, I'm in a cannonball. I'm cursing and moaning and clutching my gut because the pain is killing me. I don't know my left leg was coming out of my belly button. I expect a hard fracture to the left femur, which is what normally happened to people that eject from F-105s. I say to myself, "Well, I know I've got an aneroid barometer that's supposed to open my chute, but I'd better get my hand on the D-ring in case I'll have to pull the ripcord." So I put my hand on the D-ring and just at that moment the chute pops open.

I go unconscious again. I regain consciousness again. I'm looking down.

I will tell you, the countryside is gorgeous. I'm right on the border of North Vietnam and Laos—remember, I was thinking of making it to Udorn and landing on afterburner—and it's a spectacular scene of color and beauty.

So I come on down, and I see a stream, and long huts. I'm trying to stick my ass in a sling, and I'm, really hurting, I'm, in pain, and I say to myself, "I think you'd better let yourself go back to being unconscious again." I do. And I'm awakened again with this sensation of oscillating. My parachute is oscillating. I say to myself, "Vas, you've got to resist the urge to go under. You've got to wake up and be ready for the PLF [parachute landing fall]." And I say, "Vas, take this arm and stick it between the risers and get into a good position here, because your left leg is all fucked up."

I hit the ground hard.

Evidently, the parachute gets a sudden blast of air inside the canopy and then deflates just as I hit, so I hit the ground really hard. Thank God I still have my helmet on, chin strap and all, because now I knock myself out again from the impact. And then I come to again, lying on the ground on a 45-degree incline. The parachute comes down right on top of me, with its orange and white panels against the green foliage, flowers, and elephant grass—so I'm lying there and I'm highly visible to anyone who might want to find me, which could mean rescue forces or North Vietnamese infantrymen. I wonder if the North Vietnamese appreciate us for those bright orange panels.

Down in North Vietnam

My concern is, "Do they see me?" I haven't used a survival radio yet and haven't been in touch with anybody. I can see Leeson in his F-105 still circling on top of the terrain. I try to get to my survival radio, which is inside my harness, but I can't straighten out my damaged leg to reach the radio. After some effort, I manage to kick away the parachute restraints. Now, I'm unencumbered by the parachute, but I've got to be able to turn over to pull my radio out of its pouch. Apart from the leg, I also have a fractured knee and have no movement below it. Those are my injuries, caused by my high air speed in the F-105 when I ejected: I'm in excruciating pain, can't move, and can't pull out the radio.

I'm woozy. I'm sweating. I'm about ready to go unconscious yet again. I say to myself, "Vas, knock it off. You can't afford to go unconscious." I'm wondering whether the North Vietnamese are going to come upon me at any second.

All of a sudden, to my left, here comes this goddamned Skyraider. This was the prop plane I flew on my earlier tour, and it's also the plane that escorts and covers rescue forces, using the radio call sign Sandy. I look up and the Skyraider comes right overhead and rocks its wings, signaling that he sees me. I'm hurting real bad but now I'm smiling, too. I say to myself, "Vas, if the Sandys are here, the Jolly Green can't be too far behind." The A-1 Sandy flight and the HH-3E Jolly Green helicopter were in a holding position ready to move in if anyone got shot down today—they do that every day, throughout the entire goddamn war. Radio calls from Tom Leeson and Jim Baldwin brought them in. I guess Baldwin marshaled them in while Leeson covered me.

The pararescue jumper, or PJ, who rescues me is Mike Benno. He comes down from the helicopter, lowered by the chopper's hoist. I was never so glad to see anybody in my life. I was very badly battered—the injury to the leg has been a problem throughout the rest of my life—but when Mike (whose name I learned later) hauled me into that helicopter, I felt I was one really lucky F-105 pilot.

At Korat Army Field Hospital, I wake up and put my hand down here. And my leg isn't coming out of my belly button any longer. This doctor is standing there. I say, "Shit hot, Doc! You fixed it! How long before I can fly?" He looks at me. He says, "You kidding?" I say, "No, I'm not kidding you. You fixed it! How long before I can fly?" So he takes out a pen. And he jabs me—here, and, and here. And he says—the expression I used earlier—"There isn't a nerve, a muscle, or a blood vessel intact in that leg. If we save the leg, and that's only if we save it, walking will be a bonus." And I say to him, "I want to tell you something, Doc. I have to tell you about me. I have a secret weapon." He says, "Yeah?

Who's Who

Major (later Col.) Charles "Vas" Vasiliadis, F-105 Thunderchief pilot, 333rd Tactical Fighter Squadron, 355th Tactical Fighter Wing, Takhli Air Base, Thailand

Major (later Col.) Tom Leeson, F-105 Thunderchief pilot, 333rd Tactical Fighter Squadron, 355th Tactical Fighter Wing, Takhli Air Base, Thailand

Staff Sgt. Mlke Benno, pararescue jumper (PJ), HH-3E Jolly Green Giant helicopter

---

What's that?" I say, "I've got good, high-protein Greek blood. I'm going to fly again."

Home from War

After the doctor tells me my leg will never work, they send me to Okinawa, where my wife is. She's pregnant with number three son, Roger. I step out of the C-130 at Kadena and see my wife. I say, "You've got to be shitting me! Look at that belly!" Joannie says, "I can see from that grin on your face that you're going to be okay." They told her that I was hurt ejecting from my F-105 over North Vietnam, but they didn't describe my injuries to her. Col. Bob Scott who was the F-105 wing commander at Korat—and had been with me at the test squadron at Eglin—called her, but she still didn't know my condition.

They take me to the Army field hospital on Okinawa. I say, "I'm going to fly again. I'm going to fly the F-105 again." The medic shakes his head. My blood count is down. I'm bleeding internally. They want to give me a blood transfusion. My leg is yellow, but the skin isn't broken and there's no bleeding. And I won't let them because I don't want to dilute that good high-protein Greek blood.

In October and November 1967, we lose sixty-six F-105s in the campaign over North Vietnam. There aren't enough pilots to make the frag. So I call a friend at Pacific Air Forces and say, "I want to go back." He tells me to write a letter volunteering to return to Southeast Asia to complete a hundred missions. I write the letter. The operations officer at

Over North Vietnam, F-105s often operated in flights of four. Many of the advantages of the F-105, including its high speed, were negated when the aircraft was heavily laden with bombs. Even then, the F-105 could often survive a hit form Hanoi's dreaded antiaircraft artillery, or Triple-A.

[U.S. Air Force]

Korat Air Base, Thailand, comes and gets me and picks me up in a C-130. I didn't want to go back to Takhli because I was flying their airplane when I was shot down, so I got myself assigned to Korat. I flew again and flew again in combat, in the F-105.

Republic F-105 Thunderchief

The Republic F-105 Thunderchief, called the "Thud" by pilots, was the biggest, heaviest, and loudest warplane of its era—in many ways the "most" aircraft ever entrusted to one pilot in a single-seat cockpit.

Men who flew the Thud, or who worked on it, will never forget the throaty roar of an afterburner takeoff by this swept-wing giant. The

F-105 was an impressive sight, whether sitting on a parking apron or flying at twice the speed of sound. In time, this great fighting machine was to bear the awful burden of the Americans' 1965–68 aerial campaign against North Vietnam.

The manufacturer of this great jet is sometimes called the "Republic Iron Works" because it produced beefy, sturdy combat aircraft. The best known was the P-47 Thunderbolt of World War II, and in some ways the F-105 was a kind of latter-day " 'Bolt," conceived by an engineering team headed by the same designer, Alexander Kartveli.

Early plans to use an engine other than the Pratt & Whitney J75-P-19W turbojet foundered, resulting in delays. But the F-105 also showed innovation. Its long fuselage made use of area rule, or the "wasp waist," a new shape that channeled the airflow most effectively for good performance beyond the speed of sound.

After the first flight of the prototype, the first operational F-105 made its maiden trip into the skies on May 26, 1956.

The Thunderchief had proved itself superior to a competing design, the North American F-107, but it was plagued by early difficulties in manufacturing and flight test, which—for a time—seemed to suggest that the future of this aircraft was in jeopardy. At the very time the United States became deeply embroiled in Vietnam in the early 1960s, these early troubles were resolved and F-105s began rolling off the factory line at Farmingdale, New York.

The initial concept for the Thud had called for an internal bomb bay, capable of carrying the nuclear weapons that became so numerous during the Cold War years. After the Thud entered service in May 1960, this bay was usually used to carry a 700-gallon (1476-liter) fuel tank, while a formidable load of up to eight 750-lb (340-kg) bombs was carried beneath the fuselage and wings.

The two-seat version of the Thunderchief was 2,000 pounds (907 kg) heavier, began life as a combat-capable trainer, and evolved into a "Wild Weasel" used to suppress enemy surface-to-air missiles, or SAMs. Two-seat F-105F and F-105G Wild Weasels may have had the most dangerous mission of all when operating at low level against SAM sites: losses were high.

It is almost impossible to exaggerate the difficulties that confronted F-105 pilots after they were deployed to Thailand to begin long-range bombing of North Vietnam in Operation Rolling Thunder (1965–68).

This is a bomb-laden Republic F-105 Thunderchief on a 1967 mission over North Vietnam.

[Republic Aviation]

Republic F-105D Thunderchief

Type: single-seat fighter and fighter-bomber

Power plant: one 24,500-pound (1112-kg) thrust Pratt & Whitney J75-P-19W turbojet engine with afterburner

Performance: maximum speed, 1,390 mph (2337 km/h) or Mach 2.1 at 36,000 ft (10970 m); rate of climb 34,000 ft (10485 m) per minute in clean configuration; service ceiling 41,200 ft (12560 m); ferry range 2390 miles (3846 km)

Weights: empty 27,500 lb (12474 kg); maximum overload takeoff 52,838 lb (23967 kg)

Dimensions: wingspan 34 ft 9 in (10.59 m); length 64 ft 4 in (19.61 m); height 19 ft 7 in (5.97 m); wing area 385 sq ft (35.77 sq m)

Armament: one 20-mm General Electric M61 Vulcan, or "Gatling," cannon, with 1,028 rounds, plus up to 25,000 pounds (11340 kg) of bombs, rockets, and missiles, including the Martin AGM-12 Bullpup air-to-surface missile

First flight: October 22, 1965 (YF-105A); June 9, 1959 (F-105D)

Every mission involved aerial refueling. Bad weather was a constant. Once in battle, the F-105 pilot was far from his home base, deep into the enemy's lair.

In the first air-to-air encounter in April 1965, North Vietnamese MiG-17s sneaked up on a flight of bomb-carrying Thuds and shot down two without being seriously challenged. In their first attack on a bridge near Hanoi, F-105 pilots seethed with frustration while their Bullpup missiles bounced off the target or detonated with little effect. It became clear over time that the best weapon for the Thud was the ordinary "iron" bomb. The Bullpups were soon discarded.

As the campaign up north evolved, F-105 pilots found themselves flying against some of the most formidable air defenses in history—a lethal mix of antiaircraft guns, MiGs, and surface-to-air missiles.

Always intended for air-to-ground action, the Thud was never ideal for a dogfight with MiGs. But because of the sheer brute force and structural prowess of this big aircraft, a MiG pilot could never be certain of a kill, even after zeroing in. F-105s badly damaged by gunfire and missiles repeatedly brought their pilots home, safe and sound. And while less nimble than their skyward adversaries, F-105s shot down dozens of North Vietnamese MiGs, using cannon and AIM-9 Sidewinder missiles.

Today, the last F-105 is gone except for veterans that reside in museums. Republic Aviation Co., which manufactured 25,000 fighters, no longer exists.

Chapter Sixteen

Dragonfly Squadron

What Happened

During the Vietnam War, Air Force pilots flew an air-to-ground attack aircraft that resembled the service's familiar primary training plane. But the surest way to get a reaction from an A-37 Dragonfly pilot was to confuse his aerial warrior with the T-37 "Tweet" trainer. Although the two planes look alike, the T-37 is only a distant relative of the attack plane. It taught thousands of pilots to fly but never fired a round or dropped a bomb.

"The A-37 was bigger, bulkier, and heavier than the trainer it was derived from," said Curt Richards, who flew the A-37 with the 604th Fighter Squadron at Bien Hoa, South Vietnam, in 1970.

"Yes," confirmed Richards, "it certainly was developed from the familiar trainer. But our attack plane was something very different.

"It had a bigger engine. What they always forget is, this was a sturdy combat aircraft, not a lightweight aircraft designed to teach students."

When Albert Motley, Hank Hoffman, and Curt Richards arrived in Vietnam, U.S. troop strength was at its peak, but American policy already was aimed at having the South Vietnamese take over much of the burden of their defense. The plan was to fly the A-37 in combat for a period while waiting for the South Vietnamese to transition into the plane and take over the mission.

Captain Albert E. Motley Jr.
1970
Cessna A-37B Dragonfly
604th Special Operations
    Squadron, 3rd Tactical
    Fighter Wing
Rap 01
Bien Hoa Air Base, South
    Vietnam

Capt. (later Col.) Albert E. Motley
Jr., was typical of the men who flew
the Cessna A-37B Dragonfly on
low-level missions over South
Vietnam. Motley also flew the
propeller-driven A-1 Skyraider in
combat. In stateside assignments,
he flew the F-100 Super Sabre, the
first American fighter able to
routinely fly faster than sound in
level flight.

[U.S. Air Force]

Not everybody thought this should be the Air Force's job. The Army evaluated the T-37 trainer for a potential combat role in 1958 and was first to suggest that an attack plane be developed from the trainer. The idea foundered initially because the Air Force objected to the Army flying fast jets. The borrowed Army T-37s apparently lacked wing pylons for ordnance and conducted the tests without dropping bombs or firing rockets.

AL MOTLEY. The radio call sign for our squadron was Rat. We were flying an airplane that may not have looked like much compared to the F-100 Super Sabre or the A-1 Skyraider, both of which I also flew. The A-37 was just a plain old ordinary aircraft. We had no radar or anything like that. But despite a very ordinary appearance, the A-37 was the right weapon for Vietnam.

You sat on the left side (the other seat, on the right, stayed empty except for the rare occasions when you carried an observer), so you had excellent visibility out of the cockpit on the left side and ahead, but it was difficult seeing from the right. I would not have designed the airplane that way. I would not have wanted to be flying that plane in air-to-air situation. But we did not expect MiGs. We did not expect to be in a dogfight.

The gun was offset on the side. It was called a "mini-gun" or a "mini-Gatling gun," and it spat out rounds at a very high rate of speed. The gun was good against people if you could catch them in the open. It shot a lot of rounds per minute. We had just a plain little old mechanical reticule sight.

We caught ground fire just like everybody else did. No, there wasn't an air-to-air threat. There were no MiGs there. But this was hardly a permissive environment. When we flew missions at low level to support friendly troops, we could expect to get shot at.

CURT RICHARDS. Your first airplane is like your first love. You don't forget. I have over a thousand hours in the A-37B Dragonfly now, and I've flown pretty much everything the Air Force can throw at a pilot, but I still remember the first time in an A-37B.

Compared to the training plane it's based on, the A-37B weighs as much when empty as the trainer weighs when fully loaded: By the time an A-37B is fueled and armed and crewed, its gross weight is up to 14,000 pounds (6350 kilograms). So the A-37B had to be re-engined. It shares its power plant with the T-38A Talon, which is itself a simplified F-5, so you can see there's plenty of power there.

Apart from that, the main difference between the trainer and the A-37B is its undercarriage gear. To take the weight, it has to be a lot more massive. But strip an A-37B of its tip tanks, weapons pylons, and gun, paint it in training unit colors, and you could mistake the trainer for the fighter unless you looked real close.

Before Vietnam, there wasn't a requirement for an aircraft such as the A-37B. Then, the policy makers started to see how things were shaping up and they realized that there was going to be a hole in our capabilities to fight the Viet Cong. That led eventually to the A-10 Warthog, which was too late for Vietnam. Back then, they were trying to do it with the aircraft they had, and there wasn't one that was any damn good—not at close support the way the Army meant close support.

They tried the A-7 Corsair II, but the A-7 is an interdictor, not a strike aircraft. Sure, the guys who have two thousand hours in it, they

This is a Cessna A-37B Dragonfly of the 604th Special Operations Squadron, 3rd Tactical Fighter Wing, stationed at Bien Hoa Air Base, South Vietnam, and flying a mission fully loaded with bombs and napalm. The A-37B offered side-by-side seating for a pilot and observer. The pilot sat in the left seat (closer to camera, here) but the other seat was often unoccupied.

[U.S. Air Force]

can use it in the strike role, but then they could probably hit a goat's rear end using just about anything.

Then they tried close air support with the F-4 Phantom II, and that was a really miserable experience. The aircraft was just too big, too heavy, and didn't have anything in the way of pilot aids.

Then they went from one extreme to the other, got hold of some Skyraiders from the Navy, and called them A-1s. It was predictable, that switch from real fast to real slow. In between wars, the Air Force always wants to go fast. Then, when we have a war, they find out that a lot of the jobs that have to be done, they can only do them slow. In air combat, speed is life, but speed doesn't always get the job done, and that's where the A-37 comes in.

So they had the aircraft, and the next thing was to train the guys who were going to fly it. That meant survival school, gunnery school, and a replacement training unit where you learned to use the A-37B in its intended role. All of us, I think, followed pretty similar paths toward flying the A-37B in harm's way in Southeast Asia.

An A-37B Dragonfly of 604th Special Operations Squadron drops Snakeye retarded bombs on Viet Cong troops in South Vietnam. The A-37B was the only warplane capable of hauling its own weight in bombs and rockets.

[U.S. Air Force]

HANK HOFFMAN. After flying the B-52 Stratofortress in combat, I was on the verge of resigning from the Air Force because I wanted to be a fighter guy, not a bomber guy. My wing commander offered me a tour in F-4 Phantoms. After only a small amount of thinking and discussion with my wife, I agreed. I really did want to be a war hero, and about a month later I received my assignment to the A-37 Dragonfly. It wasn't the promised F-4, but I didn't complain. I was going to be a fighter pilot!

A historical note: In 1970, we started bombing in Cambodia. It was about time. That's where the enemy was. We were asked to keep the information to ourselves. The world would find out soon enough, and the Viet Cong, the VC, couldn't complain, or they'd have to admit to being there.

Even though our bombers were doing a great job, I left the Strategic

Air Command, or SAC, after 172 combat missions in the B-52, over three tours in a five-year period. I had over 2,500 hours in the B-52, including a thousand in combat. I had earned ten Air Medals and the Distinguished Flying Cross. I was so glad to go I'm not sure I can tell you. SAC sucked, but I was free! Free at last, free at last, great God in heaven, free at last! (Credit to Martin Luther King Jr.)

Terri and the kids again went to Phoenix. I checked out in the A-37B at England Air Force Base, Louisiana. During that period, I was aboard an airline flight when a hippie-looking college coed confronted me and called me a "baby killer" and then spit on me.

I have always been slow to anger; a good thing I think. I was more mystified than irate to begin with and I was still trying to understand what had happened, when two stewardesses grabbed each of us and turned us around. They put me up in first class, and that was enough to satisfy me. The bimbo went to the back, and I never saw her again. I suspect she still thinks she is a hero, instead of being lucky to have her very own original teeth.

The A-37Bs at England were the newest aircraft I had ever flown, since they were built just for close air support in Vietnam. Some of them actually had that "new car" smell.

The A-37B was wonderful for its purpose. It carried as much ordnance (or more) than the F-100, was only about one-third the target cross-section size of the F-100, used less gas, and was more accurate. It had two engines and only needed one. It had hydraulic, electric, and oxygen systems, but it didn't need anything but that one engine to make a safe landing. We took about a third as much combat damage as the F-100 because we were smaller and more nimble; F-100 pilots despised that and insisted that ours wasn't a real fighter. They must have used their egos for brains.

On my way to Vietnam, I was sent to the Philippines for survival school. This was in the jungle in the Philippines, and was cheerfully referred to as "Snake School." The training concluded with an exercise where we hid from the native Negritos for only an afternoon. This was easy; just get into the darkest, buggiest, wettest, snakiest hole you can find, and they will never find you. Just plan on being the nastiest guy in the hole, and give yourself the right attitude. I excelled because I took school very seriously and didn't have to suck up to anyone to pass. Trust me, you will want to be with me when the meteor hits Earth.

CURT RICHARDS. The maximum design speed of the A-37B is 70 percent of the speed of sound, or Mach 0.7. Above that, the nose tucks down, the stall goes across the horizontal stabilizer, and you have no elevator control, so you can't pull out of the dive you've just started. To the best of my knowledge, no one ever exceeded Critical Mach in an A-37B and pulled out of it.

All that installed power can make for some pretty hairy takeoffs. Even with full ordnance, you can't run up to full power and expect the brakes to hold you. You get up to about 85 percent and then you'll start to creep forward. Then, when you do start to move, you've got a large acceleration profile to the point where you'll be airborne in less than two thousand feet. To me, the A-37B gives you more of a kick in the back than any other aircraft without an afterburner. And when you do get in the air, you've got to climb out at a steep angle to keep from overspeeding the flaps and gear.

A lot of guys would put their hand on the gear-up lever, and they'd be putting pressure on it before they were off the ground so that the instant they broke ground, up would come the gear. I never thought that was too bright an idea myself, because the only thing you've got between you and the gear coming up is a solenoid interlock switch that stops you from raising the undercarriage while it's got weight on it, and if that switch fails—well, you'll raise the gear, all right, but that will have the effect of lowering the aircraft straight to the tarmac.

You learn all this training in the A-37B stateside, and you learn it again in Vietnam. In between, it's off to the Philippines for "Snake School" on your way to check in to your squadron.

HANK HOFFMAN. Less than twenty-four hours after survival school, I was on my way to Tan Son Nhut airbase outside Saigon, in the back of a C-130 Hercules, with a hangover. I hitchhiked a ride to Bien Hoa and kind of surprised my new unit with my arrival. They weren't prepared for a new captain, so I got to stay temporarily in the empty bunk of young 1st Lt. Tom Browning, who had been shot and was in Hawaii recovering and recuperating. His bloody parachute harness with a bullet hole in it hung on the back of the door. I saw it as an omen to get my mind right: *You are not paranoid if they really are trying to kill you!* I met Tom again, thirty-three years later, when he was a brigadier general and the liaison officer from the Reserve Forces to the governor of Arizona.

Capt. Curt Richards inspects a bomb under the wing of his A-37B Dragonfly at Bien Hoa Air Base in South Vietnam in February 1969.

[U.S. Air Force]

Some notes on Vietnam: It was hot and wet pretty much all the time. The vegetation was mostly jungle, just like the Philippines. After the harvest, they tended to clear the fields by burning them, and it made for extra-low visibility at times. The aircraft and most of the buildings had revetments around them to limit the damage done by mortars. We had Vietnamese women doing the cleaning and the laundry for a very low wage. We did not use the greenback money from the States. We used scrip, printed just for Vietnam and not good anywhere else, for security reasons that I don't fully remember.

In nine days, I was checked out solo, dropping bombs as a wingman. A week later, I was fully qualified. I flew solo most of the time, my bombs were accurate, and life was good. I still wanted to be a hero, and I figured the way to do that was just keep doing my duty.

Browning returned. The flight surgeon assigned to our unit went back to the States. I moved across the hall into a single room befitting my status as a fairly senior captain. These were the best quarters I had while flying combat. The toilet and bath were down the hall, and the squadron bar was next door behind the wall, but I was alone, and the air conditioning worked. The Army can have the rape and pillage; give me clean sheets and air conditioning!

Next door were two young men I would know the rest of my life: Curt Richards and John Lamb. Curt was a hell-raiser, and John ran the bar. John was on his second Vietnam tour, having flown the AC-47 Spooky gunship the year before. We met in unfortunate circumstances when he was holding court at the bar, declaiming that he had more combat time than anyone in the unit. I was new, so I asked him how much he had. The answer was four hundred plus hours, and I nodded and thought and told him I had just over two hundred hours more than twice that.

Well, I got to hear more about being a "Real Fighter Pilot" in capital letters and about how flying the B-52 didn't count. Still, the bottom line is to be careful about shooting off your mouth in public. You never know who is listening, and you may have to embarrass yourself with a retraction.

The squadron scheduler was a captain named Jim something or other. He was very nearly God, because he could give you duty officer or make you Rap 01. ("Rap" was the call sign of our birds, starting with the first flight of the day and numbered as the day progressed, and duty officer was ground duty and it sucked. We also flew as Hawk when we were scrambled from the alert pad.)

I pretty much did as I was told, but after flying all week as Rap 02, I asked him what was going on. The Rap 01 call sign had been preempted all week by a very senior figure we all called "Colonel Asshole." He had just completed an in-country checkout in the A-37. He had been flying the F-100, but those birds were all going home, and three squadrons of A-37Bs were all there was to fly. Since he was the 800-pound gorilla, he flew what he wanted to, and he wanted to be first up every day, which meant he got the number-one call sign.

My considered opinion is that he really was an asshole, but I didn't care what he flew, I just didn't particularly want to be in the same sky with him. He told me early on that I wasn't a real fighter pilot, and that all he wanted to hear from me on the radio was "Two" (The response I would make when I understood) or "Lead, you're on fire." This was a standard way to make the new guy feel unnecessary. I had heard it before, and I just considered it an ego statement, making him feel big by making me feel small. I still regret that I never got the opportunity to make that second transmission to him.

So I asked Captain Jim what was going on, and he told me that Colonel Asshole had declared the first three wingmen he had flown with "unqualified," and sent them back for retraining. The colonel liked his wingman to fly en route formation where he could easily see them. This meant practically flying in front of him, and not only was it was a pain in the ass, it was one of lots of things that could make you unqualified. Jim said that he did not have an unlimited supply of wingmen or instructors to requalify them, and since I was cutting it, he had given me a semipermanent job in the number-two slot. I was flattered, I guess, and I don't really know if the colonel got tired of flying Rap 01 every morning or he found another wingman, but I finally was moved out of that slot and got to go to the alert pad anyway and to relax a little.

CURT RICHARDS. In all of your stateside preparations before reaching your squadron, you never actually dropped a real bomb. All you dropped in practice were 25-pound practice bombs. Once or twice in training, you got to take off with a real 500-pounder on board—filled with sand, not explosive. Then, you got in the battle zone and everything was different.

The A-37B has two seats side-by-side, but you don't fly close support missions with an unnecessary life at risk, so the only time the right-hand seat gets used is for check flight. Your first time in the combat zone, it's going to be you sitting there, watching what an experienced pilot does and learning from him.

The next time, you fly the aircraft and he sits in the right-hand seat and checks you out. Now, remember, this is only the second time you've been under fire, and it's the first time you've dropped a 500-pound bomb so, all in all, it's a pretty stressful situation. You're a new guy and aren't supposed to drop closer than a mile away from friendly forces. Truth is, you'd be happy to drop in the right county, and sometimes the right country will do.

You do two missions like that and then a flight examiner will come along and check you out, and if he clears you then that's it. Those four introductory missions are a good idea. You feel you're ready to just go out there and do it the moment you land in-country, but there's a lot of local stuff to learn: radio channels, fueling and arming points, and forward air control procedures. You even need to learn the route around the airfield.

It was good to have that time to come to know a little about the local weather, too. It was pretty common out there to have 3,000-foot overcast and broken cloud down to 1,500 feet. That was common. That meant on bad days you might have to work in just a third of that, meaning 1,000-foot overcast. You'd get to the point where it was commonplace, and you'd think nothing of it, to go in at lower altitude than that to release the ordnance. I didn't like it. I don't think anybody liked it because you were a sitting duck to the antiaircraft artillery and had a bad time acquiring your own target. Sitting there, one plane in a daisy chain of four, waiting within three miles to roll in, just trying to keep the target in sight . . . that could be nerve-wracking.

HANK HOFFMAN. Being on alert was a much better deal in Vietnam than in the B-52. We got to fly nearly every day, sometimes three times a day, and it was usually the more exciting missions, like "troops in contact," meaning we were supporting friendlies who were battling the enemy. Now this was really flying!

We did a fair amount of drinking in the squadron. With no women to temper our judgment, our parties were outrageous. We gave the "Plumber" award, a wrench mounted on a piece of plywood, to the guy who was the worst pilot. ("As a fighter pilot, he would make a great plumber . . ."). We gave the "Friendship Beads," a set of phony shark's teeth, to the guy who did the best job of screwing his buddies. We gave out the "Top Glass" award to the guy with the biggest bar bill each month. His prize was a free drink.

Mixed drinks were twenty-five cents; beer was a dime a can. To win Top Glass, your bill had to be over $100 to even compete. Do the math. An A-37 pilot who had once been in a B-52 squadron with me won repeatedly; the man could drink. Of course, technically, you didn't have to drink it all to win, you just had to buy it, and we had games that could rapidly run up your bill. If you entered the bar with your hat on, you bought everyone present a drink, and that could very swiftly put twenty beers on your tab.

My next-door neighbor, John Lamb, ran the bar as an extra duty, and he said the revenue from it would have made a small Fortune 500 company. There wasn't actually much profit because we bought the beer for a dime, too, but there was enough profit from the mixed drinks to pay Miss Mai, a good-looking native who tended bar for us. She was almost always the only woman there. We always respected her (we did!), but she had to have seen a lot of naked drunks in her long career there, even though she disappeared when it got late and rowdy. Miss Mai kept score with a pencil, and her count was law. I have no idea how accurate it was; I was usually too drunk to care, and so was nearly everyone else not flying.

Our parties tended to nudity. A tradition had arisen such that if an officer was seen with a hole in his T-shirt, it was considered an unfit uniform, and the first to see such hole would put his finger into it and make it into a large hole. Most of the T-shirts had holes. We laughingly suspected the maids of running the T-shirts through the device used to break the buttons on our other shirts, but they might have come just from the strong detergent they used.

One man who cared was a staff lieutenant colonel, the "Staff Weenie," I'll call him, who got into the wrong party. Or maybe we got into his. The RUSTIC forward air controllers, who flew the OV-10 Bronco, were in the building, called a hooch, next door. They were good buddies of ours, and we all had credit accounts at their bar, too. Anyway, Kent Fister, Ken Frizard, and I wandered next door to have a quiet drink. Mr. Fixit (so called for his abilities as a handyman), a Capt. Ron Shoulars, had made a cannon of old Coke cans. He squirted lighter fluid into the end and torched it off with a cigarette lighter. It fired a tennis ball harder than you could throw it. He injected one with water, and it went through a wooden door; truly a fearsome weapon. That night, he was firing small (unshelled) shrimp out of his cannon, and we three were too mature to stay and risk punctures.

So we went next door. We were naked, except for combat boots. This caused no commotion, even from the girl tending the bar. Ken sat on their bar, which was constructed from a piece of a large helicopter blade, and placed his equipment on the bar. The aforementioned lieutenant colonel, the "Staff Weenie," took umbrage at this act and came over to tighten us up. Well, he was wearing a T-shirt, and things almost got very ugly. The RUSTICs gathered up their staff weenie, and I led my two back into the flying shrimp zone and the possibility of a Purple Heart. (The bar smelled obscenely for months afterward.) The next morning, our squadron commander, who knew enough to stay out of our bar, questioned me about homosexual tendencies in the squadron, and then he forgot the whole thing. It was funny and stupid all at the same time.

Another thing that happened at night that was not so much fun was the mortar attacks. The Viet Cong never did any real damage to us that I recall, but the sirens and the "whump, whump" of the explosives certainly got your attention. The concussion against the wall (if it was not too close) sounds a lot like someone throwing a football against it.

Drive into Town

The closest I came to real trouble also came at night only a few days after I arrived. I was at the Rap bar, peacefully drinking, when a couple of Australian nurses entered. This was rare, but not unheard of, and we also had the occasional Red Cross worker (or "Doughnut Dolly") stop by, too. One of them was going to spend the night with some forgotten member of the squadron, and the other asked me to drive her home. I said, "Sure! Where's your car?" and she explained that they usually stole the operations officer's jeep for the purpose. I was high enough to be up for it, and we started driving. It turns out she didn't know how to get back home, and pretty soon I drove under all these bright lights that turned out to be the main gate.

Well, I knew downtown was off limits at night. I had no ID card, no money, no weapon, a blood alcohol level that was impressive for someone actually able to see, and we were lost. We drove around until she finally got her bearings and we found the Aussie hospital. She invited me in for a drink (just what I needed), and then pointed the way back to the base. "Go this way for a while and then turn right," she said.

The street signs did not use our alphabet, and I couldn't tell one squiggle from another. I drove slowly and noticed the little men guarding the more affluent houses. They wore black pajamas and carried rifles of some kind. God must have helped me decide when to turn right, because a mile or so after I did, I again saw the bright lights of the base. I turned into it and a U.S. guard stopped me. I fully expected to be arrested, but I smiled at him and said, "Hi!" He looked at me for a long moment with barely disguised disgust, and then motioned me through. I guess he didn't feel like doing the paperwork.

This rear view of a Cessna A-37B shows the enormous load-carrying capacity of the aircraft: This one has four external tanks that could carry fuel or napalm. This also provides a good view of the landing gear, open canopy, and "cheese-grater" dive brakes.

[U.S. Air Force]

I never went into town again, day or night; and I swear my virtue remained intact, too, in spite of being easily led astray.

I was made a flight commander after about two months, only because I outranked the other guys, and I discovered that didn't mean that I really commanded anything, but was only required to write officer evaluation reports, or OERs, for young men I didn't know anything about. Well, everyone in the combat zone got a nine on his OER, but you had to say something, too, and I hated to just make stuff up, so I went to the scheduler and "helped" him.

I drew up a plan where each of the five flights would rotate through the duties together, giving me ample opportunity to reasonably evaluate each man, and it also ensured a roughly equal distribution of nasty jobs. We changed from days, to day alert, to nights, then night alert, and finally ground duties every six days, and you got at least a half a day off between shifts. Captain Jim liked it because it was easier for him to be fair to everyone, and he put it into effect immediately. I just love things that work efficiently.

We did some flying, too. I checked out as flight lead on September 19, 1970, and as instructor pilot, or IP, on November 7, in spite of not being a "real fighter pilot."

I had not been a flight lead for very long before I very nearly killed myself. We were on alert, scrambled on a "Troops in contact" call by a forward air controller, or FAC, out of Tan Son Nhut, but when we got to the target area, the FAC asked us to hold. He said he had a bunch of boats, but they had all run for the shore during the last set of fighters he had put in and now he could not see them.

Here was one of the remarkable qualities of the A-37, as compared to any other fighter. We could hold for a surprisingly long time by shutting down one engine and cruising at low speed. This gave you a kind of sideways vector because the rudder trim was not enough to cover the generated yaw, and your leg got too tired trying to hold it straight for thirty minutes at a time. I once logged 2.9 hours, the longest A-37 combat mission I ever heard of, by doing that.

The VC kept their heads down for about twenty-five minutes. They knew that the FACs got new air every twenty minutes or so, and when we didn't show (they couldn't see or hear us at 12,000 feet), and the guys supposedly behind us didn't show twenty minutes later, they assumed no air was coming and launched their little nautical armada.

They might also have known that the FAC was running low on fuel, since he was only good for a couple of hours on station in that O-1 Bird Dog. We never saw him after he marked the target, but he did call "Cleared hot!" on our every pass. I think he was in the traffic pattern back at Tan Son Nhut, taking care of number one.

Our load was napalm and CBU. CBU means cluster bomb unit— kind of like hand grenades that would scatter all over and were very effective against troops. The FAC had already briefed us to do napalm, CBU, and strafing, in that order, but as I was rolling in from 12,000 feet (I would normally have been at 3,500 feet), he asked if we could strafe first, with the bombs still on. Neither my wingman nor I had heard of such a thing, but we were pretty sure it was not illegal, so the answer came up yes, and we got very busy resetting switches and gun-sight settings and, oh yes, starting that other engine.

I finally rolled out on the first boat and squeezed the trigger. I was pretty sure they were shooting at us, too, although it was hard to detect any muzzle flashes in the daylight. Here I was, getting ready to shoot, and my gun wasn't working, and the Viet Cong were getting ready to blow my A-37B out of the sky.

Chapter Seventeen

Dragonfly Squadron (II)

What Happened

HANK HOFFMAN. I'm diving on this Viet Cong boat. They're shooting at me. My gun isn't working. That's when I find that I've forgotten the MASTER ARM switch.

At this point I should have pulled off dry, but I was so excited to actually see the enemy, I just pulled up to the last boat in line and slapped the MASTER ARM on and fired a burst right into the middle of the little thing, opening fire at an altitude that was far below the minimum permitted. I remember a vision of a man in the back of the boat steering, apparently unaffected by my holing the center of his craft.

Then I pulled the stick smartly aft and pushed the throttles full forward, expecting the usual quick performance climb of the bird, and the nose did go up, but the aircraft continued to sink. The A-37 maximum weight is about 18,000 pounds, and I had about an extra 4,000 pounds of ordnance on board, or about 22 percent more than usual. As it still continued to sink, I thought I was going to hit the small mast of the boat, was relieved to pass over it, only to find that I was still descending and was about to hit the water! Well, the thing finally bit, not much higher than ground effect (that would be about twelve feet above the water), and up I went into a cloverleaf strafing pattern.

**Captain Hank Hoffman
1970
Cessna A-37B Dragonfly
604th Special Operations
   Squadron, 3rd Tactical
   Fighter Wing
Rap 01
Bien Hoa Air Base, South
   Vietnam**

Capt. Hank Hoffman graduated
from the Air Force Academy in 1963
and flew the A-37B Dragonfly in
Vietnam in 1970 and 1971. He
went on to become a test pilot and
to fly dozens of aircraft. Hoffman
retired from the Air Force as a colonel in 1988.

[U.S. Air Force]

This is when I remembered that I could have cleaned the wings of those heavy bombs with a push of my finger on the JETTISON button. I had been frozen like a deer in the headlights.

We put in the rest of the strike, and landed safely, with about a dozen boats sunk. I guess sometimes it is better to be lucky than good, and I was definitely lucky, especially considering that I managed to hit myself with my own ricochet. But the moral of the story is that if I had been smart, I would not have needed to be lucky. I didn't really get scared until everything sank in after I landed because I didn't have time to think about it, but I came damn close to running that airplane into the water at 300 knots.

That pretty much describes my boat-strafing mission. Now, I'll describe standing alert. Here we are only a phone call away from going to war, only minutes away from enemy fire. That's when the phone rings.

I grab it from the wall and say, "Yeah?"

The voice from the command post says, "Scramble Hawk One!"

I say, "Yeah." And then I yell, "Scramble Hawk One! Come on, Chuck, that's us!" slamming the phone back onto the wall.

2nd Lt. Chuck "Plumber" Purcell is my wingman. He is ahead of me as we run for the first revetments to the left of the entry door of the

From any angle, the A-37B Dragonfly was a svelte fighter with clean lines that suddenly took on the characteristics of a dump truck when hauling voluminous amounts of ordnance. It was the only Vietnam-era warplane able to carry its own weight in bombs and rockets.

[U.S. Air Force]

alert facility. We don't know where we are going, but we're going to get there quick!

The A-37 looks tiny in its concrete nest designed for a much bigger fighter. I take one step over the side of my bird onto the survival cushion that we sit on, and plop my ass down on it while turning on the battery switch. The crew chief is holding the shoulder straps of the parachute and seat harness over my shoulders, and I slip into them. Just two buckles secure me, those for the parachute and survival kit. I push one button to start number-one engine even before the chief is gone from in front of it. At 15 percent power, it gets gas from the throttle. At 45 percent power, I start the other engine. As number-two comes up to idle, I pull forward outside the revetment and look for the "Plumber," who is only seconds behind me.

I speak rapidly on the radio: "Bien Hoa ground, Hawk One, scramble two!"

Bien Hoa says, "Hawk One clear to taxi." Plumber says, "Two!" and we are on our way, not forgetting to salute the crew chief. He will worry about us while we're gone.

We don't know the combat situation yet. We have only a FAC call sign, a frequency to join him on, and a radial direction from Bien Hoa. We will get the details when we get into the combat area.

I scan the engine start, before taxi, taxi, and before takeoff checklists as we taxi to the end of the runway. There is stop today for an armament check. The safety pins on our bombs were already pulled for quicker response when we went on alert.

There is a delay at the runway end, however. There is a crowd of aircraft ready to go, but we have priority and I taxi past all of them on the very edge of the cement to a position just behind a C-130 that fills the entire entry to the runway. There is also a delay for a Vietnamese A-1 that has an emergency landing in progress with a hung bomb.

Plumber and I pull to a halt just behind the C-130 wing on the very edge of the tarmac to wait for the emergency bird. In less than a minute, it touches down right in front of us, about a hundred and fifty feet away, and as it does, the "hung" Mark 82 500-pound bomb releases and drops the five feet from the wing to the runway. Clearly, it is no longer hung!

It is very loud in my cockpit, parked as I am very close to the C-130's much larger turboprop engine, but I can still hear the bomb hit the runway with a clang. Not a ringing clang, like a piece of pipe, but a dull clang. After all, it is not empty, but full of high explosive. It has fuses on the nose and the tail, and it should have been dropped "safe," without pulling the fuse wires, but then it should have been dropped on the enemy an hour ago, and not fallen here in front of us. It is also moving about a hundred miles an hour down the runway, sliding and picking up heat from the friction. How hot will it get? Will the fuses arm? They shouldn't but, I don't know; no one knows. I do know that I am in a vulnerable position on the ground, surrounded by fuel and more explosives in my own aircraft. I don't want to wait to find out.

Into the breathless silence generated by the bomb's fall in front of all eyes, I push the mike switch and say, "Hawk One, scramble, we want to take off now!"

The tower says, "Can you get around the C-130?"

I say, "Roger. Clear to go?"

He says, "Hawk One flight, cleared for take off. C-130, hold your position."

We taxi under its wing onto the runway. This is a clear safety violation in the States. I am using the best judgment I can swiftly come up with to get out of the area of the bomb, now well down the runway and already too hot to touch. I pull into position, give the Plumber the run-up signal, push the throttles to 100 percent, and check the gauges. I look back at Chuck who is showing me thumbs up. I tap my head, and as I move it forward to signal the action, release the brakes. Three seconds later, Chuck is on the roll, too.

There is no sign of the bomb, but we see lots of flashing light from ground vehicles alongside the runway. I take off, clean up my aircraft, and start a left turn for my wingman to join on me. I reduce to 98 percent power, and we are on our way to work.

I'm running the after takeoff check when I hear an alarming trans-mission on Guard radio frequency from one of the RUSTIC FACs who lives next door to us. He has been hit and is going down. He gives his lo-cation, and I do a little mental navigation and figure he is only about fifty miles away, and I decide that taking care of him could be more im-portant than blowing up some trees.

I transmit, "Hawk One, go 3-2-7 point 9," referring to our combat radio frequency. Chuck answers, "Two!" I call for our own FAC and explain the situation. I ask him how critical is the time on his target.

He says, "Why don't you check on the RUSTIC and get back to me later." Roger that, I think. There won't be a "troops in contact" mission today. Our hurry has been for nothing significant, but now we are avail-able to help our buddy.

Chuck and I go to Guard frequency, get the RUSTIC's frequency, and get his updated location from him. I compute a course to intercept him in my head, based on my radial from Bien Hoa and his.

He is still airborne, but has taken three rounds between his legs into his instrument panel and does not know how long he can remain so. I compute a rendezvous with him and soon see him headed almost right at us, trying to get back to Bien Hoa.

We do a rejoin on him, kind of an interesting maneuver since he is right underneath us. He is doing about 200 knots and we are doing about 300, but the join-up works out just fine. I used the TLAR system (That Looks About Right), a sort of educated guess for pilots. It at least sounds more precise than a WAG (Wild Ass Guess), which is also used by pilots. I visually check him over for leaks or obvious damage and find none. I have never flown formation with an OV-10, and I keep my dis-tance from those barely visible propellers.

He thought he was going to have to parachute down on top of the

The dense jungle canopy visible in this picture was often an obstacle to A-37B Dragonfly pilots trying to provide close air support to friendly "troops in contact." This A-37B of the 604th Special Operations Squadron is firing rockets at Viet Cong insurgents.

[U.S. Air Force]

very bad guys he'd been getting ready to put a load or two of bombs on. He found that his engines still worked, and we escorted him to high key over the base (really all we could do) and then contacted our FAC and put in our own strike a few minutes later than planned. No report of any kind was made of this action; I was not interested in inviting criticism. We just did what we needed to do.

We were soon involved in the everyday details of bombing the enemy. Calculations of drop altitudes and wind corrections, and random headings on the attacks were standard parts of staying alive. On the way home, during the first even-slightly quiet moment we have enjoyed, when I run the after-action checklist, I discover that I had not turned on the gun sight. This is not the first time, either. I'm not so sure how I can keep such accuracy without the illuminated pipper to mark the target, but I can. We bomb so often that it is kind of like learning to throw rocks. It is second nature. It just feels right.

The scientific explanation is probably something more like being able to feel the vector of the aircraft (and the attached bomb) and project it onto the ground. The very precise mil setting we use in the sight really just computes the amount the ordnance will fall below that aircraft vector, and looking carefully at the ground for minute movements can show the flight path vector. Your vector is the spot in your vision that does not move; all other points you can see move outward away from this central point, which simply gets closer and does not move either left or right or up or down. The new avionics systems will show that spot with a green triangle through the "head up" display, and you don't have to look so hard, but it's the same spot anyway. I say, just "be the bomb" and you'll get close.

Whatever it is, it is. We fly back to Bien Hoa, and seeing no bomb crater near the runway, we land and rearm and wait for the phone to ring again. Maybe this afternoon I'll get that great target and have the opportunity to be a hero. With the availability of an adrenaline high like this, who needs drugs? Well, maybe that's why we drank every day after flying; we needed the alcohol to calm down.

Later that night the RUSTIC FAC tells me he has never seen anything so beautiful in all his life as the sight of our two aircraft, belly up to him during the rejoin and showing him all those wonderful bombs under our wings. He felt saved right then, and I couldn't buy a beer for some time afterward. I guess the point is that we took care of each other in war. The president and the Pentagon were just concepts; your buddies kept you alive. This is why our wartime comrades are so important to us veterans. This is why young men want to leave the hospital to get back to their units.

In my B-52, we had bombed targets in North and South Vietnam, and also in Laos. This last was apparently a secret for some time, although how you could hide the enormous scar the B-52s made in the earth was beyond me. Sometime after my A-37 tour started, we received permission to bomb targets in Cambodia. This initially resulted in a great number of sorties (and new, rich targets) for us, and we were happy. So were the Cambodians. A large group of their military ended up at Bien Hoa in our bar, telling us about it. They were wonderful patriots, and I hope they are okay today, but I doubt it.

It also resulted in one of our pilots having to divert into Phnom Penh after losing an engine. Well, the Cambodians bought him whisky and offered him women and generally made a great fuss over him (as a representative of the United States helping them out) and the end result was that we all wanted to spend the night in Phnom Penh, too!

A few days later, I was totally bored, on duty as SOF (Supervisor of Flying), chatting with 1st Lt. Earl Combs, who was also screwed to the ground as squadron duty officer. We were chatting about going to Cambodia, and I was making the point that there was nothing else to talk about. I suggested that he pick up the phone, call the alert pad, and ask if anyone spoke French. I told him if they asked why, to tell them that I was talking to Saigon and that's all he knew.

Well, thirty seconds later the phone rang, and my buddy Curt's wingman, 2nd Lt. John Bradley had studied French in high school and the Great Secret Mission caper was on. I wrote some coordinates from the far side of Cambodia down from a chart along with a "secret word" and wandered over to the alert pad. It was usually pretty sleepy there until after nine or so, but *everyone* was up and practically salivating when I walked in shortly after seven. John, who would later become the major general in charge of all Reserve forces, had somehow found a French-English dictionary and was trying "hit my smoke" in French. I told him he should probably practice, "Good evening, Mr. Ambassador," and gave Curt the "secrets" I had supposedly gotten from our headquarters in Saigon.

I stepped back to avoid the crush as the entire room rushed to the map to locate the target, and immediately noticed that it was too far away to hit without stopping somewhere (Phnom Penh? Oh boy, oh boy!) to refuel. The hook was in solid. I went back to the squadron to laugh with Earl. But the hook was in too deep. They called us every twenty minutes or so to see how it was going, and I finally told Earl to tell them that the squadron would fill the mission with two staff lieutenant colonels and an enlisted guy from finance who happened to speak French. You already know that everyone despised the staff, and as pilots, these two were fine "plumbers." We also hated the finance office because our pay was screwed up from the day we arrived until the day we left, one way or another.

In a few minutes, I drove to the alert pad to see the result of my bombshell. Curt was enraged. He railed against staff weenies and finance by turns, and then he turned to me and said, "Say it isn't true, Hank! Say it isn't true!"

Now I had my cue on how to end the prank. I said, "Well, okay. It isn't true."

Curt looked at me strangely and said more slowly, "What isn't true?"

I said, "None of it. I made up this whole thing. I made it all up because I wanted to see how badly you guys wanted to go to Phnom Penh."

Curt grabbed for me, but I was ready and faster than he was. We

Not every flight ended perfectly. This A-37B Dragonfly had a nose wheel collapse and ended up surrounded by foam on the runway at Bien Hoa Air Base, South Vietnam, in 1970. The pilot was unharmed.

[U.S. Air Force]

went around the entire alert facility, upwards of a quarter mile, and he tired but showed no sign of stopping. We had just started a second lap in the 90-degree heat and 90-percent humidity, when the alert horn ended the chase with him having to figure out whether he wanted to kill me more than fly. Flying won out.

He eventually cooled off in the air and did not do violence to me, and that was the story of the Great Secret Mission and how I won the "Friendship Beads" at the next Rap Fest. I guess the point of that story is that if people want to believe what you have to say, they will suspend their suspicions.

After all my drinking stories, you might expect that we did some flying while intoxicated. In my opinion, that was generally just not the case, but I will confess to at least flying while hung over.

We had a Rap Fest, and I was scheduled to go on alert the next morning as Hawk 03 at 8:00 A.M. At about 11:00 P.M., the phone rang and the command post reported that Hawk 03 had just had their second flight of the young evening. Two night flights was all you got, so we were to report to the alert facility and take over alert duty early. Well, my wingman and I were both loaded, but we hadn't actually been asked to fly, so we went down the hill to the alert pad, blew off the briefing and preflight, and went to bed.

At 6:00 A.M., we were scrambled, and without thinking about it at all, found ourselves in the air. The FAC was a friend of mine, and he had called the strike in early as a favor to me. At 8:00 A.M., the crews for Hawk 7 and 8 would report, and they would have been given the flight instead of us. In fact, we were in their airplanes, loaded with napalm instead of the slick Mark 82 bombs on Hawk 3 and 4.

The FAC had eight structures for us as targets, and when I rolled in on the first one, I discovered that I could not make my eyes change focus quickly between the distant target and the near instruments. I missed. The first time ever. On the second pass, I discovered that if I just waited until the target filled the gunsight, I couldn't miss. Of course, that was far too low a release for regulations, but the napalm wouldn't hit you with a fragment like a bomb would, and no supervisors were present to disapprove. I got three of four targets. My wingman was oh for four.

By the time we returned to base, we were well into the hangover phase. The smell of breakfast cooking was simply nauseating, and we returned to bed.

At 10:00 A.M., we were called again, again on different aircraft. We drove to the squadron and took a pair of birds with no bombs whatsoever (armed only with strafe, our 7.62mm mini-gun) and flew that 2.9 hour mission I mentioned, escorting a ground convoy of frightened Cambodians without expending on a target. Upon return from that awful, mostly sideways, nauseating, hungover flight we were released from the alert pad and went home to bed again for the third time that day. I vowed not to drink for the next four hours, and to never again fly in such physical condition. I kept those promises, too.

On January 10, 1971, I was putting in a night strike deep in Cambodia when I heard my wingman say those dreaded words, "Lead, you're on fire!" I actually already knew that since the light was so bright in the cockpit that I could not see the ground. For night strikes we brought our own flares out on outboard stations numbers one and eight, and the lead pilot had to put out a new flare every couple of passes to keep the target illuminated, not to mention the ground. What had happened was that a magnesium flare had managed to light inside the flare pod (whether from accident or ground fire, I don't know) and those fires just do not go out. Soon it would light the other flares and maybe burn into the wing, and in the meantime it was making me into a wonderful target for the enemy.

I furiously flipped switches on the armament panel. I jettisoned the whole flaming flare pod and went back to work bombing. I would worry about replacing the foam rubber sucked out of my seat cushion later.

Night flying has special hazards. Without the actual horizon, it is pretty easy to get disoriented, particularly if the only light is a flare in a hazy atmosphere. Sometimes, one side of a flare looks as much "down" as the other. One night, I pulled off the target heading for downwind and another pass, when I noticed that my attitude indicator was 45 degrees in error in bank. When I moved the control stick to see if the indicator was stuck, I discovered that it was correct, and I would have been in grave danger very shortly. Anyway, I went back to work and didn't think of mentioning it at a safety meeting or anything. I very much regret this omission.

I was due to go home toward the end of February 1971. My classmate from England Air Force Base, 1st Lt. Jim Harris, was to rotate back about a week before me. In the argot of the day, he was the "shortest" man in the unit, or a "short-timer," and I was the second-shortest. But on February 1, 1971, Jim went to fly a night mission and his aircraft impacted the ground on the downwind leg in the target area. No ground fire was reported, and we all suspected disorientation caused his death, and I continue to wish that I had shared my experience with him, and with all the other pilots. Sometimes a word at the bar about an actual experience can be a far more effective learning experience than an hour in class.

Jim Harris was an awfully nice young man, a bachelor, and not half the drunk that the rest of us were. He did not deserve it, but war is a dangerous business, and death does not choose us based on merit. I know that I felt less worthy to live than Jim, and if God had chosen him instead of me, I just did not understand. Jim did not deserve to die. War takes the innocent and the guilty without regard, but I do believe that those with a "refuse to lose" attitude are taken later.

I was on alert for his memorial, when I realized that I was wearing a loaded pistol in a church, the only time this would ever happen. The unit did a "missing man" flyby for him immediately afterward, and I was unable to speak or make eye contact with my buddies for some time. We also did not speak in the corridor when we passed his padlocked room. That simple object was again an ominous reminder of our mortality, and I tried to keep my eyes away from it. But as men, we could not openly show our emotions. I had that ability at my grandmother's funeral, but I was now too manly. Sometimes being manly is not such a good thing, but I no longer had the choice.

Jim's demise convinced me of a couple of things. First, I was not as bulletproof as I thought I was, and second, my death in Vietnam would make no difference to the war or its outcome, only to my friends and relatives. Oh, and to me, of course.

To resolve the first point, I decided to take better care of my safety the remaining week of my assignment. Regarding the second point, it was apparent that we had the military ability to win the war, but that the politicians and the populace at home would not let us do it. We were shackled with very restrictive "rules of engagement" that really kept us from hurting them badly. No bombing Haiphong harbor or the electric generating plants or the dams for example. I was burned out and ready to go home.

I completed 195 combat missions in the A-37B, for a grand total of 377 missions and 1,605 combat flying hours spread out over a four-year period. I had never been a hero despite my growing collection of medals, including two Distinguished Flying Crosses, eighteen Air Medals, and nine stars on my Vietnam Service Medal.

I realized that combat was sweaty, intense, and intensely a man's game. It was sweaty, and unless you were fresh from the shower, your flight suit hung heavy upon you. It was intense because we were more alive being so close to death. Even brushing your teeth was memorable if punctuated by the concussion of a mortar round outside the hooch. This game was played for the highest of stakes, and to even think of losing might become a fatal weakness. It was a man's game, crowded with men torn from their homes and feminine influences. The aura of testosterone was palpable.

You will notice that I have not used the word "courage" despite having a bunch of medals that attest to my having it. I admit instead to a firm concept of duty, which served in place of courage for me. I did my duty as I saw it and did not even consider courage. And for me, courage was not so much a positive thing as a refusal to admit to the possibility of loss: an irreversible concept of duty that proved to be a very positive force for me. I was bulletproof, and when I drank enough, invisible, too!

CURT RICHARDS. Without the A-37B, no one would have flown under low cloud cover the way we did to engage the North Vietnamese like

The goal was to eventually hand over the A-37B Dragonfly squadrons to the South Vietnamese air arm as part of the U.S. government's "Vietnamization" program. These A-37Bs are being flown by South Vietnamese pilots at Da Nang in September 1950.

[U.S. Air Force]

that. The F-100s, the F-4s, they wouldn't have come down through the overcast to fight, and they damn well shouldn't have, either.

Down there at the Forward Edge of the Battle Area, or FEBA, the trick is to stay over your own guys as much as possible. The forward air controller, or FAC, will have gone in ahead of you, and you can bet that's where he's going to be—but then he's not flying at any more than a hundred knots, so he needs all the help he can get.

Exactly how you'd line up to come in, and the precise route you'd take, would be a matter of the terrain, the weather, and the troop deployments. With forward-firing ordnance and drop ordnance, you would want to release when you're parallel to your own guys, to minimize the chances of them getting hurt by mistake.

So you have these four or five aircraft flying in circles, but they're not concentric. The FAC, because he's only doing a hundred knots, is flying a tight pattern, staying over our guys pretty much all the time if he can. At one point on his orbit, he overflies the other guys, but that's on the leg that parallels the FEBA.

We're doing the same thing, but because we're pulling 300 knots, our orbit is a lot bigger, and accordingly the center of it is farther back than the FAC's. There's no point in flying an orbit that takes you into enemy territory; the guys who need your support are your guys, and you don't find them out there. The targets you want to hit are the targets they want to hit, and you're not going to find them out there.

Flying close together, in terrain that isn't just table-smooth, your knowledge and experience of the guys you're working with becomes really important. You get very used to flying with your wingman. It gets to the point where it's no big deal, the sort of close-proximity work you're doing, because you're in identical aircraft, you're tasked with the same job, and you know how he's going to go about it and he knows what you're going to do.

On top of that, you're watching out for him. You see the flash from his ordnance, you know that you can go in safely and that you're not going to run into him, because he's on the other side somewhere, limited by the characteristics of an aircraft that's just like the one you're flying, so he couldn't be coming back at you even if he wanted to.

The type of ordnance you were using would condition the way you made your passes. Slick Mark 82s, for example, you'd try to drop from no lower than 2,000 feet. You'd roll in from 6,000 feet in a dive angle of 30 degrees and release the weapon at 2,500 feet, at an airspeed of around 320 knots. Sometimes you'd have to go lower, but you sure wouldn't want to go lower than 1,500 feet, because that not only puts you into the small-arms envelope, but also into the bomb's own blast envelope, so you'd get hit by shrapnel from your own weapons.

With a high-drag bomb, where the fins come out and slow its fall, you can afford to get down lower, maybe to 1,000 feet, because you've still got time to get away before it hits the ground and goes off.

When dropping napalm and cluster bomb units, or CBUs, you could get in real close because there's not the blast to worry about. You'd normally drop napalm from 300 to 500 feet, depending on the terrain and sort of CBU.

Now, I know there were F-100 pilots who could do that and maybe there were even some F-4 pilots who could do it, but that's not the point. Any A-37B pilot could do it. He didn't need to be some sort of ace who could outthink and out-react and outperform the aircraft he was flying. He didn't need to be some sort of freak, the sort of freak you'd need to be able to get a bomb to within ten meters of your own guys, flying something that fast and that clumsy.

But that was what we did consistently. Guys who'd been in-country, on the job, for a year, they were almost always down to a circular probable error of ten or fifteen meters, and that's less than the diameter of the crater the bomb's going to leave when it explodes. That's what we call bulls-eye bombing.

Not all our bombing missions were in direct support of troops on the ground. Toward the end of my tour—I came home on December 1, 1970—we were going to Cambodia a lot. One of my academy classmates, Russ Voris, was killed in Cambodia. A pair of A-37Bs was sent to attack bridges about ten miles east of Kratie, Cambodia. Voris was pulling out from his pass on the bridge when his A-37B was hit by gunfire and crashed. Although Russ survived the crash and was rescued from the wreck by an Army helicopter, he died later in the day of his injuries. The Air Force lost a total of twenty-two A-37Bs in Southeast Asia, including five in Cambodia.

Russ was simply too low to eject, which illustrates how we often operated at treetop level beneath the cloud cover. At a hundred feet of altitude, your ejection seat wouldn't even clear its rails before you hit the ground.

The missions we flew into Cambodia were known as SCARs, for Strike, Control, and Reconnaissance. We called them Fast FACs. These missions involved distinct call signs. If you did it in an F-100, it was Misty. If you did it in an F-4, it was Stormy. And if you did it in an A-37B, it was Typhoon. The Fast FAC missions really consisted of loading the aircraft with enough fuel for three hours, piling on stores until you got to the all-up weight limit, and then going out to look for targets.

Among the most popular targets were bridges. Instead of flattening the whole structure, we'd just go in and drop one span—the southernmost or the westernmost, depending on the way the bridge was oriented. That was what it took to foul up the North Vietnamese who were operating in Cambodia.

Our bosses decided that the Cambodian town of Cam Pon Thong was "no friendlies remaining," and we went in and blew it away. Cam Pon Thong had been a town of around 100,000 people, though I guess most of them had left by the time we started bombing it. Over a period of weeks, we flattened it. Our squadron knocked down every building in the entire town. It was riddled with bunkers and arms dumps, and everybody wanted a piece of it, so every day we went over there, identified some feature, and just erased it.

Who's Who

A-37B Dragonfly pilots of the 604th Special Operations Squadron, Bien Hoa Air Base, South Vietnam, call sign Rap, 1970:

Capt. (later, Col.) Albert E. Motley Jr.

Capt. (later, Lt. Col.) Curt Richards

Capt. (later, Col.) Hank Hoffman

Capt. John Lamb

2nd Lt. (later, Maj. Gen.) John Bradley

1st Lt. (later, Brig. Gen.) Tom Browning (wounded in action)

1st Lt. James Harris (killed in action)

1st Lt. Russell E. Voris (killed in action)

Flying SCARs gave you a lot more freedom than flying close support. About half of the missions were preplanned, set up the day before, and you'd be fragged to hit a certain place at a certain time. The other half of your missions were Alerts, and that would happen when a unit on the ground got into difficulties they hadn't expected and needed a little help in a hurry.

We always had eight A-37Bs on alert, twenty-four hours a day. On the night missions—I flew nights most of my tour—you wouldn't use flares if you could possibly avoid it. They disoriented you and destroyed your night vision. We had them, and couldn't land with them, so we'd drop them out in the middle of the boonies after the mission was over.

A lot of the time, these missions were in support of "troops in contact," and some pretty wild things could happen. The worst times for me were situations like that, when you had to get so close to your own guys that you could never be sure . . .

One time I got one of those calls, and the guys on the ground told me to drop on their smoke. Normally, it would be five hundred meters away, or something like that, but these guys were being overrun and they told me to drop onto them, but only to use napalm and our small-caliber gun, which we called the Tiny Pistol. They were bunkered up, and they were sure that the napalm and the small-caliber rounds wouldn't penetrate to where they were. So I did it. It must have worked, too. I was awarded the Distinguished Flying Cross for that action.

Cessna A-37B Dragonfly

In 1962, the Air Force modified two T-37B trainers to become YAT-37D service-test ships. They were modified with 2,400-pound thrust J85-GE-5 turbojet engines, considerably heftier than the Continental engines used by the training fleet. The first YAT-37D took to the air on October 22, 1963. During tests, it was repeatedly shown to the public with wing pylons and various loads of bombs, rockets, and gun pods. Late in its service life, the Air Force gave the YAT-37D a new name as the YA-37A, the "Y" prefix continuing to connote a service-test function.

A few A-37A models were deployed to Vietnam in 1967, in part to assess their suitability for operation by both U.S. and South Vietnamese squadrons. These "A models" earned some disdain from pilots. As Curt Richards put it:

"Even when they'd become convinced there was a requirement for an aircraft like this, they still didn't go full speed ahead to build one. They got hold of a bunch of worn-out T-37 trainers, aircraft that had flown maybe two and a half times their design life already. They put bigger engines in, beefed up the gear, and called it the A-37A. They did have the gun, but they weren't air-to-air refuelable. They sent three squadrons of them off to Southeast Asia to see if they could do the job. They could, and pretty soon the B models came along and they could refuel, and that just about tied up the package."

The manufacturer, Cessna Aircraft Co., of Wichita, Kansas, began testing the definitive A-37B, which had provision for in-flight refueling, a strengthened airframe, and improved J85-GE-17A engines. Cessna built 557 A-37Bs between 1967 and 1970. The A-37 series was given the popular name Dragonfly, though pilots and maintainers rarely used it.

Air Force pilots flew air-to-ground missions, and some helped train the South Vietnamese to fly the aircraft. The A-37B received few headlines, but it was frequently on the scene for close air support when friendly troops were under attack.

Fredric Neumann, a maintainer who served with the 604th Fighter

Squadron in Vietnam, said, "The A-37 followed the KISS principle ('keep it simple and stupid'). It was well equipped for operations from primitive airfields and required little of the fancy, high-tech maintenance needed by more sophisticated warplanes like the F-4 Phantom."

With a wingspan of 33 feet 9 inches and a maximum speed of around 420 miles per hour, the Dragonfly was a modestly sized warplane, but it could carry up to 8,000 pounds of bombs, rockets, and guns.

In 1970, during a process called "Vietnamization," when the South Vietnamese were being primed to provide the bulk of their own defense, many ex-Air Force A-37Bs went to the South Vietnamese air arm. In later years, A-37Bs later became a familiar sight in Latin America, where they equipped about a dozen air forces.

Though it left active duty beginning in 1970, the A-37B became a familiar sight in Air National Guard units, beginning with Maryland's 175th Wing at Glenn L. Martin Airport in Baltimore. Late in its career, the Dragonfly acquired a forward air control mission and was renamed the OA-37B, the "O" for observation. The last of these aircraft served with the 24th Composite Group in the Panama Canal Zone until 1990.

Cessna A-37B Dragonfly

Type: two-seat fighter and attack aircraft

Power plant: two 2,850-lb (1293-kg) thrust General Electric J85-GE-17A turbojet engines

Performance: maximum speed at 16,000 ft (4875 m) 524 mph (834 km/h); maximum cruising speed at 25,000 ft (7620 m); range with maximum payload, including 4,100 lb (1860 kg) of external weapons, 460 miles (740 km)   WHAT?

Weights: empty equipped 6,211 lb (2817 kg); maximum takeoff 14,000 lb (6350 kg)

Dimensions: wingspan 35 ft 10½ in (10.93 m); length 28 ft 3½ in (8.62 m); height 8 ft 10½ in (2.71 m); wing area 183 sq ft (17.98 sq m)

Armament: one .30 caliber (7.62-mm) GAU-2B/A mini-gun; typically up to 5,000 lb (12268 kg) of Mark 82 500-lb (227-kg) or heavier bombs, napalm, or air-to-ground rocket projectiles

First flight: October 22, 1963 (YAT-37D)

Chapter Eighteen

Eagles in Desert Storm

What Happened

When the United States launched Operation Desert Shield on August 6, 1990, days after the Iraqi invasion of Kuwait, the 1st Tactical Fighter Wing at Langley Air Force Base, Virginia, under Col. John M. "Boomer" McBroom—earmarked for Middle East duty under U.S. Central Command, or CENTCOM—began deploying F-15C/D Eagles on just hours' notice. Forty-eight Eagles made the longest fighter deployment in history, flying fourteen to seventeen hours nonstop from Langley to Dhahran with six to eight air refuelings en route.

The fast-responding Langley Eagles were joined on August 12 by F-15E Strike Eagles (Chapter 20). At this juncture, because of delays in the program, the F-15E had only begun to operate with its navigation pod and did not yet have a targeting pod, so the Strike Eagle was temporarily a low-tech purveyor of "dumb" bombs. The early arrival of Eagle and Strike Eagle units—able to fit, readily, into facilities where Saudi Arabia, too, had F-15s—was credited by some with deterring Iraqi forces from moving directly against Saudi oilfields. Others claimed Saddam Hussein never had any such intention.

While the buildup was underway, the U.S. Air Force transferred twenty-four of its F-15Cs to the Saudis.

Captain Rhory R. "Hoser" Draeger
January 17, 1991
McDonnell F-15C Eagle (85-0108)
Union 3
58th Tactical Fighter Squadron, "Gorillas," 33rd Tactical Fighter Wing
Tabuk, Saudi Arabia

Capt. Rhory Draeger poses with his F-15C Eagle at Eglin Air Force Base, Florida, in 1991 after returning from Operation Desert Storm. Barely visible on the fuselage beneath the Eagle's windshield are two green stars to signify the two MiGs that Draeger shot down during the first war with Iraq.

[U.S. Air Force/Debra Millett]

McBroom's F-15C Eagles immediately began flying combat air patrols, joined by Saudi F-15Cs and British Tornado F.3s.

By November 1990, Desert Shield shifted from a defensive to offensive posture with a second wave of force buildups. Almost unnoticed, in September, the 33rd Tactical Fighter Wing from Eglin Air Force Base, Florida, under Col. Richard "Rick" Parsons, deployed its 58th Tactical Fighter Squadron, the "Gorillas," with F-15C Eagles, to Tabuk in western Saudi Arabia.

The war to dislodge Saddam Hussein's Iraqi forces from occupied Kuwait began in the early hours of January 17, 1991, after Hussein ignored an ultimatum from President George Bush. The air-to-ground action waged during Operation Desert Storm received much of the world's attention, especially when stealth warplanes bombed Baghdad—but there was also an air-to-air war. The air action was dominated by the F-15C Eagle fighter and by the 58th squadron. The engagements were not always as one-sided as they may have seemed, but no Iraqi fighter ever succeeded in touching an F-15.

Most Desert Storm aerial victories were made at long range, often beyond visual range, by the radar-guided AIM-7 Sidewinder air-to-air missile, a weapon that had been plagued by mechanical problems during the Vietnam war but performed well in the 1990s. Eagle pilots made nine kills using the AIM-9 Sidewinder infra-red air-to-air missile, and one pilot downed an Iraqi MiG-29 by maneuvering his adversary into the ground. There was relatively little of the close-quarters dogfighting at which the F-15 had been built to excel. Although the Eagle also carries a 20-mm "Gatling" cannon, the gun was never fired during Operation Desert Storm.

Several F-15 pilots shot down Iraqi aircraft on the first night of the war. One of these was Capt. Rhory Draeger, flying an F-15C Eagle (no. 85-0108), who used an AIM-7M Sparrow to take down a MiG-29 Fulcrum south of al-Taqaddum in the hours after midnight on January 17. On January 26, at the controls of a different F-15C Eagle (no. 85-0119), Draeger got his second aerial victory, a MiG-23 Flogger. Draeger was leading four F-15Cs on combat air patrol when an airborne warning and control aircraft, or AWACS, spotted three MiG-23s taking off out of H-2 airfield in western Iraq. The four-ship F-15 formation spread out line abreast, headed west, and destroyed all three MiG-23s, giving Draeger and Capt. Cesar A. Rodriguez their second kills. (Rodriguez later shot down an enemy aircraft in Kosovo in the Balkans in 1999, making him the only current fighter pilot to have three aerial victories, and the only one to have gotten kills in two wars.) Among other achievements by the Eagle squadron:

- Most combat sorties and hours for any air-to-air fighter squadron (1,182 and 7,000)
- The greatest number of pilots in one squadron with aerial victories (12)
- Most pilots from one squadron with multiple aerial victories (4).

The success of each mission relied on the hundreds of maintenance and support personnel who worked to ensure the planes and pilots were ready to fly.

RHORY DRAEGER. "What's it like to sit in the F-15C and fly it? From the standpoint of just going up and down, feeling forces on your body, it's the worst roller-coaster ride you've ever been on, multiplied by about a hundred.

Two F-15C Eagles of the 58th Tactical Fighter Squadron, the "Gorillas," on patrol during Operation Desert Storm.

[Bill Faton]

All those sensations that you get with your stomach going up and down, the G-forces that you feel at the bottom of a loop—if it's not a hundred times that bad, it's ten times. In our normal flying, we deal with high G-forces all the time, throughout the flight. On a regular basis here, I'll pull regularly nine Gs, right to the limit of the aircraft. It's not uncommon for guys to come back with eight to nine Gs on the jet. During the combat missions we flew over in Saudi Arabia, I would say the most I ever pulled over there was seven Gs, which was not much.

Because we've got a bigger wing than other fighters, we've got increased lift out there and we're not going to bleed off energy as quick as other aircraft will. Take, for example, an F-105 Thunderchief. Now that had real thin wings, very high wing loading—but for flying down at low altitude, real fast, that's what you want to have because it's going to be a real smooth ride. But when you're trying to make a turn with it, it's such a high wing loading it's going to bleed off energy at an extremely fast rate. With an F-15, we've got a big wing and low wing loading—but since it's got all that lift, it's going to be a bumpy ride out there.

It handles well on the ground, like driving a car except you don't have a steering wheel, so you steer it with your rudder pedals. You have plenty of visibility. In fact, I think that's why a lot of people get sick—there's so much visibility and there's a sense that when you make a turn, you're kind of falling out of the jet, as opposed to a normal airliner where you're looking out a window and feel secure in your little bubble. The F-15 kind of goes down to your shoulders and you get the sensation of falling. It affects people, especially those who fly in the backseat for the first time.

I was credited with two kills. On one of these, my wingman Tony Schiavi also got a kill.

My other kill, the first of the two, was on January 17th. We were sweeping out in front of a strike package. We were a four-ship. The strike package consisted of F-16 Fighting Falcons, F-4G Wild Weasels, EF-111 Ravens, and other F-15s, some of which were with us and some of which were with the strike package.

It was a morning mission, and the actual strike was around noon. It was our first combat mission. We had taken off from our air base at Tabuk, tanked, and heard AWACS calling MiGs airborne while we were on the tanker. "Union Flight, bandits southwest, Baghdad, medium altitude."

"The actual strike package is going to an airfield just west of Baghdad. As we head up there, the bandits are still there. They end up being MiG-29s. They're in a CAP, a combat air patrol, just southwest of Baghdad, around that southern lake—there are three lakes on the west side of Baghdad, and right just southwest of that southern lake is where they're CAP'ing.

We start out at about 13,000 feet (3960 m), doing a couple of turns. During that time period, we'll run—we'll close the distance from about eighty miles (130 km) down to forty (65 km), when they're coming back hot. As they turn back cold one more time, we're thinking that they're out of gas because they've been airborne so long, so we're kind of saying, "Oh, man, they're heading back toward their airfield now."

While Union Flight presses in on the MiGs, the F-15s come under heavy surface-to-air missile and gunfire, make evasive maneuvers, jettison wing tanks (while retaining centerline tanks), and dive to lower altitude. We dump our tanks off at about halfway in on the intercept. We're closer than we wanted to be to a SAM site. We've got indication that they're launching on us.

Closer to the Foe

They get just west of their airfield now and it looks like they're turning back into it, but in reality they turn back toward us. During this time period, we close it from forty miles (65 km) down to seventeen miles. And so, when they make their turn back in, at about seventeen miles (27 km), I'll lock up the western man and shoot him with one AIM-7.

Sly Magill locks one up and shoots at him with two AIM-7s. Capt. Charles J. "Sly" Magill, a Marine Corps exchange officer with the 58 Tactical Fighter Squadron, the "Gorillas," is leader of Union Flight with 1st Lt. Mark J. Arriola as his wingman. I'm in the number-three position accompanied by my wingman, Captain Tony Schiavi.

We're using AIM-7Ms. I see the missiles from the time they leave the aircraft until the time they hit. That's unusual. You normally don't see that because the rocket motor will burn out.

Because of the environmental conditions, I see it all—even though we don't have them visually when we start shooting. Very shortly after firing, I pick them up. They descend. They're at 13,000 feet (3960 m). Now they're at five hundred feet of altitude separation from us. When I actually shoot I don't see them, but at about twelve miles or so I start to pick them up. They're at low altitude, flying in echelon formation about a mile between them. And I see the missiles go right into impact. I call: "Splash two."

This means, we've got two fireballs out there and the two MiGs are destroyed. There are no Iraqi shoots. Our missiles hit them head-on and they just drop out of the sky. These are real small fireballs because they're real low on gas.

From what we can tell, they never locked us up. They may have been attempting to, but we didn't get any indications of it.

From what I can see, the MiG-29s have a camouflaged paint scheme. It's kind of in shadows, so it's hard to tell.

When we get done with our mission and we're claiming a kill, we fill out paperwork that says, "This is what happened." Each guy in the flight fills out the paperwork. Even if they didn't shoot, they verify it, so you've got witnesses. A wingman will say, "We did see a fireball," or, "We did see his missiles track to the target," and that's used to try to verify the kill. There are other means, too. The paperwork is sent up to headquarters, and a board meets. It's decided at a higher level than just a captain. They go through all the data and say either, "Yes, it was a kill," or, "No, it wasn't.'" Both of my kills were pretty straightforward, and there wasn't any doubt about who was shooting at what, or what happened.

I graduated from college, the University of Wisconsin, in 1981, and

The first of the two Soviet-built fighters shot down by Capt. Rhory Draeger was a MiG-23 Flogger similar to this one.

[U.S. Navy]

---

went to OTS (Officer Training School). First, I went to the flight screening school at Hondo, Texas, and before that, a three- to four-week course in the Cessna T-41, which was actually the roughest part of pilot training for me. I went to pilot training at Laughlin Air Force Base in Del Rio, Texas. I got an F-15 assignment out of there and went to fighter lead-in school in the AT-38B Talon—a two- to three-month indoctrination in fighters—followed by F-15 RTU (replacement training unit) at Luke Air Force Base, Arizona.

I had eighteen months at Kadena Air Base, Okinawa, and was a flight lead when I left there. I went to Langley Air Force Base, Virginia, as my follow-on assignment, also flying F-15s, during which period I went to Fighter Weapons School. I came to Eglin in November 1988.

I'm actually a member of the 59th Tactical Fighter Squadron, "Golden Pride," which did not deploy to the Persian Gulf; I'm an augmentee with the 58th, "Gorillas," during that squadron's stay at Tabuk, Saudi Arabia.

No, the F-15 isn't perfect. If I had my way, I'd say bigger engines, better radar—but the F-15C is the best in the world today. I want the ATF (Advanced Tactical Fighter, later called the F/A-22 Raptor) tomorrow. Realistically, compared to any other aircraft in the world, it will be real hard to improve on the F-15.

TONY SCHIAVI. This is how I saw the January 26, 1991, mission when I was credited with a MiG-23 kill. During this same mission, Captains Rhory R. Draeger and Cesar A. Rodriguez were also credited with MiG-23 kills—in their cases, the second kill for each man.

The mission we were on was protection—a "high asset value," or HAV, combat air patrol, which we called a "have-cap"—in this case protecting an E-3B/C Sentry AWACS aircraft. By this time in the war, we're doing so well in the air-to-air portion that we have a lot of flexibility. This is unlike earlier when, if you were tied to HAV, you were doing only have-cap. If you were doing a sweep, you did *only* that. Things were more stringent at the beginning because the threat was much higher.

We have an eastern AWACS, a central AWACS, and a western AWACS, and they all just cover their own ground. Cougar and Buckeye are the call signs for the western and central AWACS.

At this point, we're into the war about nine days, we're doing well, and we've started to get more flexibility. Maybe you're on a have-cap mission, but they'll call up and say, "Hey, there's a strike package of X number of One Elevens [F-111s], how would you like to do a pre-strike sweep for them?" Or they'll call and say, "There's a cap between a threat area and a target airfield." So you could go up on a routine HAV mission and have something good happen in terms of air-to-air possibilities.

We've been up on cap for about an hour and a half. We've just gone down to the tanker to get our first air refueling. We're eighty miles (120 kms) southeast of Iraq's H-2 and H-3 airfields, near the Jordanian border. We're a four-ship on the tanker. My two-ship is the second to fuel up. As we're coming off the tanker, AWACS calls and says, "Hey, we've got bandits taking off from H-2, a whole group of them, heading northeast." At that point in time, Chevron, our flight lead, Capt. Rhory Draeger, asks for permission to commit on them. AWACS says, "Granted. Go get 'em."

We start to commit northeast to get an intercept vector on these guys, a cutoff vector. We have to decide whether our other two-ship element can join us. In the F-15, firepower is awesome. When you get four F-15s running in a wall toward somebody, there's no way you're not going to come out victorious. So our game plan at all times, when we can do it, is to keep the four-ship together, to use that firepower. But our other two-ship is a little bit lower on gas, just because they were on cap while we were down at the tanker. We instruct them to come with us, as long as they can, as long as they have gas, and we'll go in as a four-ship up against these guys.

These guys, these Iraqis, took off from H-2 in a big, disorganized gaggle. We're coming at them. They're heading northeast, and we're trying to cut them off. They're not trying to flee to Iran which is too far from H-2 but are just moving, with no logical purpose that we can see.

About a hundred miles (161 km) away from them, we're going as fast as we can with three bags of gas. Initially, I'm thinking, "There's no way we're going to catch these guys." They're a hundred miles (161 km) away, and with our vector we're slowly starting to cut them off, but it's going to take a long time and a lot of gas." We close it to about eighty miles (128 km) and we're probably just about at the point where we need to turn back, getting too far up there, into an area where they have ground threats. So right at this point, just as we're saying, "We're not going to be able to get these guys," four *more* take off right behind them from H2— and we're *in there*, we're in a perfect geometry for these new guys.

Outguessing the Iraqis

Do they know about us? My conjecture is, the first group of Iraqis called back and said, "We're gone. We're out of here. Now you can launch the next bunch." Or, maybe the first group is saying, "Here's our chance to drag four Eagles and sandbag the sons of bitches." That was one of the things we had to think about as we started this turn into this intercept: What happens if these guys, the first group, do a 180 degree turn, so that we're caught between two groups of bogies. They could get us in a pincers. And we were obviously thinking about it. Captain Draeger was thinking about it.

Of course, AWACS can see quite a ways, so we'll have warning if they try to box us in. So we don't *know* if they're aware of us—but we always think worst case.

AWACS eventually loses the first group because they're so far away. At this time, we still don't know what types of aircraft are in either group, although in fact they're MiG-23 Floggers. So that's something else you have to think about—what airplane am I going up against? And you have to think worst case. You don't know. But of course when you're intercepting and chasing the guy by the tail, you're not worried quite as much because he's not going to shoot you while he's flying away from you.

So we're running our intercept against the second group of MiG-23s to take off from H-2. They're at low altitude. They're below a thousand feet. Our radar, as awesome as it is, isn't perfect at this distance when you're trying to paint guys who are down at low altitude.

For reasons impossible to explain, one of these guys suddenly turns around, goes back, and lands at H-2. Maybe he has an aircraft problem.

Now we're forty miles (64 km), and with this guy going back, we don't know if they're running some new tactic on us or what they're doing. But the other three continue, and we're watching them on the scope. They're coming on our radarscope in the kind of Soviet-type formation, what we call a "Bic" formation, that we've talked about all the time.

It's so funny. Here, war is happening. And it's just like training. There are three blips on your screen. They're in the standard "Bic" formation.

We're coming in about thirty miles (48 km) from the merge. We punch our wing tanks off but keep the centerline tank on. Okay, so we have better maneuverability now if we get in an engagement in this thing. If the man decides to engage us and if our missiles don't work, we'll be able to turn more tightly without those tanks.

We're descending out of the mid-twenties (20,000 feet/6096m), doing about Mach 1.1 or 1.2. The weather is overcast. We can't see the ground. We're also thinking, "We may never see these guys." We can shoot at them, obviously, but once the missiles go through the clouds, at best, we'll see a glow.

The critical decision as you get within twenty miles (32 km) is, "Okay, who's going to target whom?"

That's Captain Draeger's job as number one to decide, "Okay, who's going to take whom?" So he does that. He says, "Okay"—his philosophy is that, hey, I'm going to take the map-reader first, and that's usually the guy out front; if you kill the guy that's leading the thing, everybody else will ask, "Oh, shit, what do we do now?"—so he targets the leader, or the map-reader as he calls him.

He sets me up as number two on the northwestern trailer. Draeger and I are One and Two. Now there's only one Iraqi left, so Draeger says, "Okay, Three and Four, *both* of you take the southernmost guy. (Our head-up display "box" is used to identify bogies, relative to each other, by geographic direction.)

Draeger says, "Two, target the trailer. Three and Four, you target the southernmost." We acknowledge. I say, "Chevron 2, sorted. 270. 25

miles." It's just like William Tell—the stateside training exercise. If they were closer together, it might be necessary to refer to them by using a BRA call, meaning bearing, range, and altitude—but that's not necessary.

The other two pilots are Capt. Cesar A. Rodriguez as Chevron 3—he's the guy who got the maneuver kill earlier, the Iraqi who flew into the ground—and Capt. Bruce Till is the last guy, Chevron 4.

So we're coming in, and the other thing we're looking at is, are we spiked or not spiked (locked up by the other guy)? That's our other indication of whether they know we're there, our radar warning receiver scope. At this point, there's no indication—but you can never be sure your system is working accurately.

So the flight lead has called the target plan and now all we have to do is lock the guy we're supposed to lock, and shoot. Like I said, we got an early "Bandit! Bandit!" call on these guys at about forty miles (65 km), so we know these guys are bad, which takes a lot of the guesswork out.

We take our shots. Draeger shoots first. We're now well inside twenty miles (32 km).

He shoots. His missile comes off. I see it guiding. I shoot next, just a couple seconds after him. Because Bruce and Rico are offset from us, they have to wait a little longer before they get in range, so it's probably several more seconds before I hear Rico fire.

As the missiles start flying off, we pick up the first Tally Hos, or visual sightings, about ten miles (16 km) from the merge. We can see the Floggers running across the desert, fast. A lot of times you can see the missile, you can keep a Tally Ho on that missile.

I mentioned the weather before. At about ten or twelve miles, there's a sucker hole that just opens up. So we go diving through. So now we're in a visual environment, versus shooting through the clouds. For some reason it's just opened up, which is perfect for us.

Missile Hit

Draeger's missile hits his man. It hits him right in the back, the old Flogger running across the ground, there, and he's flying so low you can see the dust kick up around him. Draeger calls, "Splash!" Then he looks again. The Iraqi airplane flies right through the fireball and comes out the other side. It hit him but didn't knock him out of the sky. He's burning but not down. Draeger goes to a heater, preparing to fire an AIM-9 Sidewinder heat-seeking missile, to put some heat on this big fire. But

"The F 15 Eagle has the cleanest lines of any fighter in the Air Force," said one pilot. This Eagle belongs to the training squadron at Tyndall Air Force Base, Florida, that trained new Eagle pilots for the Air Force.

[Norman Taylor]

---

before he can to this, the fire reaches the Flogger's wing root and it suddenly explodes in a huge fireball. I'm so busy watching this, watching this guy blow up, so amazed by the damage the warhead did, that I've almost forgotten my own missile.

Draeger comes off. He says, "Let's come off north." First thing you do when you start blowing guys up is, you think about getting the hell out of there, fast. Once people see fireballs, that gets their attention and you don't want to be around. So Draeger says, "Let's come off north."

Right about then, my missile hits my guy. I call a second, "Splash!" There's another big fireball. After the first guy blows up, the other two guys do a hard, right-hand turn, right into us. Whether they picked up a late visual on us and saw us, or what, I don't know—but what they were doing was too late and my missile hit him.

As for what the MiG-23 Floggers looked like, they were camouflaged and they were two and a half to three miles in front of us when they actually blew up, so we saw them pretty well. Number four's missiles were maybe two seconds late, so number three, Captain Rodriguez, got the kill.

There's a road right underneath them. I think they were navigating by following the road. The first guy blows up and the other two blow up on the other side of the road, three fireballs right in a row. My guy blows up, boom, and a moment later I hear Rodriguez call the third splash.

So as we come off, our big concern now is—we're getting a voice-style warning from a device called a Bitchin' Betty on our airplanes—we're worried about Bingo fuel. We still have our centerline tank, but as we start to egress, Draeger and I punch off our centerline tanks also so we can get some speed up and get away from any ground threat (we're fairly low in here), and now our big concern is to get back.

We call AWACS and tell them that we've splashed three fireballs. AWACS says, "Say type." That's when we say, "Floggers." We didn't use any code word. We just said, "Floggers."

I think if we had gotten the more advanced AMRAAM missile during Desert Shield, if we'd had time to prepare and practice with AMRAAM, everybody would have been real comfortable with it. Now, you're talking about getting a brand-new weapon. It's got a different capability, different tactics. There were [only] eight or nine of us who had actually done work with the AMRAAM. The AMRAAM missile was employed midway through the war but was not used in any combat engagement.

McDonnell F-15C Eagle

The McDonnell F-15C Eagle was the dominant fighter in the 1991 Persian Gulf war and the flagship of the U. S. Air Force's fighter force in the 1990s. The F-15C is no longer in production (although the manufacturer, now Boeing, continues to manufacture export models), but the Eagle remains on the front line while its replacement, the Lockheed Martin F/A-22 Raptor, begins to enter service.

The Eagle remains an impressive sight. The F-15C pilot sits high atop the twin-engine fighter on a tall, almost stalky undercarriage. With its straightforward but very large wing of 608 square feet, the Eagle is one of the few fast jets that has no need for a braking parachute: it lands smoothly and gently without one. The shoulder-mounted, swept wing has a fixed leading edge and plain unblown trailing-edge flaps.

The Eagle's pilot is equipped with ACES II zero-zero ejection seat

Who's Who

UNION LEAD:
Capt. Charles J. "Sly" Magill, a Marine Corps exchange officer and F-15C pilot, 58th squadron, call sign Union Lead on January 17

UNION 2:
1st Lt. Mark J. Arriola, F-15C pilot, 58th squadron, call sign Union 2 on January 17

UNION 3, LATER CHEVRON LEAD:
Capt. (later Maj.) Rhory R. "Hoser" Draeger, F-15C Eagle pilot, 58th Tactical Fighter Squadron, call sign Union 3 on January 17, 1991; call sign Chevron Lead on January 26

UNION 4, LATER CHEVRON 2:
Capt. (later Col.) Anthony E. "Kimo" Schiavi, F-15C pilot, 58th squadron, call sign Union 4, on January 17, 1991; call sign Chevron 2 on January 26

CHEVRON 3:
Capt. (later Col.) Cesar A. "Rico" Rodriguez, F-15C pilot, 58th squadron, call sign Chevron 3 on January 26

CHEVRON 4:
Capt. Bruce Till, F-15C pilot, 58th squadron, call sign Chevron 4 on January 26

and is intended to fight in the "hands on throttle and stick" mode, the pilot getting key information from his head-up display.

The F-15 Eagle's success in air-to-air combat owes much to its powerful Hughes APG-63 radar, its maneuverability and durability, and its heavy load of diverse weaponry. The APG-63 radar is being constantly improved, and on C and D model Eagles has become lightweight X-band pulse-Doppler radar with a reprogrammable signal processor. Beginning in 1999, the Air Force introduced an improved radar that provides increased pilot situational awareness and takes full advantage of the capabilities of the AIM-120 advanced medium range air-to-air missile. This improved APG-63(V)2 active electronically scanned array radar is based on the earlier APG-63(V)1.

The F-15 can destroy enemy aircraft beyond visual range using the radar-guided AIM-7M Sparrow or AIM-120 AMRAAM, Advanced Medium Range Air-to-air Missile, which became fully operational only after Operation Desert Storm. At closer quarters, where its large wing makes it very maneuverable, the F-15 can engage with its 20-mm M61A1 Vulcan six-barrel cannon.

In a European scenario, the F-15 Eagle would go aloft to attempt to wrest air superiority over the battlefield and would fly frequent missions of short duration in bad weather. In this setting, ease of maintenance for rapid turnaround is essential. In Operation Desert Storm, Eagles flew longer missions to escort strike aircraft. On these missions, F-15Cs took off, refueled in flight, cruised at medium altitude of around 28,000 feet (8668 m) for two hours or more, typically at Mach 0.93 or 660 mph (1062 km/h), and engaged Iraqi aircraft seven hundred miles (1127 km) or more from their base. Quick turnaround was also a factor in the war against Iraq, and maintenance people reported that the F-15C met their expectations.

F-15Cs carry conformal fuel tanks that provide an additional 8,820 pounds (4000 kgs) of fuel.

Design work on the F-15 began in 1965, and the first plane flew in 1972. The series began with the F-15A and the combat-capable two-seat model, originally the TF-15A and now called the F-15B. The first two-seater made its initial flight on July 7, 1973. According to the Air Force Museum, the service acquired 365 F-15As and fifty-nine F-15Bs.

The operational career of the Eagle began with the first delivery of an F-15A to Tactical Air Command's 1st Tactical Fighter Wing at Langley Air Force Base, Virginia, on January 9, 1976. By 1985, the Air Force was in the process of fielding ten fighter wings equipped with the Eagle.

In the 1980s, the F-15A operated with TAC air defense squadrons in the interceptor role and was the carrier aircraft for the anti-satellite weapon, development of which was eventually cancelled.

From June 1979, A and B models were succeeded in production by the F-15C and its two-seat equivalent, the F-15D. According to the Air Force Museum, the service acquired 409 F-15Cs and sixty-one F-15Ds. Foreign users of the Eagle are Israel, Saudi Arabia, and Japan.

When Operation Desert Storm began on January 17, 1991, the United States had five F-15C air-to-air squadrons deployed to the Persian Gulf region. Most air-to-air engagements were fought by F-15Cs of the 58th Tactical Fighter Squadron.

No F-15C/D Eagle fighters were lost during Desert Shield/Storm. More than 2,200 missions, totaling some 7,700 hours of combat time, were logged.

The F-15C Eagle is capable of carrying a variety of weapons and missiles. This one has Sidewinder heat-seeking missiles under the wing and Sparrow radar-guided missiles under the fuselage.

[McDonnell Aircraft Co.]

Most aerial victories were achieved against Iraqi aircraft caught by chance or attempting to flee to Iran, rather than in serious air-to-air battles. F-15Cs scored thirty-two aerial kills, from a total of forty-one victories in the war. Of these, all but eight were achieved with the Eagle's beyond-visual-range weapon, the Sparrow missile. Seven kills were racked up by AIM-9 Sidewinders, and one by outmaneuvering an opponent. The AIM-120A AMRAAM was not fired in anger, although more than a thousand "captive carries" of the missile were racked up during combat missions in the final days of the war.

In the 1990s, F-15 Eagles underwent staged improvements to radar and internal systems. Although committed to the F/A-22 Raptor as its next fighter, the United States has kept in production the dual-role F-15E Strike Eagle (Chapter 20). Most F-15A and B models have now been retired, and F-15C and D models are in their third decade of service.

McDonnell F-15C Eagle

Type: single-seat air superiority fighter

Power plant: two 24,000-lb (10886-kg) thrust Pratt & Whitney F100-PW-220 low-bypass turbofan engines

Performance: maximum speed 1,875 mph (3000 km/h), or Mach 2.5 plus, at 45,000 ft (13716 m); service ceiling 65,000 ft (19810 m); combat radius, 1,000 miles (1610 km) unrefueled, ferry range with conformal fuel tanks and three external fuel tanks 3,450 miles (5520 km)

Weights: empty 28,000 lb (12975 kg); maximum takeoff weight 68,000 pounds (30600 kilograms)

Dimensions: wingspan 42 ft 10 in (13.06 m); length 63 ft 9 in (19.43 m); height 18 ft 8 in (5.69 m); wing area 608 sq ft (56.48 sq m)

Armament: one internal M61A1 Vulcan 20-mm cannon, with maximum of 940 rounds; provision for up to four AIM-9 Sidewinder missiles and up to four AIM-7M Sparrow or AIM-120 AMRAAM missiles

First flight: July 27, 1972 (F-15A); July 7, 1973 (F-15B); February 26, 1979 (F-15C); June 19, 1979 (F-15D)

Chapter Nineteen

Black Jet over Baghdad

What Happened

In a little-noticed ceremony on July 12, 1990, the U.S. Air Force took delivery of its fifty-ninth and last F-117 Nighthawk, the famous stealth fighter called the "Black Jet" by pilots and crews. The following month, Iraq invaded Kuwait.

In response, the Desert Shield buildup began. Col. Alton C. Whitley Jr., who years earlier had been the first operational pilot to fly the F-117, took the 37th Tactical Fighter Wing and its Black Jets halfway around the world to Khamis Mushait, Saudi Arabia.

Although they did not initially expect a real war, officers began plotting how the F-117 would be used against Iraq if diplomacy failed. Though it might take three air refuelings per sortie and would be grueling on pilots—every Black Jet jock had a Sony Walkman rigged to his helmet earphones to listen to music while in cruise mode—the F-117 could make a five-hour, 1,000 mile (1160 km) round-trip and deliver two 2,000 lb (907 kg) laser-guided bombs with pinpoint accuracy.

In his command facility, the "Black Hole" at Riyadh, Lt. Gen. Charles Horner planned an air campaign against Iraq—organizing his needs for refueling tracks, jamming, countermeasures, and air rescue. In October 1990, Whitley began "mirror image" combat rehearsals, named Sneaky Sultan, in which strikes on Iraq were practiced. In these

Captain Dale Zelko
January 17, 1991
Lockheed F-117A Nighthawk
(Hale 53)
416th Tactical Fighter
Squadron "Ghostriders,"
37th Tactical Fighter Wing
Khamis Mushait Air Base, Saudi
Arabia

Capt. (later, Lt. Col.) Dale Zelko
poses in 1991 with his Lockheed
F-117A Nighthawk, the famous
stealth fighter known as the "Black
Jet." Zelko flew the F-117A in
combat in Operation Desert Storm
in 1991 and in Kosovo in 1999.

[Dale Zelko]

mock tests, Iraqi defenses shot down dozens of Black Jets. That month, intelligence officer Michael P. Curphey sat in on a meeting where Horner confirmed that "downtown" (Baghdad) would be set aside exclusively for the Black Jet. Curphey emerged shaking his head. "You know," he said, "that goddamned crazy man Saddam Hussein isn't going to back down."

On the evening of January 16, 1991, an ultimatum to Saddam Hussein passed. It was time for the F-117 stealth fighter to encounter the heavy antiaircraft and missile defenses waiting "downtown"—in Baghdad. The first wave of Black Jets launched just before midnight. Capt. Dale Zelko was in the second wave.

DALE ZELKO. When we prepare for a mission, we follow the adage "dress to egress." Especially when going into combat, you're going to take that idea very, very seriously. There's always the possibility that you'll have to get out of the aircraft. There's a possibility that suddenly you're going to find yourself no longer a comfortable fighter pilot in a cozy little cockpit. You're going to have to be a guy on the ground now. I've always taken that very seriously, on peacetime or wartime missions: "dress to egress."

You wear a G-suit in the airplane: it does have an "F" for fighter

Just weeks after Operation Desert Storm, the Pentagon showed off this Lockheed F-117A Nighthawk stealth fighter at Shaw Air Force Base, South Carolina, on May 30, 1991.

[Norman Taylor]

designation, after all. Of course, the mission of the F-117 is primarily to strike deep, heavily defended, high-value, strategic targets at night. So even though the aircraft is quite capable of yanking and banking—handling-wise, it's very much like any modern fighter—there's not a lot of extreme yanking and banking during deep, strategic interdiction downtown, so the G-suit doesn't inflate often, but you have it on anyway.

During Desert Storm, we were operating down there in Khamis Mushait in the southwest part of Saudi Arabia, only about eighty miles north of the Yemeni border. It was very mountainous. It was at about 6,700 feet of field elevation. It was quite similar to Tonopah, Nevada, where my experience with the F-117 began, which was about 5,500 feet of elevation in the high desert. So aircraft performance at Khamis, on takeoff roll, that sort of thing, was quite similar to that at Tonopah. Because of the field elevation, the pressure altitude, and density altitude, and because the F-117 typically had a pretty long takeoff roll anyway, we could not take off with a full load of fuel in the aircraft, so our rendezvous with the tankers was critical.

Even though it was January, it was still fairly mild. Nights were getting cool up there in that mountainous area. It was tempting to dress pretty light because you're thinking you're going to be in the cockpit, and even when you're outside the cockpit around the aircraft shelters, walking to and from the ops building and what not, it's pretty mild. You still have to plan for, "Gee whiz, what if I'm on the ground, even for days, and during those cold desert nights, exposure . . ." So you're going to want a number of layers. My typical Desert Storm–type dress was a cotton T-shirt, a flight suit, my summer-weight flight jacket, and on top of that a survival vest. In the vest, you have the essential things for basic survival and evasion in case you hit the ground and don't have the time or the presence of mind—you're going to be in some level of shock—to get your seat kit or your hit-and-run kit. Or maybe your seat kit and hit-and-run kit are lost and aren't right there at your landing zone. So you want in your survival vest everything you'll need if you hit the ground and start running and can't gather up the other stuff.

You've got your PRC-112A survival radio. There were crates of the 112B right there in theater but we didn't have them. In the seat kit, you had a spare PRC-90, a Vietnam-era radio, as a backup. It's a line-of-sight radio with no secure voice capability. We also had a magnetic compass in one of the pockets of the survival vest. We had a couple of regular signal flares. One end of it is for day use, which is smoke, and the other is for night use, which is a flame. In the survival vest itself, you had—it was customized according to what the life support shop in your squadron provided. I believe we had the basic signal mirror. We carried a 9-mm automatic, typically with two extra clips in your G-suit pocket or, maybe, on an inside pocket of your survival vest.

Boarding the "Black Jet"

You walk to the plane with a harness on. The crew chief helps you to strap in. The parachute is actually on top of the ACES II ejection seat, which is in the aircraft. That's a standard type of ejection seat, which, on the F-117, has two side handles for actuation. The parachute risers are sticking out of the back of the seat. The crew chief helps you to wrap those risers and to fit those Koch fittings together, and now you're attached to the parachute. Then, you do your shoulder straps and your lap belt. You put your helmet on. You have to hook up your oxygen hose to the aircraft operations system. You connect the communications cord.

You start engines by following your checklist. In the Desert Storm era, our aircraft had the old B-52 INS, or inertial navigation system. We did not yet have GPS, or global positioning system. That old INS was designed before the ring-laser gyro of today, and certainly before GPS. The INS had a 43-minute alignment time. So, well before the pilot got out to the aircraft, the maintenance guy hooked up a pneumatic air system for cooling, hooked up power, and started aligning the INS. Each aircraft shelter had its own unique coordinates that you could initialize the INS with. So the system is spinning and you can't move the aircraft at all, while that INS is aligning. It took a full forty-three minutes, and you couldn't move the aircraft at all while setting the INS.

The first wave takes off in the last bits of daylight. The second and third waves take off in the night. We do a trail departure, with about 20-second spacing. The F-117 has a red rotating beacon in the bottom of the aircraft for use in peacetime, but we take that off in wartime so the aircraft can be RAM'ed up—RAM is radar absorbent material—so there's no beacon, and the only thing you have are flush wingtip lights, and they're not even on the tips of the wings, they're recessed in the wings somewhere near the tips. They're very hard to see from another F-117. So we relied a great deal on timing and altitude for spacing and deconfliction.

We take off in twos, with a 20-second trail departure. Once the number-two guy gets airborne, he maintains a distance behind number one, his lead, and an altitude split, but he also tries to acquire number one visually—which is very difficult. We fly like that, in that sort of formation, to rendezvous with tankers coming out of Jeddah or Riyadh. We use "storm-type" radio call signs, like Thunder and, I think, Lightning. After we meet the tankers, we'll await our push time—the preapproved moment to go over the fence into Iraqi territory—and then we'll be confronting Saddam Hussein's antiaircraft artillery and surface-to-air missiles for a prolonged period.

My journey to the F-117 stealth program and to Operation Desert Storm began when I joined the Air Force after picking up an Academy brochure in high school. I was born in 1959 in Colorado and graduated from the Air Force Academy in 1981. After pilot training in flying class 82-07, I stayed at Vance Air Force Base in Enid, Oklahoma, as a T-37B Tweet flight instructor in the 8th Flying Training Squadron. After that, I transferred to the 355th Tactical Fighter Squadron, an A-10 Warthog outfit, at Myrtle Beach, South Carolina, what I have jokingly called a "hardship" tour. I say that with tongue in cheek. Being assigned to a resort area to fly the A-10 was fantastic. I'm not a golfer, though, and my fellow aviators told me it was wrong to assign a non-golfer to Myrtle Beach. I never gave in to the pressure to become a golfer.

After three years honing my skills as a mud-moving "Hog" driver, I was picked as a candidate for the "black world" F-117 Nighthawk community. The existence of the stealth, or radar-evading, F-117, sometimes called the "Black Jet," had just been publicly acknowledged by the Pentagon, and I joined one of two operational units at the Tonopah Test Range, located in the high desert of Nevada just 140 miles (225 km) northwest of Las Vegas

Black Jet Program

The F-117 Program was an incredible accomplishment for the U.S. Air Force. What was so impressive about it was how we were able to keep it a closely held secret. Before anyone knew the F-117 existed, we not only tested and developed the aircraft, but we had two fully operational squadrons of those planes as far back as 1983. The Air Force only acknowledged the existence of these aircraft in November 1988.

To select new pilots, the leadership at Tonopah contacted fighter units asking for candidates with a minimum of a thousand hours in fighters and who possessed a special operational maturity that would allow them to fit into this very selective community. The group at Tonopah at that time was very senior, mostly majors and lieutenant colonels. I was a mid-level captain then and one of two in my particular training class.

And, wow, what a program. We had five retired Air Force Vietnam veteran fighter pilots as classroom and simulator instructors, for the two of us. They took great care of us. We lived in Las Vegas and commuted from Nellis Air Force Base every Monday via Key Airlines, a contract commercial airline. We had our own rooms up at Tonopah, where we'd spend the next five days. It was almost like going remote every week. We would fly two waves Monday night, three on Tuesday, Wednesday, and Thursday nights and then we would all head back to Las Vegas on Friday.

At Tonopah, we flew only at night on operational training missions. At that time we were really in the vampire mode. I went into work about 3:30 P.M. and got done at about 3:30 A.M.

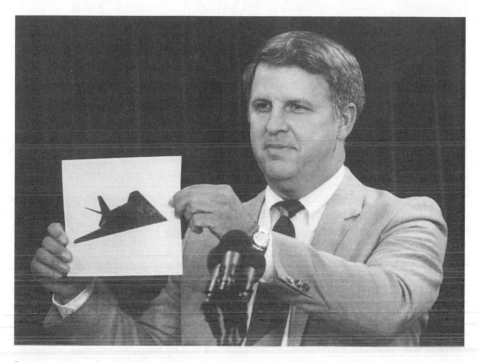

For many years, the F-117A was so secret that the Air Force did not even acknowledge its existence. The public got its first glimpse in November 1988 when Pentagon official J. Daniel Howard revealed a single picture—heavily retouched—of the plane. Three years later, Capt. Dale Zelko was flying the F-117A over Iraq.

[Department of Defense]

One of our squadrons deployed to Saudi Arabia around September 1990. My squadron deployed for Desert Shield in December. We were based at Khamis, up in the high mountains. January 17, 1991, is when Desert Storm kicked off, and as everybody knows, the F-117s dropped the first bombs. At 2:51 A.M. on January 17, an F-117 dropped the first bomb of the Persian Gulf War, a laser-guided GBU-27 that destroyed half of the Iraqi air defense center at Nukayb. A second F-117 blew away the other half. Ten more F-117s headed downtown to Baghdad. I was in the second wave and was heading for the tanker, preparing to refuel and enter Iraqi airspace.

We rendezvous with tankers who were dedicated to us about a hundred miles north of Khamis. It was about twenty to twenty-five minutes from takeoff to tankers. The total mission time, on average for an F-117 guy in Desert Storm, is about five and one-half hours. You were in Iraq itself for probably sixty to seventy minutes, which is quite a long time in Bad Guy Country.

The bomb load is two 2,000-lb (907-kg) bombs, GBU-10s or GBU-27s. We carry a varied mix of those. We had to take off with a significantly reduced fuel load because of the weight factor, including the weight of the bombs, and the takeoff roll. The temperature, the field elevation, and the density altitude were all factors. So we needed our tanker. And it wasn't a whole lot of time before we got up on the tanker. Tankers were absolutely vital. They were vital for everybody, really, but particularly vital for us in the F-117. You can't do anything in theater without tankers.

Each two-ship F-117 flight had its own tanker. We flew up as a cell—two F-117s—up to a point fairly close to the Iraqi border and refueled. We make our linkup with the tanker based on timing and on our schedule. We're in a combat mode now. The tankers are operating with very reduced external lighting, which makes it extremely challenging. When we get to the border, the lighting gets even dimmer. We were "comm out" with them, meaning radio silence, until we hooked up with the boom operator, and then we used intercom. We had an intercom that ran through the refueling boom. So we could talk to the boomer or the tanker cockpit on the interphone. Other than that, we were "comm out" unless there was some kind of emergency.

Refueling En Route

The tanker would enter an orbit up there in the northern part of Saudi. That's when we stopped being a two-ship. Just before each F-117 pilot hit his push time—the scheduled time to go over the fence into Iraqi territory—he got up on the boom and topped off with gas. You absolutely had to have that gas. We put fuel into every square inch of those internal fuel tanks. Before you pushed off the tanker, you got every last drop of gas possible because when you were post-strike, coming out of Iraq back to Saudi, you would be very close to minimum fuel.

After leaving the tanker, each F-117 is by itself. We drop off the tanker, individually. We go on our way. Before we cross the Iraqi border, we "stealth up." Once we cross the border, we're not talking and we're not squawking.

During the cruise portion of the mission, before you enter Iraqi airspace, you don't have a lot of duties to perform. Some pilots listened to music tapes. I actually did not listen to music. I preferred the silence and the solitude. It's the right antidote when your mental, emotional, and psychological state is at a pretty high level of intensity.

At the same time, though—and this is personality dependent—my personality is laid back and calm. I found that even though the intensity level was jacked up about a thousand notches in combat, my calm became even calmer. I went into an ultrahigh state of calm, if you will. I found that cruise time—if there's clear weather, you have a good visual on the tanker and on your wingman—there is a lot of time to think. I did a lot of reflecting and thought about my family a lot. There I was in that tight little cockpit on the other side of the world from my family and loved ones, and I actually found the solitude quite rejuvenating and restorative.

Was I scared? I will tell you, there was one moment on every combat mission when I was terrified. It wasn't a feeling of, "Gee whiz, I might get hurt or killed, and wouldn't that be bad for me?" It wasn't, "Boy, I'm scared for myself."

That moment happened when I came off the tanker, stealthed up, and was just about to cross the border into Iraq. At just about that time—I was well aware that this would happen—I had this kind of wave, this flush of terror that would come over my body. I would let it have its way, and it wouldn't last long. What it was, I would think about my family. I would think about my mom. And my sisters. And my kids. I wasn't thinking about me. I was thinking about, what if something did happen to me? What about the suffering, the anguish, and the sorrow my family would feel? It was horrible to think about their mental emotional suffering, anguish, and sorrow. But I was very disciplined, not only as pilot, but with my emotions: I let myself have that moment, and then I balled up that emotion into a tiny little speck and stuck it away somewhere, in a little corner inside myself. And I didn't let myself have another moment after that. That's what discipline is about. And the best way to describe my state once I entered Iraqi territory is, I was emotionless.

I don't mean that I was some hardened, emotionless killer. But I recognized that if I focused on those emotions, it would be distracting, possibly to the point of being debilitating, detracting from my success in the mission. I realized how important it was for me to get my target. I realized how much the F-117 targets meant for the whole rest of the war and what it would mean if we didn't hit our targets. Once I got down to the business end of why I was there, I was very successful at being able to do that. I don't know how I compared to the other F-117 pilots, but I flew twenty combat missions and hit thirty-some targets, and I did not miss a target. I was very proud of that. I was able to engage and take out my targets, and discipline was a part of that.

The weather was always a factor. The generic combat mission in the F-117 was intense enough, but if you throw weather in there, particularly during the tanker phase, it's very challenging and exhausting. It's mentally and physically exhausting. In bad weather, all your attention is focused on staying on the tanker, avoiding spatial disorientation, and avoiding a mishap. I remember coming out of Iraq trying to find the tanker in the middle of very stormy conditions. That was challenging. Remember, we came out of country very, very close to minimum fuel. Our fuel state was so low that typically we had just a matter of minutes to find and rejoin with a tanker and hook up and start getting gas.

In Desert Storm, we did a real good job of shutting down, or at least severely crippling the Iraqis' integrated air defense system. The Iraqis had great equipment and were well trained, but we hammered them from the very first moments of the war. Our Special Ops forces were the first ones in country taking down the early warning radars on the borders. The Wild Weasels (F-4G Phantoms equipped to attack missile sites) were really effective keeping the heads of the surface-to-air missile, or SAM, operators down, and that certainly made it easier for us "low observable" (stealth) folks to operate and survive.

Iraqi Gunfire

Their antiaircraft artillery, or triple-A, was wicked. It was unbelievable. Most people probably assume we were flying high above the antiaircraft fire. That's not true at all. We flew most of our combat target runs right smack in the heart of some of the worst triple-A, 23-mm and 37-mm mostly. And even when not vulnerable to 23-mm and 37mm, we were operating well within effective reach of the low, medium, and higher altitude airburst triple-A. Throughout the whole war it never got better.

You might think that downtown Baghdad was the worst for antiaircraft fire. It was bad, but it was just as bad, if not worse, in other areas. For example, I remember targets in and around Al-Taqqadum and Tallil

Once the Air Force revealed the existence of the F-117A stealth fighter, it also released photos like this one, showing two of the "Black Jets" on the ramp, seemingly ready for action.

airfields where the triple-A was just fierce. They were putting up barrage fire, curtain fire, sector fire, and you just had to drive right through it. The best description of the triple-A in Desert Storm that I've ever heard came from one of the pilots on my wave that first night. He said, "You know, it was like a little kid trying to run through a sprinkler and not get wet." I remember flying through that stuff and thinking, "There's no way I'm not going to get hit and downed by this stuff. Boy, I hope I live! I just can't see how it's possible that I'm going to get through this target run and still be flying."

We saw SAM launches, but most of the SAM launches that I saw, even the ones that were fairly close, seemed like they were unguided shots. Almost as if they were shooting them off like rockets, trying to get lucky.

Coming back out of Iraq, crossing into Saudi airspace, we have a rendezvous. There are preapproved refueling coordinates that the F-117 will use. A single F-117 will rendezvous with another F-117 at an exact second, at an exact spot, with a predetermined altitude split, and the two of them will go and find the tanker. Interestingly, it typically was a different F-117 than the one you started with. We were very highly

Who's Who

HALE 53

Capt. Dale Zelko, F-117A Nighthawk stealth fighter pilot, 416th Tactical
Fighter Squadron "Ghostriders"

trained and practiced, not only at going out into the middle of nowhere
and putting a bomb right on the spot, but we spent equally as much effort practicing timing, which was so crucial for the F-117. Timing was
especially crucial during the Desert Storm era when you didn't have
GPS, and you weren't talking with anybody, and you had this old INS.

By the way, if you lost that in flight, you could not restart it. You
could not re-spin up that INS back up again and realign it. If you lost
INS, the aircraft went into emergency, raw, navigational backup mode.
That meant find your way to the nearest airstrip and land.

That didn't happen very often. The INS was extremely reliable.

Our leaders expected us to have heavy losses, especially in the first
few nights. It is absolutely unexplainable that we didn't lose an F-117
during Desert Storm.

F-117 Nighthawk Stealth Fighter

Starting with the U-2 spy plane in the 1950s, Lockheed's "Skunk
Works" at Burbank, California, worked to become the industry authority on foiling detection by radar—through stealth.

In studies that began in 1975, Lockheed mathematician Bill
Schroeder developed a computer program that predicted the radar signature of an aircraft shaped with flat panels, or facets. This led to a concept called "the hopeless diamond," which in April 1976 helped
Lockheed win a contract to build the Have Blue stealth demonstrator.

Lockheed built two Have Blues. The Have Blues were completed at
Burbank within months.

Have Blue was an ugly, subsonic, single-place aircraft powered by
two J85 turbofan engines borrowed from Navy T-2B Buckeye trainers.

Have Blue was like nothing that had ever flown. Restrictions imposed on its designers by "low observable" requirements—that is, by the need to attain stealth—were unprecedented. Initial engine runs were accomplished on November 4, 1977 at Burbank. To maintain security, the aircraft was parked between two semitrailers, over which a camouflage net had been drawn.

The Have Blue aircraft was taken to remote, concealed Groom Lake via C-5A Galaxy on November 16, 1977. This was the first time a C-5A operated from Burbank; morning traffic was congested as people rubbernecked the giant transport.

Lockheed test pilot Bill Park made the first flight on December 1, 1977. During Park's thirty-sixth flight on May 4, 1978, he attempted to make a landing slightly faster than optimum speed—and experienced the plane's handling difficulties and general instability. One of his landing wheels hit the runway too hard. Park went skyward and attempted to free the jammed gear. As his fuel supply waned, he was ordered to climb to 10,000 feet (3096 m) and bail out.

Park blew the canopy and ejected. He struck his head and was knocked unconscious. He was still unconscious when his chute lowered him to the ground. He sustained back injuries severe enough to dictate an early retirement from flying.

The second Have Blue flew on July 20, 1978, apparently piloted by Lt. Col. Norman "Ken" Dyson. The second plane, too, was lost in a mishap, and Dyson had to bail out.

The Air Force moved quickly to the next step, a stealth fighter contract in November 1978 code-named Senior Trend. Lockheed test pilot Hal Farley made Senior Trend's first flight June 18, 1981.

Groom Lake in the early days of Have Blue and Senior Trend was the most secret military airfield in the United States. Security was incredible. Aircraft were kept indoors when Soviet reconnaissance satellites passed overhead. Weapons were ready for use against intruders who broke widely published rules and flew within visual range of the base. There was no town nearby. People came and went by air. Anyone who asked questions about Senior Trend was hustled into interrogation with federal officers. The feds, themselves, did not know what was going on at Groom Lake. One thought the Air Force was developing a time machine.

In 1982, Senior Trend was named the F-117. Its flying unit, the 4450th Tactical Group, was uprooted from Groom to Tonopah.

Security features at Tonopah, too, seemed to come from a science-

This is a Lockheed F-117A Nighthawk stealth fighter on ground at a desert airbase, circa. 1991. During Operation Desert Storm, the F-117A was the only U.S. warplane operating in the skies over Baghdad.

[Department of Defense]

fiction movie. Barbed wire appeared atop double-row fences, like those at a penitentiary. Badges were color coded, to indicate how deep into the layers an individual was allowed to go. Those in the inner sanctum reached the most secure areas only by gaining entry with number codes and palm prints.

Pilots were housed with their families at Nellis Air Force Base, 190 miles (305 km) away. They commuted by air to work on Monday and returned home on Friday, an unusual transport job handled by Boeing 727s belonging to civil contractor Key Airlines.

By the time of the move to Tonopah, the size and shape of the F-117 was well established. The aircraft employs radar absorbent material, or RAM, on external surfaces and chisel-edge, angular features that reduce its radar cross-section, or RCS, by scattering radar returns back in multiple directions.

The F-117's primary weapon is the laser-guided bomb. The F-117 has a slender, center-hinged bomb bay with two weapon-bearing hoists, or trapezes. Opening the weapon bay makes the aircraft less stable than it is already. Instead of conventional bomb racks, trapezes offer the most efficient way for armorers to load up the Black Jet. The hoists are lowered below the fuselage silhouette to release a bomb.

In 1985, the 4450th Tactical Group was alerted for a secret mission to "decapitate" Libya's Colonel Khaddafi. The mission was cancelled for reasons unknown.

Air Staff officers and others, eager to strip away the barriers that prevented them from including the aircraft in everyday operations, welcomed the "coming out" of the F-117 in 1988. The following year, the 4450th was redesignated 37th Tactical Fighter Wing. Col. Anthony J. "Tony" Tolin was now commander.

December 1989 saw Operation Just Cause, the U.S. assault on Panama. On December 19, 1989, two F-117s were launched to support a never-disclosed Special Operations "snatch" of strongman Manuel Noriega—which was called off only as they approached Panamanian airspace. Two other F-117s were backups, and two flew a mission to "stun, disorient, and confuse" Panamanian Defense Forces, or PDF, at Rio Hato. Their target was a large, open field alongside a barracks housing two hundred elite PDF troops.

Six F-117s flew from Tonopah and refueled five times during the round-trip to Panama. The pair of Rio Hato F-117s dropped two 2,000-

---

Lockheed F-117A Nighthawk

Type: single-seat strike aircraft

Power plant: two 10,800-lb thrust (48.04 kN) General Electric F404-GE-F1D2 non-afterburning turbofan engines

Performance: maximum speed "clean" at high altitude approx. 623 mph (993 km/h) or Mach 0.9; maximum rate of climb 2820 ft (860 m) per minute; service ceiling approx. 43,000 ft (13105 m); combat radius approx. 690 miles (1112 km) with maximum ordnance

Weights: empty weight approx. 30,000 lb (13608 kg); maximum takeoff 52,500 lb (23814 kg)

Dimensions: wingspan 43 ft 4 in (13.20 m); length 65 ft 11 in (20.08 m); height 12 ft 5 in (3.78 m); wing area approx. 1,140 sq ft (105.9 sq m)

First flight: December 1, 1977 (Have Blue); June 18, 1981 (Senior Trend/F-117A)

lb bombs, both of which exploded near their intended target. Lead pilot for the attack was Maj. Greg Feest, who later dropped the first bomb on Baghdad. Four of the F-117s returned to Tonopah with bombs still on board.

Desert Storm followed. First, there were weeks of missions against high-value targets. And then, F-117 pilots began returning, sometimes, with undropped bombs when conditions would not permit the standard of accuracy they were charged with meeting. When they dropped, targets were taken out with surgical precision. Black Jets struck the main Baghdad telephone exchange without harming the Mustashfa Faydi hospital just across the boulevard. A bomb from an F-117 destroyed an Iraqi Adnan-2, a Soviet-built Ilyushin Il-76 transport converted into an early warning aircraft.

The F-117 represented only 2.5 percent of the shooters in Desert Storm yet hit 31 percent of the targets. Forty-five F-117s and sixty pilots flew 1,271 sorties and dropped 2,000 tons of bombs. Not a single F-117 was touched by Iraqi fire. Gen. John Loh, head of Tactical Air Command, told the Senate the F-117 had been eight times more efficient than "non-stealth" warplanes. In the immediate postwar era, the F-117 unit moved to Holloman Air Force Base, New Mexico, and became the 49th Fighter Wing. It continues to serve.

Chapter Twenty

Strike Eagles vs. Al Qaeda

What Happened

The highest-ranking member of Al Qaeda to be killed by U.S. forces in combat was Mohammed Atef, the number-three man in the terror network: He was killed during a U.S. air strike in Afghanistan in 2002 by a satellite-guided bomb launched from an F-15E Strike Eagle. Strike Eagles have also flown combat missions in the Persian Gulf and the 1999 war over Kosovo.

The big, sleek Strike Eagle made its combat debut in the Persian Gulf during Operation Desert Storm and was later used in Kosovo before appearing in the war in Afghanistan. Following the September 11, 2001, attack on the United States by Al Qaeda fighters who had trained in Afghanistan, the United States began combat operations in that country on October 7.

It was not the war for which the F-15E had been designed. Early in the fighting, Air Force Gen. Richard Myers, the chairman of the Joint Chiefs of Staff said of the Taliban regime in Kabul, "We're taking down their integrated air defense network" with air strikes. In fact, as everyone knew, the Taliban did not have an integrated air defense network or any of the other Soviet-style, Cold War systems the F-15E was meant to defeat. Instead, it had small numbers of highly mobile, lightly armed fighters who were adept at hiding from American air power, even the

**"Captain John" (last name withheld)
April 2002
McDonnell F-15E Strike Eagle
336th Expeditionary Fighter Squadron
Dobby 32
Ganci Air Base, Bishkek, Kyrgyzstan**

This could be a photo of "Capt. John," the first-name-only pilot who flew the F-15E Strike Eagle on combat missions in Afghanistan. Those could be the wintry mountain ridges of Pakistan below. In fact, this portrait of an F-15E pilot was taken earlier in a different location, but it shows the openness and visibility of the Strike Eagle's cockpit, from the viewpoint of the backseat weapons systems officer.

[U.S. Air Force]

"net-centric" air power of the twenty-first century. Fighting them required some of the old tools, including troops on the ground who could guide fighter-bombers. But when they could be found, the new, high-tech weapons were effective against them.

Many of the details of Strike Eagle operations against the Al Qaeda and the Taliban were widely published, including the locations of air bases and the names of U.S. military people. Still, for a period of time, the Pentagon instructed U.S. airmen to provide their first names only and ask that they withhold some details, including the types of ordnance being used. "Capt. John" was one of those first-name-only interview subjects.

Although he left the Air Force in 2005 to take up an airline job, "Capt. John" said the Pentagon had never released him from the requirement to withhold his full name and certain other details when discussing the F-15E Strike Eagle mission. In his narrative, "Capt. John" was cagey about the type of weapon being used in a strike mission against apparent Al Qaeda fighters in Afghanistan. Was he dropping "dumb" Mark 82 bombs, which rely mainly on gravity, perhaps with help from global positioning coordinates? Was he using the costly and controversial AGM-130 air-to-ground missile, which can be guided to its target? Or was he using the latest generation of satellite-guided "smart" bomb, known as the Joint Demolition Attack Munition, or J-DAM? The F-15E pilot said that all three of these weapons would involve similar mission profiles, so that leaving out a few details would not detract from his account.

"CAPT. JOHN." Even though it's no longer the newest thing in the sky and even though it's now very familiar to me, I still feel a sense of awe when I see an F-15E Strike Eagle parked on the ramp. I still turn around to look when an F-15E is making a takeoff on afterburner. We love this airplane. Supposedly, crews have nicknames for the F-15E Strike Eagle, calling it the "Beagle" (for Bomb Eagle), or the "Mud Hen," or simply the "E." The truth is, most of the time we just call it the F-15E.

When we arrive in South Asia to begin flying combat operations over Afghanistan, memories are fresh of the September 11, 2001, attack on the United States that killed almost three thousand of our countrymen and left the World Trade Center in smoking ruin. We begin flying missions immediately over parts of Afghanistan where the Taliban government allowed Al Qaeda terrorist camps to operate. I still have my name tag on my flight suit (it is quickly removed after the first mission or two), and the name of our airbase in a South Asian country appears in many newspapers, but we are asked not to identify either and to use first names only. So my name is just "Capt. John." I sit in the front seat of an 81,000 pound (36740 kg) plane that can carry a variety of high-tech weaponry, including a guided bomb, the AGM-130. In the backseat, operating our navigation and targeting equipment, is my weapons systems officer, "Capt. Fred." Today, we're going to operate over an area where we expect friendlies on the ground to identify a target for us.

Do I ever have fantasies about being the pilot whose bomb would go right into the cave and blow up Osama bin Laden? Of course I do. I think every American would like to pickle that bomb. But we don't do a lot of thinking about the bad guys down there.

Today, our radio call sign is Dobby 32 and we're part of a two-ship formation that will be available for targeting in the Takur sector of Afghanistan. We do our briefing, go "stepping"—preparing for the

An F-15E Strike Eagle doing it the old-fashioned way, dropping "dumb" iron bombs on a desert range in the United States. In Afghanistan, F-15E crews could choose from a variety of smarter weapons but the mission remained the same—bomb the target while being ready to fight in air-to-air combat if necessary.

[U.S. Air Force]

---

flight—in the life support section where they keep our helmets, oxygen masks, and harnesses, and ride out to the aircraft. The F-15E looks a little like a praying mantis getting ready to pounce, sitting in its parking slot attached to the auxiliary power unit.

As "Capt. Fred" will be the first to tell you, climbing into the jet is a poignant reminder that this was a single-seat aircraft reconfigured for a strike mission requiring a crew of two. The reminder comes when climbing the ladder that attaches to the front-seat cockpit. To get into the rear, "Capt. Fred" needs to step awkwardly atop the air inlet for the port engine (gingerly missing a "no step" area near the lip of the intake), then bend like a contortionist to wriggle into the backseat

With help from our hard-working ground crews, we strap in, start up, and taxi out. When you're carrying bags and bombs—"bags" is what we call external fuel tanks—the F-15E loses some of its sex appeal during taxi.

When taxiing on the ground, the F-15E feels a little stalky with its relatively narrow main-gear track.

When we arrive at the "last chance" hammerhead at runway's end, armorers scurry over our two F-15Es, checking connections, arming bomb fuses, and doing a visual safety check of the aircraft. The "arm, de-arm" troops have to squint at everything hanging from the plane. The weather's okay today but we often launch at night and in deteriorating weather, so these airmen scrambling under our wings have a really tough job. I don't know a single pilot who thinks he could do his job without the dedication of dozens of hardworking enlisted airmen.

The bombs speak of the job for which the McDonnell F-15E Strike Eagle signed on with the U.S. Air Force—delivering ordnance, often at considerable distance, with precision accuracy. Once they've been checked and armed, I receive the okay to taxi out onto the active runway and line up for takeoff.

Close behind comes our second F-15E (88-1702), call sign Dobby 34, piloted by "Major Bill." In the back is "Lt. Col. Andy," a weapon systems officer (WSO) with instructor/examiner skills and the most experienced man in Dobby flight.

Clamped into my Strike Eagle's ACES II ejection seat, I'm wearing helmet, visor, oxygen, CWU-27/P flyer's coverall, harness, survival pack, and G-suit. I'm attached to the aircraft in ten places—a lap belt with one buckle; an attachment to the seat kit with two buckles, one on each side; a shoulder harness, with one Koch fastener on each side; a plug-in for the G-suit; and separate attachments for oxygen hose and comm cord. Just before taxiing out, I flipped a switch next to my left hand to arm the ejection seat.

"We're set to go," Fred says on the intercom.

I go into full afterburner for takeoff power. Our big F-15E hurtles forward as if kicked in the pants. Because it always carries conformal fuel tanks, which add substantially to weight and marginally to drag, the F-15E always takes off with afterburner—and causes eyes to turn. We begin to rotate at 130 knots. At 165 knots, with my gloved hand very gently on the stick, the Strike Eagle flies itself off the ground.

The panorama of our air base rushes past and quickly falls away. Visibility from the cockpit of the F-15E is spectacular. Our takeoff, with "Major Bill's" Dobby 34 breaking ground twenty seconds behind us in trail, affords a sensational view of the base and of the region around it. Some day, I hope to be able to describe it in detail.

The base is home to the 336th Expeditionary Fighter Squadron, the deployed version of the 336th Fighter Squadron, the "Rocketeers," headquartered at Seymour Johnson Air Force Base, North Carolina, as part of the 4th Fighter Wing. The wing was the first user of the F-15E. In Operation Desert Storm in 1991, the wing flew 6,671 combat sorties and lost two Strike Eagles in combat, plus a third in a mishap.

During liftout, the ride in the F-15E is a little rough. That's a characteristic of the airplane and it's something the older guys, who flew the F-111, always criticize. The F-111 in flight had the stability of a block of concrete. The Strike Eagle is a lot more nimble. When we pop up to get over a hilltop, you can feel the forces working on the airplane. It doesn't happen every day, but it's routine for crews to get airsick and vomit once in awhile. During our flight, my roomy cockpit offers comfort and visibility, but the trip is bumpy.

I turn to our assigned flight heading, waggle my wings, and allow "Major Bill" to ease up to our left wing and tuck into a tight, two-ship formation. Once he's in place, his right wingtip is just a foot or two from our trailing edge, a vivid reminder of how close we stick to each other.

Even on missions of short duration, but especially on flights over Afghanistan where we may need loiter time, we always refuel in flight.

Somewhere near us, another two-ship formation, Waco 24 and Waco 26, is already on the tanker. Using the four multipurpose displays on my instrument panel, I lock up the tanker on our APG-70 radar, and we head up to refuel. Our flying gas station is a KC-10A Extender, call sign Petro 81.

Our wing and our squadron are supposed to be the spearhead of the new "expeditionary" Air Force of the twenty-first century, able to deploy as a self-sufficient package to any world trouble spot.

But we wouldn't fly anywhere, or accomplish anything without air-to-air refueling.

Once acquired visually, Petro 81 rushes up at us. The KC-10 looks a little ragged in its outdated lizard-green camouflage scheme. I use just a little stick and throttle to fly straight toward the spot where an F-15E from another flight, Waco Flight, has just finished gassing up. I take po-

The sheer size of the F-15E can be discerned by looking at the flight-garbed figures standing in front of it. Author Robert F. Dorr (left) prepares for a backseat orientation flight with Lt. Col. Steve "Mad" Hatter, commander of the 90th Fighter Squadron, the "Dicemen," at Elmendorf Air Force Base, Alaska, in 1999. The 90th squadron later became one of several fighting in Afghanistan.

[Robert F. Dorr]

sition off the KC-10's right wing, watch the receiving F-15E depart, and allow "Major Bill" in Dobby 34 to slide up beneath the boom next. A few minutes later, it's our turn.

In the old days, the fighter pilot would have talked at length with the tanker's boom operator ("a little to your right, sir; okay, that's good, now nudge it back just a little"). Years of practice have proven this unnecessary. Moreover, we're operating under "emcon" (emissions control), so we want to minimize radio communications. I simply slide our Strike Eagle up beneath the KC-10's "flying boom" and, without a word, allow the boom operator to find our receptacle, located six inches behind "Capt. Fred's" left shoulder, or about ten feet behind my back. The colossal KC-10 fills the sky in front of our Strike Eagle. We take on 5,000 pounds (2270 kg) of fuel without comment.

We watch the boom go up. We separate from the tanker. Now, we're heading for the fight.

"Capt. Fred" acknowledges completing a "fence check," which means that he's set up his radar warning receiver and chaff and flare dispenser, and has made another check of our ordnance. I don't know an F-15E pilot who wouldn't agree that the weapons systems officer in the backseat is worth a mint in combat. I mean no disrespect for "Capt. Fred," but having an old hand like "Lt. Col. Andy" in our companion F-15E is especially helpful—a valuable, extra pair of eyes worth a fortune in a fight.

"Lt. Col. Andy," by the way, is the only veteran of 1991's Operation Desert Storm among the four men who are rushing into harm's way today. Compared to the way he and other veterans describe the fighting in Desert Storm, our combat mission over Afghanistan will probably sound a little boring, a little like an anticlimax. After all, we fly high and drop bombs on people. That's it.

Way back in the 1970s, when McDonnell was pushing the F-15E (in competition with the General Dynamics F-16XL) for a place as the Air Force's next strike fighter, much was made of its air-to-ground capabilities. Even the Strike Eagle name was derived to separate this ship from the F-15A, B, C, and D Eagles used in air-to-air action. The F-15E performed well, air-to-ground, in Desert Storm, but its potential for battling other warplanes does not often receive enough attention. In both roles, I would call the Strike Eagle a "Cadillac of the skies."

Once we've refueled, we're "hot" for this mission and our controller directs us toward an area where American paratroopers are engaging a group of Al Qaeda fighters. "Capt. Fred" and I may be sucking in oxygen and tooling along at Mach .8, prepared to break things and kill people, but those American soldiers on the ground are the real heroes. In April in Afghanistan, it is still bitter cold, the terrain down there is rough, and there is no infrastructure to support the movement of our troops. Compared to what they face, an F-15E crew has a pretty good deal.

Nevertheless, and because higher headquarters has never ruled out the possibility of surface-to-air missiles being used against us, we're in a dense, task-saturated environment. There's no way we can fly a precision strike with fewer than two guys in the airplane. Our LANTIRN (Low Altitude Targeting, Infra Red for Night) targeting system is a tremendous system, and we have excellent coordination with other assets in the battle space, but no pilot would want to do it alone. When you actually ingress to the target and pickle off, the adrenaline is churning full-time. You've got to have confidence in your equipment and your people, and I always do.

I have to be a little careful in describing how we communicate with friendlies on the ground. As we approach a mountainous region that has been designated a "kill box," I'm in communication with an air liaison officer on the ground with the 2nd Battalion, 505th Parachute Infantry Regiment of the 82nd Airborne Division. The ALO is an Air Force officer, call him "Capt. George," who wears Army battle dress uniform, wears a Kevlar "Fritz" helmet, and is humping around in that remote, difficult terrain with a small, fluid group of American paratroopers. His radio call sign is Kershaw. They have backed a bunch of bad guys onto a reverse slope above a ravine. They would like Dobby 32 and Dobby 34 to help make it bye-bye for the bad guys. I have a way of communicating with "Capt. George" that doesn't require using voice transmissions in the clear. He has a way of passing details about the bad guys to me and my backseater while we're still at high altitude, looking down through a light haze.

Kershaw passes the global positioning coordinates. To get us lined up for a drop, I use a little stick and rudder to bank to the right, going into a gentle turn with Dobby 34 off my wingtip. We can see white vapor trails streaking back from the wingtips of the F-15E in the cool air. Kershaw and I do something called an "authentication exchange." In the backseat of my F-15E, "Capt. Fred" does some last minute jiggling with our ordnance.

This is what the Pentagon calls "net-centric" warfare. Everybody on our side is connected. The paratroopers chasing the bad guys down that slope are each connected to global positioning, to each other, and to our ALO. The air controllers for our sector of air space are in communication with everything that flies in this sector of Afghanistan. The paratroopers are feeding us not only a description of the bad guys' movements but the exact coordinates. Some of this stuff is going up to a satellite and coming down to us. We're connected. So, yes, we can see some guys moving down there on that slope, but most of this attack is being carried out with instruments.

I'm signaling to the pilot of Dobby 34, and our two F-15Es assume a "spread" while our backseaters do their final adjustment on the ordnance. This is nothing like what I've heard about Vietnam, where pilots go down into the trees and come face-to-face with the bad guys. I'm being a little vague here about how we set up, aim, and drop the ordnance, but on most missions in Afghanistan we're at relatively high altitude when we release. We've been given conflicting information about whether Taliban soldiers and Al Qaeda fighters have any capability to reach up and touch us, but on some missions we do see muzzle flashes. On one, my backseater thought he saw a rocket-propelled grenade being fired in our general direction.

Today, we've got the Al Qaeda fighters' command post locked up. Even though the guy in the backseat is, in effect, the bombardier of the F-15E, the pilot is in command, so I'm the one who toggles the pickle switch. We feel only the gentlest sort of change as the bombs leave their stations and begin their journey toward the ground. Now, "Capt. Fred" and I are very busy, indeed, trying to achieve two contradictory goals. We want to do our part to guide our ordnance to the target, but we also want to get the hell out of there.

Remember I said this is a bit of an anticlimax? Today, our two F-15Es are releasing at the same time, against the same target. It's going to be very unpleasant down there for somebody.

Dobby 34 releases its bombs. Using hand signals rather than radio communication, "Major Bill" rejoins formation with me. I take us into a slight bank, now, so we can attempt to see the result down there, through the haze. With the naked eye, we can see figures in motion, a couple of structures, and then four explosions—just a hint of a flash followed by a lot of black cloud and flying debris—as the bombs from both F-15Es go exactly where we wanted them to go.

While I'm not going to discuss the manner in which our precision-guided ordnance reached the bad guys—it's no secret that some weapons are laser-guided, others are satellite-guided, and some are just plain "dumb," but I'm not going to say—I will say that each bomb has a 1,000-pound (454-kg) warhead, which is in the middle of the range of conventional weapons carried by the F-15E. Obviously, we don't hear any detonations or feel any impact from high altitude, but I have had the experience of being on the ground observing a bomb drop. I can tell you that four 1,000-pounders don't make quite as much noise as you'd expect. The sound is very loud but very brief. However, they do inflict devastation over a wider area than you might expect.

On the intercom, "Capt. Fred" utters a two-word comment that says it all: "Good job." Again using hand signals, I direct our two-ship formation to turn for home.

If the enemy had any fighters, we would be able to take them on in our F-15Es. In fact, we're carrying ammunition for the cannon and "hot" missiles. But that isn't a threat in this war, at least not for now.

Later, we will be informed that we did, in fact, hit the target exactly as we were supposed to.

Our return to our airbase, our low-level pass over the base, and our approach to landing add more anticlimax to a mission that was pretty straightforward although certainly not without risk. We're cleared for landing and go into the airfield pattern. During final approach, I hold the F-15E between twenty and twenty-two units of AOA (angle of attack), a moderately nose-high posture, which equates to touching ground at 145 knots. You can aerobrake the airplane by pulling the nose up so that the wing slows it down. The F-15E has no brake parachute and needs none.

In contrast to its rough handling during takeoff and climb-out, an F-15E landing is like gossamer. The huge, "barn door" speed brake enables me to put the aircraft into a standard letdown, nose-high, and the Eagle virtually flies itself to the runway.

Our landing is routine, and I taxi toward the parking spot. Mercifully, "Capt. Fred" spares me his joke about how, "It's Miller time." We will debrief and return our flight gear to the life support (short) but we won't be drinking a brew. Having a beer is not part of our life at this location.

SHACK?

McDonnell F-15E Strike Eagle

Quite remarkably, the F-15E was an aircraft that almost did not happen.

In the late 1970s, with a large fleet of A-10 Warthog and F-111 Aardvark aircraft, the Air Force was not eagerly shopping for an air-to-ground weapon.

The F-15 series, which had been around for several years by then, had always been "wired" for air-to-ground combat but was being used only in the air-to-air role. To transform the single-seat F-15 fighter into a ground attack plane, experts believed that a strengthened airframe and a backseat weapons operator would be essential.

Who's Who

DOBBY 32-A
"Capt. John," F-15E Strike Eagle pilot, 336th Expeditionary Fighter Squadron

DOBBY 32-B
"Capt. Fred," F-15E weapons systems officer

DOBBY 34-A
"Major Bill," F-15E Strike Eagle pilot

DOBBY 34-B
"Lt. Col. Andy," F-15E weapons systems officer

KERSHAW
"Capt. George," Air Force Air Liaison Officer, or ALO, on the ground with the 82nd Airborne Division

"But nobody was buying it," said James Hart, a former employee of the plane's manufacturer, then known as the McDonnell Aircraft Co.

"We knew the F-15 was highly adaptable to the deep-interdiction mission with heavy ordnance," said Hart in an interview. "But the Air Force was more interested in dogfighting than in 'mud moving.' We knew we were going to have to work hard to sell our concept."

Using its own funds, McDonnell modified an F-15B to serve as a demonstrator prototype for the projected F-15E Strike Eagle. In its new configuration, the plane made its initial flight at the manufacturer's St. Louis, Missouri, factory in August 1981. About 30 percent of the original F-15 structure had to be redesigned to create the F-15E.

"At that point, it was strictly a private venture by McDonnell and the subcontractors," Hart remembered. "There was a lot of interest but no assurance the investment would redeem itself."

Gradually, the Air Force took an interest.

One reason was not evident to the public. Gen. Wilbur Creech, commander of Tactical Air Command from 1978 to 1984, wanted a backup for the forthcoming F-117 Nighthawk stealth fighter (Chapter 19), then a supersecret "black" program. If the F-117 were to suffer systems integration problems, for example, Creech wanted an alternative aircraft optimized for attacking mobile, high-value targets—a task for which

This is a formation of F-15E Strike Eagles. These aircraft belong to the 391st Fighter Squadron at Mountain Home Air Force Base, Idaho, one of several F-15E squadrons that fought in Afghanistan and Iraq.

[U.S. Air Force]

the A-10 and F-111, which lacked high-tech, air-to-ground surveillance sensors, were less than ideal. For many other reasons as well, Creech, a much-respected combat veteran, wanted a version of the F-15E that could break things and kill people.

Although the F-117 worked out fine, the worldwide proliferation of mobile missile sites and other potential targets justified a new air-to-ground warplane, and the Air Force proclaimed a need for a replacement for the F-111. The service narrowed its choice to two aircraft, the F-16XL Fighting Falcon, which would have been designated F-16F if used operationally, and the F-15E Strike Eagle. Insiders said the competition really was no contest at all: The F-16XL had technical and cost problems, while the F-15E seemed right from the start.

The target-designator pod carried by the F-15E, coupled with an ergonomic, two-crew cockpit designed by McDonnell's Eugene Adams, assured that the Strike Eagle would be deemed the better of the two aircraft.

On a realistic mission, the F-15E carries up to a maximum of 24,250 pounds (11000 kg) of tactical ordnance, including 1,000-lb (454-kg) bombs, AGM-65 Maverick missiles, and GBU-10, GBU-15, and GBU-

The F-15E Strike Eagle, now fighting in Iraq and Afghanistan, will be in service for many years to come. But the Air Force has staked its future on the Lockheed Martin F/A-22 Raptor, which it calls an "air dominance fighter." This is one of the first operational Raptors at Tyndall Air Force Base, Florida, in 2004.

[Norman Taylor]

28 guided weapons. The F-15E doesn't have the range of the F-111 it replaced, but pilots who flew both aircraft say they would never give away the air-to-air capability the F-15E has and the F-111 lacked.

The service eventually picked the F-15E and ordered it into production. Following test work with the company-modified prototype, the first production F-15E made its first flight on December 11, 1986, flown by test pilot Gary Jennings.

"You went from a 'steam-gauge'-oriented cockpit in the F-15A [air-to-air fighter] to a true digital cockpit in the F-15E," said Washington defense analyst John Gresham. "The initial order was very modest, for only fifty aircraft, but the Air Force knew it was getting an excellent machine with the Strike Eagle."

In 1988, the 405th Tactical Training Wing at Luke Air Force Base, Arizona, became the Tactical Air Command's replacement training unit for the F-15E Strike Eagle aircraft. Soon thereafter, the first operational F-15Es were delivered to the 4th Tactical Fighter Wing at Seymour Johnson, replacing the F-4E Phantom.

On August 12, 1990, as the United States began Operation Desert Shield in response to the Iraqi invasion of Kuwait, F-15E Strike Eagles from Seymour deployed to Al Kharj Air Base, Saudi Arabia. During Desert Storm, F-15Es were assigned strike missions against a variety of targets, including five- to six-hour sorties in search of Scud missile launch sites.

The 1991 missions often involved low-level terrain avoidance in order to avoid Iraqi surface-to-air missiles. They sometimes involved a real or potential threat of intervention by Iraqi fighters. For those reasons, and also because of the difficulties posed by desert conditions, the Desert Storm mission was in many ways a more difficult one than those that followed in Afghanistan a dozen years later.

Pratt & Whitney, with its superb F100 series of low-bypass turbofan engines, has a "lock" on the Strike Eagle population. The F100-PW-229 began production in 1989 as an increased-performance version of

---

McDonnell F-15E Strike Eagle

Type: two-seat, dual-role air superiority fighter and strike fighter

Power plant: two Pratt & Whitney F100-PW-220 afterburning turbofan engines rated at 29,340-lb thrust (125.52-kN), or two Pratt & Whitney F100-PW-229 afterburning turbofan IPEs (Improved performance engines) rated at 35,600-lb thrust (151.24-kN)

Performance: maximum speed 1,875 mph (3000 km/h), or Mach 2.5 plus, at 45,000 ft (13716 m); service ceiling 65,000 ft (19810 m); combat radius, 1,200 miles (1920 km) unrefueled, ferry range with conformal fuel tanks and three external fuel tanks 4,000 miles (6400 km)

Weights: empty 31,700 lb (14380 kg); maximum takeoff 81,000 lb (36740 kg); fuel capacity, internal: 13,125 lb (5952 kg), external: 21,645 lb (9820 kg)

Dimensions: wingspan 42 ft 10 in (13.06 m); length 63 ft 9 in (19.43 m); height 18 ft 8 in (5.69 m); wing area 608 sq ft (56.48 m)

Armament: one internal M61A1 Vulcan 20-mm cannon, with maximum of 512 rounds; provision for up to four AIM-9 Sidewinder missiles and up to four AIM-7M Sparrow or AIM-120 AMRAAM missiles; thirteen ordnance stations for up to 45,000 lb (20385 kg) of bombs or missiles at minimum range, or 24,250 lb (11000 kg) of bombs or missiles at long range

First flight: August 1981 (modified F-15B); December 11, 1986 (F-15E)

the F100 series, delivering around 5,000 pounds (2267 kilograms) more thrust than the original engine. The PW-229 has the best single-engine safety record of any fighter engine in history.

The F-15E itself has a superb safety record. Through mid-2005, it suffered 1.54 losses per 100,000 hours flying time.

General Electric—which believes its F110 turbofan would improve performance for the Strike Eagle—demonstrated its 24,000-lb (10886-kg) afterburning thrust F110-GE-129 engine on the F-15E, but after extensive tests the Air Force wasn't buying.

Ultimately, the Strike Eagle's manufacturer, which became Boeing in 1995, produced 236 Strike Eagles for the Air Force.

Index

Page numbers in *italic* indicate photographs; those in **bold** indicate aircraft specifications

RF-86A reconnaissance aircraft, 169
Rhee, Syngman, 207
Rice, Raymond, 100
Richards, Curt (Lt. Col.), 250, 252–253, 256, 257, 257, 258, 259–260, 273–274, 277–282
Ritchie, Andrew, 176
Robertson, T. D. (Gen.), 238
Robinson, James (Capt.), 30
Rodriguez, Cesar A. "Rico" (Col.), 286, 291, 294, 295, 296, 297
Rogers, Robert J. "Bob" (1st Lt.), 3, 10, 14
Rolls-Royce Merlin engines, 18, 81, 101
Ronca, Bob (Capt.), 179, 180–181, 185
Roosevelt, Franklin D. (President), 46, 61, 71
Root, Gene, 215
Roth, Russell M. "Rusty" (test pilot), 235
Royal Air Force, Britain (RAF), 1, 4, 13, 14, 17, 22, 52–53, 81, 100–101, 160

Sabre. See F-86A Sabre; F-86F Sabre
Sanders, Lewis M. (1st Lt.), 9
Saudi Arabia, 284, 307, 331
SB2C Helldiver "Beast," 116, 118
SBD Dauntless, 118
Schiavi, Anthony E. "Kimo" (Col.), 288, 289, 291–296, 297
Schick, William R. (1st Lt.), 11
Schirra, Walter (Lt.), 153
Schmidt (Capt.), 32, 32
Schmued, Edgar, 100
Schroeder, Bill, 312
Schweinfurt-Regensburg raid, 102
Scott, Bob (Col.), 245
Self, Sir Henry, 100
Senior Trend, 313
September 11, 2001, 319
Seven Mile, 27–28, 38, 38
Seymour Johnson Air Force Base, 199, 322, 330, 331
"Shark Fin" flights (Cold War reconnaissance missions), 218, 220
Shokaku (carrier), 8
Shomo, William A. (Maj.), 106
Shooting Star. See F-80C Shooting Star
Short, Walter C. (Lt. Gen.), 1–2, 4, 5
Shoulars, Ron (Capt.), 261
"shuttle," 112
Silver Star, 195
single-seat, carrier-based attack aircraft. See AD Skyraider
single-seat air superiority fighter. See F-15C Eagle

single-seat fighter. See F6F Hellcat; F-80C Shooting Star; F-86A Sabre; F-86F Sabre; P-38 Lightning; P-39M Airacobra; P-40B/C Tomahawk
single-seat fighter and fighter-bomber. See F-105 Thunderchief; P-51D Mustang
single-seat fighter-bomber. See F-84E/G Thunderjet
single-seat jet fighter. See F9F-3 Panther
single-seat strike aircraft. See F-117A Nighthawk Stealth Fighter
Sinuiju, 127, 140, 179
Sisley, Bill (Lt. Comdr.), 114, 116, 122
Skeen, Kenneth L. (Capt.), 150–151, 153
Skliar, William (1st Lt.), 142, 153
"Skunk Works," 135, 136, 312
Skyknight. See EF-10B (F3D-2Q) Skyknight
Skyraider. See AD Skyraider
Slaughter, William W. (Capt.), 140
"Sled," 235. See also F-105 Thunderchief
Smiley, Al (1st Lt.), 163, 165, 181, 182
Smith, Jack, 132–133
Smith, John L. (Maj.), 68–69
Smith, S. M. (1st Lt.), 27
"Snake School," 255, 256
SNB Expeditor, 115
Sneaky Sultan, 301–302
Soryu (destroyer), 67
South, Mike (Lt.), 114, 116, 117, 119, 122
South Korea, 107, 208
Soviet MiG. See MiG
Soviet Union and atomic bomb, 208
Sprague, Charles A. (Maj.), 78
"Staff Weenie," 261
Stanley, Robert M. (test pilot), 135
Starnes, Edsel R. (Lt.), 131–132
stealth fighter. See F-117A Nighthawk Stealth Fighter
Stearman N2S-1 (PT-17), 207
Stephens, Evans G. (Col.)
    islands and P-39M Airacobra, 20, 21, 21, 25–29, 35, 79
    jet-vs.jet battle (history's first) and F-80 Shooting Star, 126, 127–128, 128, 129, 131, 132, 134
Sterling, Gordon H., Jr. (2nd Lt.), 9
straight-wing fighters, 166, 167
Strategic Air Command (SAC), 141, 142, 155, 254–255
Stratton, William T. (Maj.), 233
Straub, Bob (1st Lt.), 163
Strike, Control, and Reconnaissance (SCAR) missions, 280, 281

Robert F. Dorr, a veteran and retired American diplomat, has written more than sixty books on air operations, including *Chopper* and *Marine Air*. He lives in Oakton, Virginia, with his family and Labrador retriever.